BERG

Oxford • New York

First published in 2002 by
Berg
Editorial offices:
150 Cowley Road, Oxford, OX4 1JJ, UK
838 Broadway, Third Floor, New York, NY 10003-4812, USA

Berg is an imprint of Oxford International Publishers Ltd.

Library of Congress Cataloging-in-Publication Data
A catalogue record for this book is available from the Library of Congress

British Library Cataloguing-in-Publication Data
A catalogue record for this book is available from the British Library.

ISBN 1 85973 514 2 (Cloth)
1 85973 519 3 (Paper)

Contents

Contents

Acknowledgements

This book has gradually taken shape over several years of reading and teaching, and has been encouraged by the influences and support of far too many people to mention here. However, special thanks must go to Euan Hague, Andrew Samuel, Viv Kinnaird and Kevin Hannam who have organised conferences and seminars, where I have presented papers on some of the themes featured here. Also, several colleagues have helped by sharing work in progress with me, including Helen Watkins, Rhys Jones, Dan Knox and notably Julie Nugent. Stimulating conversations and correspondences with a range of colleagues, including Cameron McCarthy, Mick Smith and John Urry have also fuelled the project. I want to extend particular appreciation to Wendy Hamilton and Ed Williams who helped my research into the 'Self-Portrait' zone of the Millennium Dome, the subject of Chapter 6, and likewise to Elspeth King and Steven Paterson who provided gratefully received assistance in my examination of William Wallace and his legacy. Respect is due to the staff at Berg who encouraged me with the project and efficiently facilitated the production of this book. And I'd also like to thank Malcolm Henson and Zhang Pinggong for their valuable help. First and foremost, the book would not have been possible without the contribution of the many cultural studies students whom I have taught over the past few years, and the support of colleagues at Staffordshire University. Finally, I would like to thank my family for their patience and encouragement: Rosemary, Jim, Lopa, Ji, Jay and Kim – ta very much. And most of all I must pay tribute to Uma Kothari for her intelligent and stimulating contribution to the project and for acting as a check on excessive academic pomposity.

Preface

National identity persists in a globalising world, and perhaps the nation remains the pre-eminent entity around which identity is shaped. In this book, I want to explore the relationship of national identity to popular culture and everyday life. For although there have been numerous studies of nationalism, few have examined the more mundane aspects of national identity. Dominant theories of the nation are concerned with political economy and history, and the national cultural elements they refer to are either in the realm of high culture, are the 'invented traditions' and ceremonies concocted many years ago, or are versions of folk culture. These are reified notions of culture, which, while certainly still relevant, are only a small part of the cultural matrix which surrounds the nation. Curiously, despite the rise of Cultural Studies as an academic discipline, few have attempted to address the more dynamic, ephemeral and grounded ways in which nation is experienced and understood through popular culture. And similarly under-explored, the habitual, unreflexive routines of everyday life also provide fertile ground for the development of national identity. Thus the cultural expression and experience of national identity is usually neither spectacular nor remarkable, but is generated in mundane, quotidian forms and practices. As Bennett asserts, Cultural Studies is concerned with 'practices, institutions and systems of classification through which there are inculcated in a population particular values, beliefs, competences, routines of life and habitual forms of conduct' (1998: 28). And yet these concerns have rarely focused upon national identity.

The existing literature on national identity provides little guidance in exploring this dense and murky cultural realm and so it is necessary to utilise a different set of theoretical tools. I have chosen a range of ideas that have recently emerged in social and cultural theory to try and suggest that the national is still a powerful constituent of identity precisely because it is grounded in the popular and the everyday. I have thus drawn upon contemporary theoretical insights from studies into identity, space, performance, material culture and representation. The book is organised around these key themes, and, while I do not want to claim that these are evidently the most appropriate foci for the exploration of national identity, I believe that they provide a useful range of interrelated contexts which suggest that national identity is dynamic, contested, multiple and fluid. This might suggest that if it is so protean then it must be weakening. I want to emphasise that this is far from the case, and that this diversity, the multitudinous cultural effects, and the flexible symbols of the national produce an enormous cultural resource that is not a monolithic set of ideas adhered to by everybody but a seething mass of cultural elements. Accordingly, I consider national identity to be constituted out of a huge cultural matrix which provides innumerable points of connection, nodal points where authorities try to fix meaning, and constellations around which cultural elements cohere. Culture, according to this conception, is constantly in a process of becoming, of emerging out of the dynamism of popular culture and everyday life whereby people make and remake connections between the local and the national, between the national and the global, between the everyday and the extraordinary. For as Cubitt remarks, 'however institutionalised [nations] become, and however well established the symbolism that denotes them, nations remain elusive and indeterminate, perpetually open to context, to elaboration and to imaginative reconstruction' (1998: 3).

The focus in this book, then, is on the dense spatial, material, performative, embodied and representative expressions and experiences of national identity which are inextricably interlinked with each other, which constitute a shared compendia of resources, akin to a vast matrix into which individuals can tap to actualise a sense of national belonging. By using the metaphor of the matrix, I can emphasise the complexity of the cultures of national identity, and highlight the multiple connections which exist between cultural spheres. I can also account for the innumerable routes towards expressing identity that exist within this matrix, a matrix within which some branches wither, are renewed, transplanted or emerge.

These ongoing processes all feed back into each other, consolidating the apparent naturalness of modes of understanding and enacting national identity. These dense series of associations between spaces, acts, things and forms of representation form the ground for epistemological and ontological notions about the nation: to unpick and unpack the threads of such a densely grounded identity is thus difficult. But the fact remains that those who attempt to fix the meanings of nationalism cannot incorporate the whole matrix, they must necessarily concentrate on a few selective, symbolic dimensions to suit their purposes.

However, because national identity is not only a matter of will and strategy, but is enmeshed in the embodied, material ways in which we live – in the rich realm of 'thick description' (Geertz, 1993) – it is in many ways inaccessible to the politicians and campaigners and their circumscribing manoeuvres. This is, of course, not to say that such appeals are not effective in mobilising people to fight for causes – recent history suggests otherwise – but that the sheer complexity of these associations offers hope that the increasing ambivalence of national identity might militate against exclusive and reified versions.

Chapter 1 develops the theoretical framework for this study, critiquing previous conceptions of national culture, proposing an approach to the key concepts of popular culture, everyday life and identity, and explicating my argument that national identity is being redistributed in a cultural matrix.

Chapter 2 examines the different levels through which the nation is spatialised. I first look at symbolic and ideological landscapes, moving on to consider iconic sites. These two spatial constructs have admittedly been the subject of much analysis but I then go on to consider a range of other spaces intimately concerned with national identity – namely, places of congregation, 'taskscapes' and familiar, everyday landscapes, and more homely spaces. I emphasise the sensual and unreflexive forms of dwelling within national space in contradistinction to the iconic and the spectacular.

Chapter 3 focuses on modes of performance. Commencing with an assessment of the contemporary effect of large formal ceremonies and invented traditions, I move on to examine more popular forms of overtly national performance, notably in sport, dance and carnival. I then investigate the ways in which the nation is increasingly dramatised and staged through tourist productions, before exploring the everyday performances which often unreflexively consolidate national identity. By identifying popular competencies, embodied enactions and synchronised habits, I show how national identity is grounded in quotidian practices.

Chapter 4 considers how we might conceive of the material culture of the nation. After a theoretical outline of the ways in which objects can contribute to the constitution of social relations through their affordances, commodification, habitual emplacement, semiotic meaning and biographies, I will develop an exemplary analysis of the automobile and the ways in which it is loaded with national significance. Primarily concentrating on British and American car cultures, I will look at their iconic importance to national industry, the 'motorscapes' they produce, the practices which centre upon them, the sensual experiences they afford, and the ways in which they are represented.

Chapter 5 investigates the ways in which nations are represented. Taking the example of *Braveheart*, the Hollywood blockbuster which tells the story of medieval Scottish hero William Wallace's battle against the occupying English, I consider how this global product was received in Scotland. My argument critiques those who suggest that the disembedding of cultural production necessarily reproduces stereotypical forms of national identity, for I show the diverse affective and political responses that the film stimulated in Scotland. In fact the film is merely the latest retelling of an important myth, which has been appropriated and utilised by different groups, represented in numerous ways, and fed back into complex debates about contemporary Scottish identity.

Chapter 6 acts as a conclusion by summarising the points I have made through-out the book by assessing the representation of Britishness in the *Self-Portrait* zone at the Millennium Dome in London. Particularly concentrating upon the *Andscape* feature of the zone, I show how a dynamic British identity is enmeshed in the popular and the everyday, continually domesticates the nation by making links between the local and the national, is highly contested and variable, and suggests a host of interconnections and constellations.

Popular Culture, Everyday Life and the Matrix of National Identity

Theories of Nationalism: Reductive Cultural Perspectives

The literature on nationalism and national identity has been dominated by a focus on the historical origins of the nation and its political lineaments. Nevertheless, so powerful is the allure of the nation that is has proved to be 'an imaginative field on to which different sets of concerns may be projected, and upon which connections may be forged between different aspects of social, political and cultural experience' (Cubitt, 1998: 1). Strangely, however, the nation has been subject to very little critical analysis in terms of how it is represented and experienced through popular culture and in everyday life. This absence masks a supposition that 'nation' is equivalent to 'society', a popular assumption that also afflicts social scientists and cultural theorists. For as James avers, 'the concepts of the nation, *this* society, and *this* community are often used as coterminous' (1996: 123). Accordingly, notions of society remain 'embedded within notions of nation-state, citizenship and national society' (Urry, 2000: 6) and, as Billig further elaborates, 'the "society" which lies at the heart of sociology's self-definition is created in the image of the nation-state' (1995: 53). Thus despite appearances to the contrary, not least at the level of common sense, the nation persists as a pre-eminent constituent of identity and society at theoretical and popular levels. Despite the globalisation of economies, cultures and social processes, the scalar model of identity is believed to be primarily anchored in national space. Partly, then, the space in which culture and everyday life operates is conceived to be indisputably the nation, and this has resulted from a lack of enquiry into how such cultures are (re)produced and experienced, how they are sustained to succour the illusion that the nation is somehow a natural entity, rather than a social and cultural construct.

At the level of culture, then, there is a reification of the nation, as if different cultures can be identified, ticked off according to a preconceived set of national characteristics. Bounded and self-evident, a nationally rooted culture is not imagined as 'the *outcome* of material and symbolic processes but instead as the *cause* of those practices – a hidden essence lying behind the surface of behaviour' (Crang, 1998: 162). For instance, in a recent account of national identity, the contention was advanced that the nation 'represents the socio-historical context within which culture is embedded and the means by which culture is produced, transmitted and received' (Guibernau, 1996: 79) This, of course, considers culture (and national identity which expresses it) to be singular and fixed instead of multiple and dynamic. But as Clifford declares culture is not 'a rooted body that grows, lives, dies', but is rather a site of 'displacement, interference and interaction' (1992: 101).

Thus whilst there are many studies of particular 'national' cultural forms and practices (many to which I will be referring), at a general theoretical level, the idea of popular culture seems to be mysteriously absent. And paradoxically, although it is believed that discrete national cultures exist, a sophisticated account of how popular culture is manifest and expressed as national has not been attempted. As I will shortly discuss however, there are the stirrings of a more considered approach, and there have been several highly suggestive accounts that have not yet been utilised.

The aim of this first section is to explore the ways in which some of the best-known writers on nationalism and national identity, namely Ernest Gellner, Eric Hobsbawm, Benedict Anderson, Anthony Smith and John Hutchinson, have considered the cultural and its relationship with the national. I will argue that these accounts are seriously distorted in their consideration of 'high', 'official' and 'traditional' culture to the exclusion of popular and everyday cultural expression, and that their conception of culture is rather undynamic.

Ernest Gellner

Ernest Gellner's work on nationalism has been enormously influential. Yet his emphasis on the essentially modern origins of nations utilises a particular perspective towards culture. He maintains that the institutionalisation of cultural norms shared over a large geographical area, and the dissemination of national ideologies, can only occur in modern, mass societies. Thus the nineteenth-century bureaucratisation of education, hygiene and medicine, the rise of organised, rational recreation, and the rise of centralised institutions of scientific knowledge which classified criminals, insanity and nature are part of a wider reorganisation of social and cultural life (Lloyd and Thomas, 1998). Primarily, the authority for organising this transformation is national, and responsibility for establishing common adherence to centralised policies, structures and norms devolves to regional and local authorities to reinforce the cultural homogeneity demanded by the centre to facilitate nation building. Gellner's account of this drive towards the modern formation of national identity focuses upon the establishment of what he terms 'high cultures', defined as 'a school-mediated, academy supervised idiom, codified for the requirements of reasonably precise bureaucratic and technological communication' (1983: 57). More specifically, these are referred to as 'garden cultures' (ibid.: 7), which are presumably surveyed, tended and codified by specialist experts. Thus a mass education system binds state and culture together, canons are devised, museums are established, official histories written, scientific bodies set up to subtend the propagation of 'official' knowledge, so that specific bodies of knowledge, values and norms are ingested by all educated citizens.

Crucially, for Gellner, the extension of an authoritative knowledge to all denizens of the nation marks a break from the cultural differentiation in medieval worlds, where, for instance, it was not imperative for the inhabitants of regions to communicate with each other, or for the peasantry to share the language of the elite; indeed, distinct courtly cultures were designed to differentiate elites from masses. Instead, with 'standardised'

> homogeneous, centrally sustained high cultures, pervading entire populations and not just elite minorities, a situation occurs in which well-defined educationally sanctioned and unified cultures constitute very nearly the only kind of unit with which men [*sic*] willingly and often ardently identify. (ibid.: 55)

For Gellner, nationalism is a function of modernity and the process of modernisation, where education, technologies of communication and bureaucracy, the very structure of the modern state, are driven by rationalist, administrative imperatives rather than any manipulating caste. Nations are thus the forms which are best suited to carry these modernising imperatives. Whilst plausible, the account tends to focus on the Appollonian features of modernity – the rational elements – whilst ignoring other dimensions such as the continual change and fluidity which challenges the ordering processes that nations, amongst other agents of rationality, attempt to reinforce. This incessant transformation of economic, social and cultural life means that bodies of thought and knowledge are inherently unstable, open to challenge as new adaptations are sought by individuals and institutions. Therefore, national organisations must keep pace with change whilst simultaneously reinforcing authoritative cultural delineations if they are to retain their authority. I am suggesting that Gellner's account overemphasises the rigidity of (national) cultures – and indeed, processes of modernity.

This also raises the issue as to whether all subjects willingly give up their cultural values in the face of the nation? Perhaps, as Smith argues as part of his argument that nations are based on pre-existing *ethnies*, in certain cases, selective ancestral cultures have been adopted as official cultures by nations (1998: 42). The position of the state towards already existing cultures is complex, for certain cultures may be eradicated (especially in the case of ethnic or religious particularity), or they may be adopted and adapted by the cultural establishment. Questions are also raised about who is left out of the national culture, how are ethnicity, religion, language and region accommodated by the state and who is marginalised or rejected as unsuitably national. Gellner's assertions seem to suggest that subjects passively accept knowledge and identities, are effectively interpellated by all-powerful national cultural organisations. However, the struggle for inclusion is an ongoing battle which cultural guardians cannot always control. For example, the British state permits freedom of worship but has insisted upon the provision of compulsory teaching of Christianity in primary and secondary education. Nevertheless, heterodox and dissenting religious cultures have abounded and church attendance has dwindled despite the preferential conditions provided for this official cultural consolidation.

Moreover, we must be careful that we do not assume that the educationalists, academic bodies and arts organisations are composed of an homogeneous membership. For instance, as Smith argues, many national education policies are shaped by a desire to transmit cultural diversity via multicultural education strategies (ibid.: 41) rather than reinforcing rigid cultural norms.

Most serious in my opinion, however, is Gellner's focus on 'high' cultures as those which contrast with the 'low' cultures of the majority – what Gellner refers to as 'wild' cultures, local, spontaneous and unreflexive. There is no doubt that historically, in the first instance, there were attempts to formulate a nationally codified body of knowledge which foregrounded 'high' culture. However, once the nation is established as a common-sense entity, under conditions of modernity, the mass media and the means to develop and transmit popular culture expands dramatically, and largely escapes the grip of the state, being transmitted through commercial and more informal networks. The rise of popular forms of entertainment, leisure pursuits, political organisations and a host of vernacular commonalities is not generated by national elites but is facilitated through the mobilities engendered by advances in transport and communication technologies. Whilst I concede that Gellner's account has historical salience, it is important that strong contemporary parallels are not drawn, for a cultural elite propagating high culture is but one aspect of the production of national identity.

In fact, the 'wild', vernacular, 'traditional' and regional cultural elements, ignored or reviled by national cultural elites, have returned as repressed knowledge and have been reconstructed as part of alternative kinds of national identity. Cast into what has been called the 'cultic milieu', a resource into which rejected ideas are deposited, they have been reclaimed by 'alternative' groups, partly because the rational, establishment organisations against which such groups react disdained their utility. In some cases, these cultural elements have been curiously re-enchanted with a nationalist slant. Goddess and tree worship, druidic rites and pagan sites are celebrated as epitomising the spirit of a pre-Christian Britain, as containing alternative origins of a national spirit in contrast to 'official' Christian and over-rationalist constructions of national identity.

Eric Hobsbawm

In *The Invention of Tradition*, Eric Hobsbawm and co-editor Terence Ranger also contend that the nation is essentially a modern construct. They focus upon the ways in which the powerful 'invent' traditions to create the illusion of primordiality and continuity, to mask the fact that nations are invariably of recent vintage, to 'inculcate certain values and norms of behaviour by repetition, which automatically implies continuity with the past' (1983: 2). The traditions they and their contributors discuss focus particularly upon the large-scale pageants and rituals devised in the nineteenth century by European elites for a range of purposes: to symbolise a cohesive sense of belonging; to legitimise the power vested in institutions, elites and ruling authorities; to transmit ideologies which sustain common values and beliefs.

I will discuss these rituals in greater length in Chapter 3, but here I want to take issue with some of the implicit cultural assumptions in Hobsbawm and Ranger's account. The identification of a historical process whereby national elites try to construct culturally an ancient national lineage is undoubtedly valuable. The (re)staging of ceremonies, and attempts to encode selective cultural forms and practices as evidence of primeval traditions, remains an important theme, and persists in the contemporary cultural constructions of national identity (for instance, see Vlastos, 1998).

However, the cultural assumptions of Hobsbawm and Ranger reveal a Frankfurtian understanding that the masses are drawn together by such ceremonies, and are powerless to resist the overwhelming appeal that they impart, passively ingesting ideological messages. Rather than the culture industries, it is the cultural elite who bewitch them with their designs. And these elites are always assumed to be concerned with developing fiendish tactics to control the masses, to bend them to their will. Thus, too much credence is given to the idea that they are primarily concerned with ideological manipulation rather than issues of authenticity and spectacle, to control rather than notions about protocol. Again, there is a conspicuous dearth of cultural dynamism in the assertion that these cultural productions achieve elite objectives in pacifying the masses and coercing them into line with the national project. The popular seems to be collapsed into the ceremonial traditions they discuss, for these cultural expressions are foregrounded as key to the formation of national identity and the vernacular and the everyday is conspicuously absent from their analysis

However, a theme of this book is that the meaning of symbolic cultural elements cannot be determined or fixed. In fact, particularly powerful symbols need to be flexible in order to retain their relevance over time and their appeal amongst diverse groups. As Guibernau says, 'symbols not only stand for or represent something else, they also allow those who employ them to supply part of their meaning';

they do not impose upon people 'the constraints of uniform meaning' (1996: 81). For instance, she discusses how the Catalan flag is wielded for different purposes by a range of groups, socialist, nationalist, republican and right wing. Individuals are required constantly to reproduce established symbols in accordance with changing circumstances. This is a dynamic process whereby the identification with such symbols needs to be continually worked upon to safeguard meaning.

The idea of the *invention* of tradition also overemphasises the novelty of national cultures by failing to identify earlier cultural continuities. For instance, Morgan's chapter on the nineteenth-century revival of the Welsh eisteddfod in Hobsbawm and Ranger's (1983) volume undercuts the idea that such traditions were new, but reveals their small-scale popularity across Wales before they were revamped. The basis for their co-option by the state already existed because they were grounded in popular culture. While vernacular and popular elements may have been codified by national folklorists, dragooned into anthologies and given ceremonial status, it hardly means that they have not had enduring popular appeal, merely that they are restaged on a larger scale. More crucially, a focus on large-scale spectaculars and easily identifiable traditions ignores a host of other 'traditions' which are grounded in everyday life; in leisure pursuits, work practices, families and communities, as I will show.

There is an implicit assumption that a dynamic modernity repackages aspects of a reified tradition. This misconceives tradition *contra* modernity. For rather than being ossified and archaic, traditions are continually *reinvented* in a range of different contexts. As Pickering argues, 'when vibrant, traditions are always in the process of being recreated . . . and subject to evaluation in terms of what they bring to a contemporary situation' (2001: 105). For instance, as Thompson remarks, tradition has become 'deritualised' but is re-installed in contemporary societies in the media, which 'provides a form of temporal continuity which diminishes the need for re-enactment' of the ceremonial kind Hobsbawm and Ranger discuss (1995: 195). As I will discuss in greater detail in Chapter 3, although large-scale ceremonies frequently aim for fixity, this can be difficult to attain given that each performance needs to mimic exactly the previous, minutely detailed sequence of actions. Thus tradition can be dynamic, contested and claimed by different groups at different moments in time. And this has always been the case: to conceive of societies which precede modernity as 'traditional' is to reify the past, as if traditional rituals were endlessly replicated for centuries, denying improvisation, change and contestation. Given that tradition was not recorded in oral societies, it is hard to imagine that locally rooted tradition progressed without change (Giddens, 1994).

Benedict Anderson

Benedict Anderson also adopts a set of assumptions about culture in his famous notion that the nation can be considered an 'imagined community', united by a 'deep, horizontal comradeship' (1983: 7) whereby national co-fellows are believed to constitute a bounded, 'natural' entity. While some have complained that Anderson's focus on the imagined seems to ignore the socio-political realities of power and the organisational structures of the state, perhaps a more nuanced understanding is to consider that nations emerge out of contexts of social and cultural experience which are imaginatively conceived.

The key to Anderson's argument is the invention of the printing press and the subsequent rise of print media, which provided a technological means for the widespread dissemination of the idea of the nation. Anderson remarks that the regular, synchronic shared reading of the daily or weekly newspaper produced the idea that readers shared a set of interests – the content and focus of the news for instance – in which they were explicitly and implicitly addressed as co-nationals. The experience of the nation is rooted in the quotidian, for, as he pronounces, the newspaper bolsters the assumption that 'the imagined world is visibly rooted in everyday life' (ibid.: 36). This is very suggestive. Rather than the periodic displays of spectacle, the staging of tradition and the academic urge to classify races, customs and nature, this cultural process operates at a more mundane level. For the idea of what constitutes the 'national' interest is part of that which grounds national identity in unreflexive forms of 'common sense'.

I am much persuaded by Anderson's idea of the nation as imagined community. However, his excessive focus on literacy and printed media proffers a reductive view of culture. Whilst the historical importance of print is important, it is curious that there is no reference to the multiple ways in which the nation is imagined in, for instance, music hall and theatre, popular music, festivities, architecture, fashion, spaces of congregation, and in a plenitude of embodied habits and performances, not to mention more parallel cultural forms such as television, film, radio and information technology. For instance, as Barker says, 'imagining "us" as "one" is part of the process of nation building and there is no medium which has been able to speak to as many people in pursuit of that goal as television'. Citing a list of sporting events, political and royal ceremonies and soap operas, he argues that 'they all address me in my living room as part of a nation and situate me in the rhythms of a national calendar' (Barker, 1999: 5–6). Anderson's focus on the idea that the nation is reproduced and represented textually tends to efface the spatial, material and embodied production of communal identities. Although there is a tacit recognition that national culture is both popular and everyday, his analysis remains rooted in a historical perspective which reifies the sources (literature) through which the nation is (re)produced and thereby reduces the rich complexity of cultural production to one field.

Anthony Smith

Anthony Smith has been particularly critical of Hobsbawm's and Gellner's insistence on the modernity of nations. His argument is chiefly based upon the idea that nations are founded on, and emerge out of, pre-existing 'ethnies' – ethnic communities or groups – which shape the nation. This thesis is clearly based upon Barth's notion of ethnicity as a mode of distinguishing self from other, an ascription integral to the formation of boundaries. Ethnic symbols provide evidence which distinguishes 'us' from 'them'.

There is much that is useful in Smith's approach. He does not make the mistake of homogenising elites, acknowledging that the selection of national symbols is frequently the source of much conflict between different powerful groups. Furthermore, he maintains that there is no blueprint for constructing an official culture. For instance, he distinguishes between 'national' intellectuals organising a 'vernacular mobilisation' or an aristocratic elite perpetrating 'bureaucratic incorporation' as different forms of national cultural construction. There is also some subtlety in Smith's acknowledgement that where no common set of symbols seem apparent, it may be imperative to select 'multiple' symbols so that diverse groups may be encouraged to confirm their allegiance to the national project (Smith, 1998: 155). Thus certain nations must draw on a diverse selection of cultural resources to construct cultural 'common denominators' (Eriksen, 1998) whereas others are able to draw on a more generally shared set of resources. He also points out the historical inconsistencies where different ethnic traditions are brought together, and others are neglected or expunged. Yet importantly, he recognises that such cultural elements must be credible, must speak to common sense, if they are to be accepted by national subjects. There is, then, a suggestion that a national cultural hegemony must be *achieved*, must offer plausible points of identification, rather than being enforced by a cultural elite to whom a helpless mass is in thrall. Rather, such elites (re)construct 'a conceptual language within which members of pre-existing ethnic, linguistic or political communities could express a sense of their collective being' (Cubitt, 1998: 2).

Smith is explicit in his understanding of culture as 'both an inter-generational repository and heritage, or set of traditions, and an active shaping repertoire of meanings and images, embodied in values, myths and symbols that serve to unite a group of people with shared experiences and memories and differentiate them from outsiders' (1998: 187). It is useful that culture here is presented as dynamic. Although Smith perhaps downplays invention and the malleability of cultural symbols, he offers a version of national identity in which he identifies practical and discursive connections rather than primordial ancestry and enduring cultural commonalities.

Nevertheless, despite these virtues, the overwhelming focus on myths of common ancestry, shared historical memories, religious beliefs, customs and languages postulates a reductive view of culture. The huge emphasis placed on the ways in which language, traditions, emblems, festivals and sacred places epitomise continuity offers an overly historical approach which may well capture the processes undergone in some cases, but cannot account for the extremely dynamic and ambiguous contemporary constructions of national identity.

Smith almost seems to acknowledge this deficit, for he refers to a 'common, mass public culture' (1991: 14), more explicitly identifying a range of cultural elements such as capital cities, oaths, passports, national recreations, the country-side, popular heroes and heroines, forms of etiquette and 'all those distinctive customs, mores, styles and ways of acting and feeling that are shared by the members of a community' (ibid.: 77). This is a suggestive passage where, besides the official, customary and traditional collective symbols and practices, Smith refers to the popular and the everyday. Yet the emphasis in his work continues to be on the historical and the traditional and official. For instance, he asserts that 'national symbols, customs and ceremonies are the most potent and durable aspects of nationalism. They embody its basic concepts, making them visible and distinct for every member' (ibid.). This stress on the obviously identifiable, tangible, spectacular cultural effects obfuscates the everyday, taken for granted, cultural commonsensical practices as well as the popular forms circulated in a mass culture. This distortion also becomes clear when Smith talks of the key role of intellectuals in forging national cultures: they have a 'seminal position in generating and analysing the concepts, myths, symbols and ideology of nationalism' (ibid.: 94). These writers, classifiers, artists, historians and scholars and folklorists have no doubt contributed to official and high culture, to education systems and public exhibitions. But again, this over-stresses the role of high cultural arbiters. Partic-ularly in contemporary times, any identification of national cultures would have to include a range of other cultural producers – pop stars, advertisers, tabloid hacks, marketers, fashion-designers, film and television producers and sporting heroes – as well as a host of popular cultural practices including dancing, sports-spectatorship, common pastimes, holidaying and touring.

The cultural ingredients Smith recites certainly remain important elements in the constitution of national identities. But notions about forms of 'national genius', the indivisibility of the nation, and its authenticity, are now under stress as nations become more complex, mobile and culturally hybrid. The traditions now hold less weight. They have become part of popular mediascapes, are commodified, or become more diffused amongst competing groups.

John Hutchinson

Finally, I want to consider a more specific account of the relationship between culture and national identity in the work of John Hutchinson, who, partly to counter excessive political definitions of nationalism which often purvey an image of an instrumental, bureaucratic state elite, has put forward the contrary idea of *cultural* nationalism. Cultural nationalists, according to this formulation, generally seek a 'moral regeneration' (1994), although he links the emergence of such a movement as a tactical response to the thwarted aspirations of political nationalists – as a strategy to continue the battle by other means. The leaders of cultural nationalist movements are typically 'historical scholars and artists' rather than 'politicians or legislators' (1992: 110). He describes them as 'moral innovators' who rely on national media to spread their message, which typically stresses primordial myths, histories, traditions and rituals, geographies, natural histories and folksongs, to raise national sentiment and bring the diverse cultural parts of the nation together. Again, history is over-stressed: nations are 'creative personalities continually evolving in time, and it is to history that its members must return to discover the triumphs and tragedies that have formed them' (ibid.).

His most recent formulations draw a distinction between 'modernists' and 'ethno-symbolists'. The former espouse the idea that the creation of a (homogeneous) national culture is the work of an elite, instrumentally delineated and controlled, whilst the latter focus on the nation as historically constructed, 'embodied in myths, symbols and culture' (Hutchinson, 2001: 76). Ethno-symbolists – among which Hutchinson includes himself – again insist on the pre-modern, ethnic basis of the nation. The contrast is useful in that it provides a model (contra the 'modernists') which questions top-down versions of national cultural identity. However, Hutchinson's account again essentialises culture by foregrounding the historical elements. Moreover, culture is inferred to be used entirely for instrumental reasons, to overcome blocked political advancement and further the aims of nationalists.

Whilst all the writers discussed above have made significant contributions to the understanding of national identity, they are all guilty of several reductive assumptions about culture and its relationship with national identity. First of all, culture cannot be subsumed by that which is consciously wielded as symbolic, for it is ingrained in unreflexive patterns of social life, stitched into the experience and the assumptions of the everyday. There is an overwhelming emphasis on the spectacular and the historic. Secondly, the only kind of popular culture discussed is that identified as 'folk' culture – that is, pre-modern – and often considered as worthy in contradistinction to mass culture. Instead, 'high' and 'official' culture is assumed to be triumphant, and is uncritically absorbed by the masses. These national cultural values organised by a national elite, cultural guardians who alone delineate what is national, propose a top-down view of culture and wholly ignore popular and vernacular cultural forms and practices. There is little sense of contestation, alternative constructions and cultural dynamism. Thirdly, the accounts are far too historicist, generalising about national identity and disregarding contemporary formulations. Hobsbawm and Gellner overemphasise the modern cultural origins of nations, and Hobsbawm compounds this by misconceiving tradition as reified. Anderson's insights are never applied to contemporary forms of identification and Hutchinson understands cultural nationalism as a purely instrumental movement. However, there have recently been a number of accounts which have suggested that any contemporary analysis of national identity needs to address a different set of issues which are grounded in popular culture and the everyday. Most important amongst these has been Michael Billig's work, *Banal Nationalism* (1995).

Billig suggests that the 'whole complex of beliefs, assumptions, habits, representations and practices' (ibid.: 6) which (re)produce national identity are reproduced in the banal realm of the everyday as part of the 'endemic condition' of nations. Critiquing the obsession to comprehend national identity as only evident in spectacular displays, and at times of national crises like war – or that it is an 'extremist', 'irrational' manifestation of less 'civilised' places' – Billig maintains that 'the concept of nationalism has been restricted to passionate and exotic exemplars' (ibid.: 8), overlooking its routine and mundane reproduction. As a metaphor to conjure up this unspectacular reproduction, he refers to the 'unwaved flag' of the nation, to suggest the numerous signifiers and reminders of the nation that form part of everyday spaces, routines and practices, as opposed to that which is wielded during overt displays of nationalism. Crucially, this routine flagging is 'mindless' rather than consciously engaged in (ibid.: 41).

The reproduction of national identity, according to Billig, is grounded in the habitual assumptions about belonging that permeate the media, where the term 'we' is unreflexively used as a signifier of 'us' as members of the nation, by politicians, sports writers and broadcasters, and even academics. No qualification is needed in this routine deixis. It is assumed that we – the readers or viewers – are part of the nation – '*the*' economy, government, countryside is *our* economy, government, countryside. This constitutes part of the way in which nations are 'naturalised', absorbed into a common-sense view about *the way the world is*, and invested with moral values, which elevate the national over other social groupings. Moreover, it produces an unquestioned and unreflexive understanding that we live in a world of nations, which although it 'has been divided up into a hotchpotch of bizarrely shaped and sized entities' (ibid.: 23), and diverse political, ethnic and cultural forms which defy any classificatory logic, is considered to be part of the natural order of things, a 'universal code of particularity' (ibid.: 72–73). Yet it is surprising, given the rich suggestions he offers, that so few have taken up the invitation to explore nationalism and national identity in its mundane manifest-ations. Billig admits that his work is a preliminary study, and his focus on unreflexive linguistic practice in media, politics and academia neglects the material, spatial and performative dimensions of the everyday. This work has partly been undertaken to explore in more detail the characteristics of banal nationalism that Billig sketches.

I have been critical of seminal theories about nationalism and national identity because whilst they implicitly assert its importance, they marshal extremely reductive notions about culture. What is missing from the above accounts is a sense of the unspectacular, contemporary production of national identity through popular culture and in everyday life. The next two sections are intended to provide a grounding and an elaboration of these far from unproblematic terms, to anchor the themes I will later discuss.

Popular Culture and National Identity

'Traditional' cultural forms and practices of the nation are supplemented, and increasingly replaced in their affective power, by meanings, images and activities drawn from popular culture. I do not want to suggest that the tradition-bound ceremonies and other cultural ingredients which most analysts of national identity have concentrated on are now irrelevant, but that their power is now largely sustained by their (re)distribution through popular culture, where they mingle with innumerable other iconic cultural elements which signify the nation in multiple and contested ways. In order to shift the focus to an exploration of national identity as expressed and experienced through popular culture, we firstly need to define popular culture.

Discussions about *culture* have been bedevilled by an inability for theorists to agree on a common definition, for it has remained a fluid term. Culture continues to suggest a host of overlapping meanings: being 'cultured' in a sophisticated and knowledgeable fashion; a collective noun to describe to works of recognised artistic and intellectual endeavour hierarchically adjudged to have attained a particular level of value; a range of practical orientations in relatively circumscribed social spheres (for example, corporate culture, particular youth *sub*-cultures); and a common, particular way of life (Giles and Middleton, 1999: 10).

Cultural Studies emerged as a discipline to counter class-ridden assumptions that what was worthy of study was 'high culture' – in Matthew Arnold's (1960) terms, 'to make the best that has been known and thought in the world current everywhere', an aim motivated by the 'study of perfection'. Arnold's baton was taken up by F.R. Leavis, a huge influence in the early years of Cultural Studies, whose arguments have provoked much reaction. Despite his championing of 'high' culture, Leavis insisted on the necessity of studying 'mass', 'popular' culture in order to ascertain the harm he believed it was doing to the British nation. Advertisements, films, pulp fiction and other popular cultural forms needed to be interrogated to tease out the damaging hypnotic receptivity they perpetrated. These elements of mass culture were distinguished from an idealised 'folk' culture, which was conceived as embodying a spirit that kindled a sense of belonging, of knowing one's place in an organic world, a pre-urban *gemeinschaft* where one's identity was part of an ingrained and unquestioned way of being. The arguments of Leavis imply a necessity of a national guardianship over culture, and mobilise a particular view of England still familiar in nostalgic productions and ideologies.

Since Leavis's campaign on behalf of 'high' culture, the notion of *popular* culture has attracted a range of meanings – from that which is 'widely favoured or well liked by many people' (Storey, 1993: 7), to those inferior cultural forms and practices which are left over after 'high' culture has been identified, reinforcing the Leavisite boundary between 'good' and 'bad'. It has also been vilified as 'mass culture', invariably commercial and homogeneous, and carrying suggestions of the harmful hypnotic, addictive qualities identified by Leavis, but instead such critiques have come from the left, notably in the arguments of Adorno, Horkheimer and other members of the Frankfurt School. Briefly, the mechanised rhythms of pop music and the addictive qualities of popular fiction and film are seen as homologous to the patterns of work and leisure required under industrial capitalism. Furthermore, this mass culture further subdues the spirit and intelligence of the 'people' by the ideological messages it transmits, shaped around values which assert the benefits of materialism, glamour and individualism. Such culture, then, is *devised* to pacify the masses and accommodate them to the needs of capital. Whilst it seems foolish to deny the powerful impact of certain heavily promoted images, ideals and themes, such accounts reify and homogenise popular culture as inherently harmful. This completely ignores the changing and dynamic nature of popular culture, its protean characteristics, and recognises its production only in what are disparagingly called the 'culture industries', the commercial enterprises that sell culture to the masses. There is no sense of the vernacular production of culture, no notion that culture alters as it circulates through daily life. In the fluid network of the everyday, cultural meaning cannot be pinned down but is negotiated over, applied in wildly different contexts. New forms evolve, meanings are challenged, alternative uses are found for apparently hegemonic cultural material, and scraps are combined and reassembled. In a seminal paper, Hall (1980) highlights the ways in which culture is encoded and decoded, and subject to 'preferred', 'negotiated' and 'contesting' meanings. Yet even this is insufficient, for it suggest a rather instrumental use of cultural forms and practices which are often consumed in unreflexive or distracted fashion, which also, nevertheless, may confound the purposes to which they were intended.

As I have mentioned, in another formulation especially pertinent to the construction of national identity, *popular* has been considered to be that culture which is prevalent amongst the 'people'. Prominent here is the nostalgic celebration of folk cultures – a more valorised, seemingly 'authentic' collection of cultural forms and practices which are being erased by modern mass culture. Whether such ideas emanate from a conservative or radical milieu, the argument is laid down that such rooted, traditional culture reflects the true nature of the national or regional context in which it is set; it grows out of the area and reflects the cultural mores of its people, and is located firmly 'in place'. The idea of uncommercial, ritualised and time-honoured folk practices, as argued above, is largely mythical and fails to recognise the dynamism and syncretic nature of culture. And it also reifies it as historic so that the notion of folk tends to exclude new vernacular practices and styles of gardening, knitting, cooking, joking and telling stories.

Generally, these ideas about popular culture construct cultural producers as invariably motivated by commercial greed and a common ideological mission, an assumption which elides the varied motives and ideals of those involved in the culture industries, and their artistic independence. Moreover, rather than a conspiratorial science where producers plot how to conquer markets by persuading the masses to consume their products, making and marketing culture is an inexact science. For instance, record companies are unable to second-guess the tastes of consumers, as is indicated by the numerous failed investments which are made in unsuccessful artists and musical products. The 'hit record' remains an elusive prize.

It should be clear that the view I am criticising here resonates in the conceptions offered by Gellner, Hobsbawm, Hutchinson and Smith discussed above. To reiterate, the view of culture offered in most theories of national identity, though central to the debates, has almost completely concentrated on 'high' and 'official' cultures, presumably because popular culture has been considered to be trivial and shallow, or at least unconnected with questions of national identity. However, the threat to national identity by 'mass' culture has been a frequently aired concern in other accounts, where all too often 'mass culture is synonymous with American culture. The colonising power of 'Americanisation' and the belief that it is displacing authentic folk culture or communally oriented 'working class' culture (for instance, as argued by Richard Hoggart in his famous *The Uses Of Literacy*, 1971) conceives of American popular culture as inherently colonising. Of course, studies since have shown the picture to be far more complex, including those which have explored how the TV series *Dallas*, a programme seemingly indelibly marked by American mores, fantasies and style, has been domesticated and utilised according to widely varying contexts of reception and consumption (Ang, 1995; Liebes and Katz, 1990). Without lurching into a rather uncritical, cultural populist celebration of the everyday subversions perpetrated by the weak, as in the work of writers such as Fiske (1989) and Willis (1990), it is important to consider the cultural contexts which constrain and enable interpretations and uses of particular cultural products.

National elites, governments and patricians continue to perpetrate the idea that 'high' culture is something that the nation must be associated with, as a form of international prestige. The national badges of high culture – national galleries, opera houses and international concert halls, national theatres, learned societies and high cultural institutions – remain marks of status. Governments are often happy to lavish funds on such cultural flagships. Yet whilst such institutions remain at the heart of statist versions of national self-image, they have been unable to retain their hierarchical pre-eminence. For the decentring of high cultures has resulted from the 'endowing of an increasing range of activities and cultural fields with national significance' (Cubitt, 1998: 14). The international success of popular writers, film-makers, television stars and sporting heroes has ensured their place in the pantheon of nationally important achievers. As I write, the British tabloid press have been celebrating the success of Anne Robinson, presenter of television quiz show *The Weakest Link*, in fronting an exported version of the programme in the USA. Other examples include pride at the international acclaim bestowed on Indian novelist Arundhati Roy, and the fame brought to Croatia by their football team and tennis champion Goran Ivanisevic.

In fact, many nations now are riven with debates over the relevance of high culture and the cultural guardians who support and represent it. For instance, in the UK and the USA there are ongoing disputes over the content of national education curricula concerning whether there can be anything resembling a national literary canon. In the UK, a furore broke out over a recent decision to grant a huge governmental subsidy to the Royal Opera House yet the Labour government also allied itself with the pop phenomena known as 'Cool Britannia'. Such challenges to high culture are countered by the widespread fear that there is a cultural 'dumbing down'. The argument is too complex and multifaceted to go into here, but the controversies over cultural and educational policy highlight the insecurity of the bastions of high culture resulting from the challenge to the notion that the treasures they elevate and guard epitomise cultural quality and authority. In fact, as Featherstone (1991) has written, the values expressed by the old cultural guardians have been challenged by what he terms the 'new cultural intermediaries', a contemporary fraction of the middle class who possess knowledge of pop music, film, and other manifestations of popular culture, and claim status on the basis of this expertise. Thus the national-cultural terrain is now characterised by a plethora of interest groups, 'experts' and aficionados who champion a bewildering range of cultural forms and practices

In this cultural contestation, where the formerly despised has been reconceived as valuable, what is important, as McGuigan points out, is not the rarefied aesthetic debates about quality and cultural values of certain cultural forms vis-à-vis others, but 'the sociality of value' (1997: 146). Whereas previously assertions about the superiority of 'high' over 'low' culture might have persisted, now popular culture itself has become a prime site for contestations of value embedded deep within fields such as television and film criticism, popular music and 'modern' art. There are constant attempts to achieve a hierarchical status through battles for distinction between 'pop' and 'rock' fans, or viewers of 'quality' drama and soap opera enthusiasts. A further complicating factor has been the increasing commercial-isation of culture, formerly assumed to be rampant in the vilified realm of the popular but now extended across cultural fields. Frow goes as far as to argue that high culture is no longer the dominant culture but 'is rather a *pocket* within commodity culture' (1995: 86). It seems unlikely that the British television series *Civilisation*, made and presented by patrician Kenneth Clark, would be able to make the kind of uncontested claims about the irrefutable cultural superiority of the classical art works he chose, or indeed that such a programme espousing cultural authority whilst addressing the nation would be made. For forms of cultural authority have multiplied and fragmented, and can no longer masquerade as being of national importance.

At the level of the nation, the debate becomes even more intense. A national(ist) imperative has been to bring together different regional and ethnic differences by identifying national high cultural points as common denominators, relying on elite cultural arbiters to make these selections and distinctions. However, increasingly, the state must arbitrate between different lobbyists and adherents of education strategy, of artistic movements, of sporting provision and of festivals and decide where funds should be provided. In doing so, it must rank the tastes and desires of particular classes, ethnic groups, regions and so on – all in contradiction of the spirit that the nation is best imagined as a composite or the notion that valuable ('high') culture is clearly identifiable.

Perhaps we might assess cultural value by the *utility* of cultural forms, especially those which lend themselves to a multitude of different uses in a pluralistic, multicultural society. This emphasises the practical application of particular forms, and the ways in which they can be used in the ongoing construction of meaning. While perhaps this suggests an undue degree of instrumentality, it captures the multiple uses and ever-changing notions which centre upon certain cultural forms, and testify to their symbolic flexibility. The ambivalence which emerges out of the dialogue and contestation over such cultural forms stresses that the power of such symbols lies not in any fixed meaning they may carry but in the fact that they are widely shared. However, as I will continually emphasise, the very production of ambivalence leads to a counter tendency to fix the meaning of time-honoured, popular symbols and thus cultural identity.

It might seem that if I am arguing that there is no longer any dividing line between popular/low/folk culture and high culture, that I am negating the very notion of popular culture. I do not want to reinforce any dichotomy between high and low culture but rather focus upon those cultural forms and practices which have commonly been regarded as 'popular'. However, I want to draw out certain features that the term 'popular' conveys to show how the cultural ingredients of national identity are increasingly mediated, polysemic, contested and subject to change. If we concentrate on those cultural elements commonly ascribed as popular, it will be clear that formations of national identity utilise a huge and proliferating resource that has emerged with the decentring of official, 'high' culture, so that cultural guardianship is no longer such an important feature of national culture (and it was never as important as has been claimed). For culture is not fixed but negotiated, the subject of dialogue and creativity, influenced by the contexts in which it is produced and used. A sense of national identity then is not a once and for all thing, but is dynamic and dialogic, found in the constellations of a huge cultural matrix of images, ideas, spaces, things, discourses and practices

The multiple, changing and contesting meanings that surround popular cultural forms and practices contrasts with a national identity that is commonly presented as 'weighted towards "heritage" and the "common past" rather than to the "common future", or . . . even . . . the "common present"' (Roche, 2000: 75). This temporal cul-de-sac has bedevilled accounts of national identity which have ignored the things we watch and read, the places we visit, the things we buy and the pictures we display. Popular culture, then, has subsumed and represented, reformulated and reproduced cultural forms in a process of 'de-differentiation' (Lash, 1990) so that forms of national cultural authority are no longer clearly identifiable.

Everyday Life and National Identity

Thus far, I have argued that writers and researchers on national identity tend to draw attention to the spectacular, the 'traditional' and the official. However, it is part of my contention in this book, following Billig's notion of 'banal nationalism', that besides these overt displays and self-conscious cultural assertions, national identity is grounded in the everyday, in the mundane details of social interaction, habits, routines and practical knowledge. It is startling how, more generally, theorists of identity have neglected the quotidian realms experienced most of the time by most people, since it is here that identity is continually reproduced in unreflexive fashion (although recently, a few attempts to theorise the mundane reproduction of national identity have been published; for instance, see Palmer, 1998; Thompson, 2001). The everyday basis of national identity is aptly drawn out by Mary Chamberlain, in discussing Caribbean migrants to Britain:

migrant lives were prosaic, concerned with the daily round of work, home and family. Perhaps it is precisely in the mundane that the culture of migration can be observed for it is within the everyday, within the family and the workplace, the home or the street, that family values and cultural practices are transmitted, contested, transformed and where identities evolve. (1999: 260)

Perhaps part of the problem in defining the everyday is that it is too apparent; by virtue of its 'second nature' it does not readily lend itself to analysis, and is commonly assumed to be uninteresting by social theorists. Perhaps this is precisely why we might consider the everyday to be important and interesting, since it reflects a widespread understanding, no less shared by academics, that we can take the quotidian much for granted. Apparently, its low-key, humdrum passage does not contain the exciting moments in which decisions are made, identities enacted and displayed. Because the everyday tends to be contrasted with the time of celebrity, of holidays, of exceptional and symbolic events, it is believed to be static: little changes during the playing out of repetitive acts necessary to sustain reproduction. Change occurs on a grander stage. However, I argue that the everyday is far more dynamic than this complacent view suggests, whilst at the same time it also contains enduring consistencies through which identity is grounded.

When we consider that there have been several important accounts of the importance of temporal schemes to the construction of national identity, it is all the more curious that the everyday has not been considered. In the era of romantic nationalism, the idea that national origins are lost in the mists of time was proposed, constructing nations as primordial. On the other hand, modernist national projects also adopt temporal notions which assert that nations are constantly in the process of becoming, whether construed as industrial, technological or social progress. Indeed, the process of identification whereby boundaries are drawn and 'others' constructed can be seen to strike these modernising chords. For instance, colonising nations frequently compared themselves with the places they colonised. Because they were asserted to be both rooted in history and in the process of developing modern characteristics, colonial missions and colonising adventures could be justified. For those being colonised were conceived to be suffering from a historical lack and therefore were bereft of any hope for the future. They were 'the people without history' (Wolf, 1982) who dwelt in 'the time of the other' (Fabian, 1983). Such representations continue to resonate through Western popular culture as well as in debates within development studies, anthropology and political economy, whilst previously colonised nations aim to recapture pre-colonial glories through modernisation policies.

Thus the primordial origins of nations and their future orientation, the idea of being and becoming, are neatly brought together by the idea that nations may become that which they once were in some mythical 'golden age'. Tom Nairn (1977) talks of the 'janus face' of the nation, simultaneously looking backwards and forwards, and Homi Bhabha (1990) similarly proffers the national(ist) sense of 'double time' in the focus on the past and the future. As is abundantly clear, these temporal conceptions ignore the present; most specifically, they neglect the everyday, which I will show is equally important in establishing a sense of national identity. We need to supplement ideas about the time of the nation with a renewed focus on cyclical time – that which reproduces identity and sustains 'our way of life'. The flux of life, the speed of change, particularly in contemporary times, means that a need for stability is sought, a degree of fixity and sense of belonging, that enables some purchase on the world to be gained. This terra firma is achieved and established in the realm of the everyday as much as in the appeals of ideologues to the immemorial traditions that national subjects supposedly share.

Despite the lack of attention towards the everyday, certain theoretical insights enable us to develop a critical approach to the ways in which identities are reproduced, mutate and are challenged. Raymond Williams's assertion, 'culture is ordinary', is often approvingly quoted by cultural theorists. Williams develops this assertion, reasoning that 'culture' describes a particular way of life 'which expresses certain meanings and values not only in art and learning but also in institutions and *ordinary behaviour*' (1961: 57, my italics). Ordinary, everyday life is perhaps most appositely captured in Williams's notion of the 'structure of feeling', a potentially rich concept, if rather vague. Williams describes the structure of feeling as 'firm and definite as "structure" suggests, yet it operates in the most delicate and least tangible parts of our activity' (ibid.: 63). In one sense, this structure of feeling is the culture of a period: it is 'the particular living result of all the elements in the general organisation'. The emphasis on the 'least tangible' is important here, as I have inferred.

A structure of feeling seems to suggest a communal way of seeing the world in consistent terms, sharing a host of reference points which provide the basis for everyday discourse and action. This resonates with Hall's definition of culture as partly 'the contradictory forms of common sense which have taken root in and helped to shape popular life' (1996a: 439). When people share similar habits, assumptions and routines, and when a reflexive sense evolves that this is a recognisable shared pattern and is intersubjectively communicated, this the 'beginning of institutionalisation' (Jenkins, 1996: 128). Institutionalisation can be understood in two senses: firstly, as the property of particular organisations; secondly, as the organisation of everyday life, and the solidification of everyday practical knowledge and value. In both cases, predictability is installed and bodies, things and spaces become subject to ordering processes. And the small everyday orderings can be subsumed under larger national orderings, merging the local with the national. Moreover, the persistence of such common patterns over time underpins a common sense that this is *how things are* and this is *how we do things*. There is thus an interweaving of conscious and unreflexive thought which typifies everyday practice and communication. Most actions are habitually (re)enacted without reflection, but occasionally they are subject to surveillance from community members, or to self-monitoring to ensure consistency and the upholding of values and practical norms.

The notion of structure may be somewhat problematic – perhaps a more processual noun is required – as is Williams's emphasis on class – one might also talk about gendered, ethnic or sexual structures of feeling. Another useful dimension of Williams's argument is that he allows for change and contestation, although as Swingewood (1998: 81) notes, this competition is generationally oriented – that is, the general cultural pattern changes as younger generations react against parent cultures. Williams also offers a dynamic reading of culture where 'dominant', 'residual' and 'emergent' cultures co-exist and compete (1981: 204–205), although the interpenetration of such categories might be more fluid than he surmises. Moreover, as I will continue to stress, a shared sense of feeling need not mean that there is common accord, rather that certain objects, concepts and symbols are shared but used and interpreted in different ways. Nevertheless, we can identify shared meanings, habits, rituals and ways of speaking which comprise resources that facilitate communication and establish a sense of national belonging. Such resources combine affective and cognitive appeal, are grounded in spatial, material, performative and representational dimensions of everyday life. I will explore this in Chapter 3 by considering whether there are identifiable forms of national habitus.

I want to consider how there might be national structures of feeling. Thus I argue that the national is constituted and reproduced, contested and reaffirmed in everyday life, and each chapter will focus on these often unreflexive identifications. In a very practical sense, national identity is facilitated by the state's legislative framework, which delimits and regulates the practices in which people can partake, the spaces in which they are permitted to move, and in many other ways provides a framework for quotidian experience. The state lays down broadcast regulations, employment rights, environmental measures, the paying of taxes, parking laws, the national education curriculum, and so on. The state is thus responsible for enforcing and prioritising specific forms of conduct, of inducing particular kinds of learning experiences, and regulating certain 'good' habits amongst its citizens. But in addition to this legal, bureaucratic framework there are familiar places and generic landscapes, which I will turn to in Chapter 2; there are a multitude of shared conventions, habits and enactions, which I will look at in Chapter 3; there are a plethora of familiar commonly used objects in households, communal spaces and in the world of commodities which constitute material commonplaces amongst national subjects, which I focus on in Chapter 4; and there are shared narratives and representations which circulate throughout quotidian life, in the media, in convivial talk and in politics, as I will show in Chapter 5. These numerous cultural forms and practices provide an epistemological and ontological basis which foregrounds the nation as a hegemonic, common-sense entity.

Of course, one could equally focus on the reproduction of locality, gender, ethnicity, class and sexuality in everyday realms, which may predominate according to time and place. Here the focus is on national identity, and yet other modes of quotidian identification are invariably imbricated within routine ways of being national. For instance, as Felski (1999) has pointed out, the everyday tends to be associated more with women then men. Men go out into the world to adventure, to engage in what Featherstone terms 'the heroic life' (1992). Women are entrusted with the more mundane responsibility of the daily upkeep of the household, and, moreover, are (in a biologically determinist assumption) related more to 'natural' cyclical temporalities through menstruation. In terms of the nation, these suppositions mesh with the reproductive roles assigned to women in rearing future national subjects (the national 'race') and also as transmitters of culture via their everyday expertise in imparting values to children, cooking and housekeeping.

As far as local quotidian worlds are concerned, it is necessary to connect them with nationally shaped cultures, to recognise the ways in which national identity is differently *scaled*. Local rhythms are often co-ordinated and synchronised with national rhythms, local customs may be considered part of a national cultural mosaic, national institutions penetrate local worlds, and national news systems collect information from the localities which make up the nation. There are multiple, overlapping networks of experience, and the interpenetration of domestic, local and national processes produces moments of dissonance, also occasioning mutual reinforcement where domestic life slides into the local, which in turn merges with the national. This interrelational process shapes shared sentiments and sensations, forms of common sense, and widely disseminated representations to provide a matrix of dense signification.

Throughout this book I will elucidate the unreflexive construction of national identity, its embeddedness in the everyday, by looking at how reflexive awareness can result from disruption – either by forms of common sense being interrogated by strangers or migrants, by familiar spaces, things and practices coming under threat from social and economic change, and most graphically by the habituated, embodied national subject being displaced or situated in an unfamiliar context. The following anecdote hopefully introduces the disorientations that testify to the power of ingrained, embodied, unreflexive nationally constituted identity.

During my first visit to India some years ago I stayed at a small village in Gujarat for six weeks. Having no experience of travelling outside Europe at this time, I was continually struck by what seemed like the radical difference of everything at an everyday level. The sounds of the buffalo, unfamiliar birdsong, agricultural machinery, and other unidentifiable noises provided a completely different soundscape to any that I recognised. The rich smellscape combining dung, dust and incense and other powerful unidentifiable aromas was similarly strange. And the taste and texture of the food, the heat and the 'atmosphere' added to the sense of unreality. Domestic arrangements were equally unfathomable. The house's interior was undecorated and functional to my eyes, and it served as a thoroughfare for the family who lived in a dwelling behind, as well as for anyone else who happened to be passing. For instance, my sense of private space was confounded by the grandmother from next door coming to sleep on the bed whenever she wanted to in order to seek refuge from her family. Many social interactions were impossible for me to read, even to make assumptions about. The familiar caste structures in the village were a mystery, although they formed part of the everyday understanding of the villagers. Forms of know-how I wielded comfortably and unreflexively at home were out of place here and were subject to mocking laughter from village children. To cook, wash and shop required a certain amount of coaching and advice. How should I eat, make small talk, laugh and sit? I could extend this account, but I have tried to indicate the levels of unfamiliarity and how virtually all my everyday, unreflexive enactions and assumptions, habits and sensations were rendered out of place in the everyday world of others.

Now it might seem as if I have just written a rather conservative account of otherness, of my intrepid adventures in a spectacularly different and indelibly inaccessible realm. But the point I want to draw out is how habituated are an enormous range of understandings, practical actions, sensations and embodied habits which are grounded in familiar milieus. In such situations, what is usually unreflexive is dramatically brought to the surface, is rendered irrelevant or impractical. And potentially this has the effect of revealing the fixtures and contexts of identity, its cultural and spatial location. The familiar settings, the cornerstones of everyday situatedness, are realised as not so much natural as cultural, raising questions about what is the normal way of being and doing. Part of what constitutes this difference, and what enables us to distinguish it from our way of life, is the national context – in the case cited above, the Indianness, as well as village-ness, of the situation. For there is a continuum of familiarity which stretches from the local to the national, so that even if such rural settings are unfamiliar to Indian city dwellers, for instance, they will probably be partly cognisant of modes of social interaction, will have seen a great number of representations of rural settings in a range of cultural forms, will probably be familiar with tales of village life and have met rural compatriots.

Nevertheless, I should add that what initially appeared intensely peculiar about the village became embodied and enmeshed in a new sense of everyday-ness, so that the reflexivity engendered by unfamiliarity dissipated to be replaced by modified habits and procedures. This is well exemplified by the ways in which the disruption to the familiar habits of everyday life caused by migration can lead to their reinstatement, often in 'purified' form, in new national contexts, as I will discuss in Chapter 2. Similarly, attempts to exclude incomers or ethnic groups from sharing national identity also often hinge on the threats perceived by habits:

ways of cooking, clothing, working, talking, moving, as well as the fears dramatised by unfamiliar forms of popular culture such as music and films.

To conclude this section, I want to question the suggestion that everyday life is inherently conservative and inimical to (revolutionary) change. Marxist writers have argued that the everyday realm suffers from the institutionalisation of human degradation under industrial capitalism, enforcing rhythms which pacify subjects, who thereby organise their lives around regressive forms of common sense. Likewise, modernist art has often attempted to jolt people out of what is often regarded as hypnotic drudgery and uncritical attitudes installed by habits. Another manifestation of the critique of everyday life is exemplified in the current academic celebration of nomadism and fluidity which can potentially disrupt an established domestic and routinised life.

However, everyday life is not merely full of robotic and rigid praxes but contains a multitude of other potentialities. According to Gardiner, the everyday is also 'polydimensional: fluid, ambivalent and labile' (2000: 6). Citing Lefebvre, Bakhtin and de Certeau, and the actions and manifestos of surrealists and situationists, he shows that the everyday contains 'redemptive moments that point towards transfigured and liberated social existence', and it possesses 'transgressive, sensual and incandescent qualities' (ibid.: 208). Likewise, Harrison says that 'in the everyday enactment of the world there is always immanent potential for new possibilities of life' (2000: 498). This emergent quotidian process is open-ended, fluid and generative, concerns becoming rather than being, and is a sensual form of experiencing and understanding that is 'constantly attaching, weaving and disconnecting; constantly mutating and creating' (ibid.: 502). Thus the immanent experience of the everyday – daydreams, disruptions and sensual intrusions – constantly threatens to undermine the structure laid down by habit. According to Gardiner, we should be attuned to 'the transgressive, sensual and incandescent qualities of everyday existence, whereby the entire fabric of daily life can take on a festive hue and be considered akin to a "work of art"' (2000: 208). Clearly, we need to recognise the patterns laid down in the everyday without forming a restrictive view concerning the potential for change, for the contemporary dynamism of national identity is embedded in everyday life, changing subtly as well as dramatically.

Conceptualising Identity

Having discussed popular culture and everyday life, it is now time to focus on the notion of identity, particularly insofar as it is articulated with ideas about national belonging. The focus on identity in this book stresses the ways in which it is shaped through shared points of commonality in popular culture and in its grounding in everyday life, but it is necessary to briefly cover some pertinent theoretical issues that have emerged in recent years in order to establish a stronger foundation for the forthcoming chapters. There has been an outpouring of writing on the concept of identity in recent sociological and cultural studies publications (for example, Giddens, 1991; Hall and du Gay, 1996; Sarup, 1996; du Gay *et al.*, 2000). The term has proved to be a potent tool through which to explore diverse social and cultural transformations across political, economic, gendered, ethnic, work and leisure, sexual and local spheres. Yet national identity has remained rather immune from these explorations, testifying to its assumed naturalness even amongst social and cultural theorists. This is despite the fact that, as Cubitt emphasises, 'we live in a nationalised world. The concept of the nation is central to the dominant understandings both of political community and of personal identity' (1998: 1).

Drawing Boundaries: Inclusive and Exclusive National Identities

We distinguish between ourselves and others at a collective and individual level, and express, feel and embody a sense of national identity. In modern times, the nation has been a focus for identification and a sense of belonging, and persists as such. Here I want to argue that the dichotomy between social and individual identities is not helpful, and rather than being understood as distinctive entities should be conceived as utterly entangled, for individual identity depends on thinking with social tools and acting in social ways, whether reflexively or unreflexively. This also helps to understand that identity is a process, not an essence, which is continually being remade in consistent ways, through an 'internal–external dialectic' involving a simultaneous synthesis of internal self-definition and one's ascription by others (Jenkins, 1996: 20). As I have already inferred, the dynamic process of identity formation, or identification, occurs in mundane life as well as in more spectacular collective gatherings, in the enaction of practical knowledge as much as in the overt assertion or celebration of communal values and character-istics, which are equally part of a larger social dimension of experience, thought and action. Identity, as Sarup asserts, is a 'mediating concept between the external and the internal, the individual and society . . . a convenient tool through which to understand many aspects – personal, philosophical, political – of our lives' (1996: 28). Crucially then, national identity, like other identities, is about using 'resources of history, language and culture in the process of becoming rather than being: not "who we are" or "where we came from", so much as what we might become' (Hall, 1996b: 4). Nevertheless, essentialised notions about who 'we' are as opposed to 'them' can proffer exclusive national identities in contrast to more ambiguous inclusive formulations.

A key element of the process of identification – especially in the case of national identity – which will be recurrently exemplified throughout this book, is the drawing of boundaries between self and 'other'. For identity is conceivable through identifying difference, but, again, this is an ongoing process of identification rather then the reified continuation of absolute antipathy, even if it involves the same others continuously being distinguished from the self. Unlike recent formations of identity which engender a more contingent, reflexive approach to the construction of subjectivity – such as New Social Movements and New Age groups with their emphasis on self-actualisation and the promotion of reflexive tools – national identity is often sought to protect oneself from the anxiety of uncertainty, as Craib puts it, by 'closing down internal space' (1998: 170–171). This can involve an overdetermination of the other which clearly reflects how it is constitutive of the self – of the expulsion of that which it fears and the suppression of that which it desires. It is worth exploring, then, the boundary-making processes which operate within national identities, ways of delineating who and who does not belong to the nation, for battles over exclusion and inclusion are always ongoing.

Authoritative, exclusive versions of identity have been perpetrated by the selection of national 'high' cultures in assertions about cultural value. And as I have inferred above, a common way of defining who belongs is by drawing attention to what are often asserted to be 'key' cultural similarities and differences, notably by distinguishing habits and everyday practices, and tastes in popular culture. But sometimes the treatment of 'difference' involves the selective incorporation of local, regional and other differences within the nation, a process whereby difference is represented as the variety inherent in unity. What is admitted into national belonging varies enormously, but it seems as if Western secular nations are increasingly required to stretch notions of cultural inclusion to incorporate those previously regarded as other. Thus national identity is in reality 'cross-cut by deep internal divisions differences, and "unified" only though the exercise of different forms of cultural power' (Hall, 1992: 68) to provide an illusion of commonality. Thus religion, ethnicity and culture are utilised to assign in-group similarities and the differences of others.

Attempts to draw boundaries may mobilise reified notions of history and roots, cultural traditions, and often exploit popular symbolic images, rituals, sites and objects. In a world of multiple others boundary drawing becomes difficult, and must reify difference, essentialise and fix it as rooted in space and for all time. Sarup argues that this has increasingly produced an 'entropic' obsession with the past and fixed cultural aspects (1996: 98). But the mobilisation of such symbols is usually fraught with complexity, for they increasingly tend to be highly adaptable, can stand for competing identities and meanings. Thus attempts to exclude by brandishing particular cultural symbols can coincide with more inclusive manifest-ations which use those same symbols. For instance, the British flag (Union Jack) has been brandished by unthinking patriots as a symbol which connotes imperial power, tradition and national pride, most evidently by the far right groups, the

British National Party and the National Front in the assertion of exclusionist, racist policies. But it has also been adopted by anti-authoritarian youth subcultures, notably mods, and was wielded in the 1960s to convey progressive modishness, an iconic practice rehashed by the late 1990s Britpop music scene. Thus the Union Jack has become both traditional and fashionable, spanning contrary desires to keep things the same and transcend tradition. Racist England football fans waved it as they sang 'Stand up if you won the war' during the 2000 World Cup defeat by Germany, but the flag was also waved at the recent Sydney Olympics by victorious black British athletes. This display of patriotism perhaps partly echoes Roland Barthes famous description of a 'negro' soldier saluting the French flag, ideologically signifying a supposedly non-racist France (1993: 116–117). Some commentators argue that the flag is irredeemably tainted by this exclusive nationalism, but I would argue that it is a mythic, polysemic symbol which is used to transmit very diverse meanings and qualities. I will point out similar condensation symbols throughout this book; iconic places, objects, rituals and heroes which are used to establish national(ist) boundaries but are liable to be claimed and employed by other groups. Herein lies the power of such cultural symbols – ideas about their import may be shared, but they can be claimed by a multitude of different identities for various purposes.

In some cases, it seems as if essentialist attempts to draw cultural boundaries between inhabitants of different nations have never been more tenuous. This fragility is particularly evident in the drawing up of national cultural policies. An interesting development in this area has been a series of recent debates around the idea of 'cultural citizenship' and 'cultural rights'. As Stevenson asserts, it has been the 'remit of cultural racism to argue that access to citizenship criteria depends upon particular cultural persuasions' (2001a: 1). To counter this, it is envisaged that cultural rights could be legally identified. The right to cultural difference and its parameters within a national context raises the right to carry out non-majoritarian cultural practices and the necessity of respecting those of others. Here, then, the codes of cultural and civic normality are being challenged by more inclusive versions of cultural belonging which 'seek to rework images, assumptions and representations that are seen to be exclusive as well as marginalising' (ibid.: 3). Stevenson fleshes out the notion of cultural rights by citing inclusive policies designed to facilitate equal access to cultural resources, via public education and media (ibid.). In such instances, the state provides spheres of communication such as public spaces, public events, media forums, educational and experimental spaces, and generates the dialogic conditions necessary to mutual respect for difference and opportunities for creative initiatives.

The proliferation of claims for inclusion within a cultural rights and citizenship agenda by disability groups, gays and lesbians, ethnic groups, women, third-age organisations and youths (all in Stevenson, 2001b) resounds with the advances made through identity politics which challenge the centrality of exclusive national identities. In an interesting example, Roche argues that in the case of Britain membership of the European Community has the potential to erode defensive cultural nationalism, particularly through an interweaving of popular culture at a European level. He argues that this is already happening through the development of particular forms of media, constructions of a common European heritage (through shared experience of world wars, for example), and especially through sport, notably football. European football competitions threaten the centrality of national contests, large numbers of professional players increasingly hail from outside the nation in which they play, and media enterprises extend their coverage of these European games. Each of these processes is subject to defensive reactions which lament the dilution of national characteristics of football and the disembedding of the game from localities and nations (Roche, 2000: 89–90). Even the British government has ensured that certain national symbolic events must remain broadcast by terrestrial television (ibid.: 92), flagging up and safeguarding that which is 'traditionally' consumed within a national sphere. Lifestyles seem to be evolving which are based on a wider notion of sociality and consumer choice and taste than can be confined by the national, so that the formation of 'multiple forms of identity within Europe' (Urry, 1995: 165) is potentially encouraged.

National Identity in the Global Cultural Matrix

Theories concerned with accounting for the changing conditions generated by globalisation, or those heralding a postmodern epoch, have focused on the decentring of identity, in contradistinction to previously bounded, coherent modern identities – like national identity – which are being superseded. Greater social and actual mobility, the fragmentation of classes, the growing importance of consumption and the rise of 'identity politics' have increasingly influenced identity formation. This has been accompanied by theoretical frameworks which emphasise linguistic, Foucauldian, psychoanalytical, feminist and deconstructive approaches which decentre assumptions about the formation of subjectivity (Hall, 1992). Moreover, supposedly mobile identities increasingly move promiscuously across various sites, amongst different people, and in diverse cultural contexts. Thus identities are 'increasingly fragmented and fractured; never singular but multiply constructed across different, often intersecting and antagonistic, discourses, practices and positions' (Hall, 1996b: 4). Old notions about identities being embedded in place or self-evidently belonging to particular (national) cultures and societies seem to be repudiated by vast, expanding cultural networks. Group and individual identifications are thus becoming stretched out in proliferating locations in diasporic, political, and cyber networks. Thus identity is becoming nationally deterritorialised, and locally and globally, even virtually, reterritorialised. Such fluidity seems to be mirrored in popular culture, where iconic figures such as Madonna and Michael Jackson apparently possess mutable identities. Moreover, television becomes more the site of multiple channels originating from local, national and global sources, far different from the days when a limited number of national channels were on offer (Barker, 1999: 7).

It may appear, then, that national identity is a waning force. Yet there are several reasons why this is not quite so. Firstly, the apparent fluidity of identity and the lack of spatial and cultural fixity can provide a discursive and affective focus for reclaiming a sense of situatedness. Any sense of uncertainty requires that terra firma be sought, and national identity provides an already existing point of anchorage. Fears like these provide fertile ground for recursive political nationalists to capitalise upon, for the threat of fully decentred identities might seem to lead to epistemological chaos. Thus regularities and consistencies help to secure a sense of social belonging. Yet if we accept that we also live in an era where subjects are endowed with enhanced reflexivity (Giddens, 1991), then perhaps such awareness means that identity has to be recreated continuously to achieve what Gilroy calls the 'changing same' (1994). This interweaves with wider socio-economic processes, where, for instance, in a globalising world, it is imperative for states to attract capital (as it is for regions, cities and localities) by broadcasting their specialisms, by advertising their specific national wares on the global market. Cultural identity is also reconstituted in global consumer culture, where the exchange of commodities and information about them all 'draw on and add to existing imageries of people and places' (Cook and Crang, 1996).

Secondly, and importantly for the argument advanced in this book, identity is not necessarily, or even mainly, shaped by reflexive, self-conscious identification, but, as I emphasised earlier, by 'second nature', the barely conscious set of assumptions about the way 'we' think and act. There is a theoretical overemphasis on strategic instrumental jockeying for position in a continual battle to express identity. This is akin to what Craib describes as the ways in which sociologists have neglected 'experience'. In these sociological conceptions, 'cognition dominates people's lives, that we only have ideas, and those ideas come to us from outside, from the social world' (Craib, 1998: 1). Instead, there is the 'unthought known', 'the precognitive and extra-cognitive knowledge' which is partly affect, the feel of things, embodied sensual experience, and which when it enters into consciousness, often 'comes as a surprise' (ibid.: 10) but is nevertheless part of a fundamental emotional subjectivity which grounds identity in shared, unreflexive feelings. As I have argued, and will exemplify throughout this book, these unreflexive bases of identity are often realised only in conditions of disruption or dislocation.

Thirdly, in their endeavours to construct the postmodern condition, many theorists have tended to neglect the continuities which tether identities in time and space, continuities which paradoxically mutate and hybridise but can nevertheless be identified by discursive themes and practical consistencies. In everyday life looms the national, a common-sense framework which provides a certain ontological and epistemological security, a geographical and historical mooring, and a legal, political and institutional complex which incorporates (and excludes) individuals as national subjects. A wealth of shared cultural resources complement this array of consistencies. In fact, this framework supplies a highly flexible resource which can accommodate multiple national identifications, so that proliferating identities can be contained within, as well as outside the nation – an obvious point but an important one. National identity does not equate with homogeneity; nor is it inherently defensive, conservative or tradition-bound. There are a multitude of social and political investments in the nation, across political spectra, ethnicity and class, for as a process, identity may weave cultural resources into its constitution according to contingency, as I will show.

Globalisation promotes the mutation of national identity resulting from 'the imposition of the conceptual grid of nationality on exchanges and interactions in the global arena' (Cubitt, 1998: 14). For instance, I will discuss in Chapter 5 how images and narratives of nations circulate globally but can be reclaimed and worked over anew. It is also apparent that national identity has become detached from the nation-state, proliferates in diasporic settings far from its original home, appears in syncretic cultural forms and practices and exists in 'hyphenated' identities. Thus globalisation and national identity should not be conceived in binary terms but as two inextricably interlinked processes. Global processes might diminish a sense of national identity or reinforce it. However, as global cultural flows become more extensive, they facilitate the expansion of national identities and also provide cultural resources which can be domesticated, enfolded within popular and everyday national cultures.

Identity is always in process, is always being reconstituted in a process of becoming and by virtue of location in social, material, temporal and spatial contexts. The fluidity of identity does not mean that there is no coherence, but rather that this has to be continually reproduced to ensure fixity. As Renan says, the continued existence of the nation depends on 'a daily plebiscite' (1990: 19). In the next section I want to explore how points of identification continuously move through different nexuses, and how in the contemporary world these nexuses have proliferated through the propagation of points of contact, cultural influences and mobilities. In a world of others, there remain numerous points of convergence.

Rorty considers that rather than being centred, we should conceive of identity as 'a centreless and contingent web' (1991: 193) constituted by 'networks of beliefs and desires' (ibid.: 191) and multiple other points of association. As I will now elaborate, identity is best conceived as a process of continually weaving together fragments of discourse and images, enactions, spaces and times, things and people into a vast matrix, in which complex systems of relationality between elements constellate around common-sense themes – one such being the national.

The Redistribution of National Identity

In order to reconsider sociological understandings of national identity, I want to disembed the common-sense idea that the nation is the fundamental basis of society, and therefore self-evidently the organising principle around which sociology is organised. This I will do by taking up some recent work which possibly suggests the lineaments of a reformulated sociology. In such work, attention is being directed to flows, processes, mobilities and 'horizontal' interconnections, rather than to vertical, hierarchical structures, and metaphors such as rhizomes and networks are being utilised to look at the complicated, uneven relationships between places, people, things and discourses. Recognising the intricacies of the social world requires that it be conceived as 'a complex, heterogeneous nexus of entities and flows' (Michael, 2000: 1), where power and identity are simultaneously transformed and reproduced, where new connections are made, and old constellations solidified. Such processes thus produce both heterogeneity and homogeneity, a host of disjunctions and ruptures as well as reifications and continuities. I want to suggest that national identity is now situated within an ever-shifting matrix, a multi-dimensional, dynamic composite of networks. Such a metaphor emphasises the relationality of the social without subjecting it to an overarching, systemic order, and insists on an ever-increasing multitude of connections and chains of relation-ality. Within such a matrix, national identity is being continually *redistributed.* For emphatically, the evolution of multiple connections does not necessarily dissipate the power of national identity, although it undoubtedly decentres the authoritative formations consolidating around high culture, official political power and national meta-narratives. Rather, points of identification with the nation are increasingly manifold and contested, are situated within dense networks which provide multiple points of contact.

Castells (1996) has put forward the notion of a 'network society' emerging from processes of globalisation, comprising economic, political and technological flows, and Appadurai (1990) has offered a highly influential scheme which suggests that globalisation is characterised by disjunctive flows of people ('ethnoscapes'), technology ('technoscapes'), information ('mediascapes'), ideas and ideologies ('ideoscapes') and money ('financescapes') which undercut nationally organised modes of distribution and control. Such ideas challenge bounded notions of society, since a host of interconnected flows and pathways impact in uneven ways in varied contexts. Barker proposes that these flows 'should not necessarily be understood in terms of a set of neat, linear determinations', but instead viewed as a series of 'overlapping, overdetermined, complex and "chaotic" conditions which, at best, can be seen to cluster around key "nodal points"' (1999: 41).

Other interesting work on networks has come out of actor-network theory, whose proponents have attempted to show how meanings and practical actions are secured through the relational arrangements of people and 'non-humans', such as animals and plants, objects and representations. The crucial element of such studies is that they emphasise the relationality of the elements in the network, which produces agency as an effect, 'distributed through an heterogeneous arrangement of materials' (Hetherington and Law, 2000: 127). A problem with most of the work which has been carried out within actor-network theory is that it has remained somewhat parochial. In the desire to identify particular actor networks, there has been a tendency to somehow seal these off, as is they are self-contained systems. As Lee and Brown (1994) have argued, all too often nothing stands outside the network. However, each element within any one network is inevitably connected, or potentially connected, to other epistemological and practical networks. This raises problems regarding agency, for instance, in that it may be inspired by a whole set of influences from outside the network under study. Despite this system-atism, most actor-network theorists have usefully acknowledged the instability of networks. Vitally, they have to be constantly activated in order to secure their epistemological and practical stability, although this might downplay the ways in which they can be contaminated or destabilised by external influences. Another difficulty is that there is little sense that ambivalent objects and people are incorporated into networks; that there is ambiguity, discontinuity and disjuncture (see Hetherington and Law, 2000). More seriously, questions of power have been conspicuous by their absence. Which actors have greater leverage within these networks? Are more able to sustain them? And for what purposes? The more complex notion of the matrix is required, an intersecting network, with multiple points of connection and constellation, is certainly better suited to my aims, for through an evermore complex matrix we can identify multiple connections which reaffirm and decentre the idea of national identity.

At one level, the extension of matrical relationships is paradoxically under-mining forms of identity formation based around the nation. In a number of ways it is true, as Urry claims, that 'flows across societal borders make it less easy for states to mobilise clearly separate and coherent nations in pursuits of goals based upon society as a region' (2000: 36). Flows and networks of technologies, mobilities, information, money, commodities, ideas and images advance the ability of many to make connections, form groups and communities which are inter-nationally organised. Travel insinuates a familiarity with forms of supposed otherness, and 'exotic' commodities are routinely traded in everyday worlds. The ability to sustain 'invisible networks' is crucial to the tactics of many internationally constituted new social movements (Melucci, 1989), and a host of affective groupings, collectivities organised around 'identity politics', and fan cultures keep in touch via globalising technologies, including, of course, in cyberspace, where 'virtual' communities are established. Likewise, Massey observes that youth cultures are increasingly 'a particular articulation of contacts and influences drawn from a variety of places scattered, according to power relations, fashion and habit, across many different parts of the globe' (1998: 124). These youthful forms of social and cultural relations cut across many of the hierarchies of scale – such as the local, the national and the global – which are held to identify spatial particularities, and are organised into 'constellations of temporary coherence' (ibid.: 124–125).

In one sense, time is increasingly desynchronised, challenging the consolidation of shared national routines and habits. 'Time space compression' (Harvey, 1989) brings the world closer, ameliorating the separate experience of nations, their emplacement in a distinct temporal scale. Television schedules and the keying in to global events undercut the mass national experience of time, and cybertime – a temporal system which takes no cognisance of national time systems – connects global users of the internet. But in another sense, there is a multiplication of time, so that the range of different lifestyles, shopping plans, work schedules becomes more complex, and also decentres a commonly experienced national time (see Adam, 1995; Nowotny, 1994). We might also refer to the speeding up of ephemeral culture, where novelties, fashions, crazes and commodities attain obsolescence evermore rapidly.

As far as space is concerned, notions about fragmented spaces, 'third' spaces or 'spaces on the margins' put forward ideas about postmodern geographies which challenge the primacy of national space. Important amongst these is Doreen Massey's (1993) conception of a 'progressive sense of place' in which places are characterised by their multiple connections – do not intrinsically locally or nationally reflect some essential character, a genius loci, so to speak – but are constituted by the processes and flows which centre upon them in myriad and differently scaled ways. Moreover, romantic metaphorical figures such as the nomad, who moves through space but belongs nowhere, have been tendered as epitomising contemporary forms of spatial identity, are part of a general root-lessness which effaces the old, reified links between space and identity. Such de-nationalised identities are perhaps best explored in diasporic modes of dwelling. Paul Gilroy (1994) has notably put forward the idea of the 'Black Atlantic', a spatial imaginary which bears no allegiance to any nation, but is constituted by the historical migrancy of Black people between the Caribbean, Africa, America and Britain, as well as by contemporary cultural circulations between these spaces. Such diasporic spaces are, of course, also made up of practical and familial networks, summarised by Brah as specifying 'a matrix of economic, political and cultural inter-relationships which construct the commonality of a dispersed group'

(1996: 196). These syncretic, creolising and diasporic identities thus contest national spaces, add to the profusion of connections which are consolidated in everyday life and the complexity of the life-world, rendering old dichotomies of 'self' and 'other' more ambivalent.

There is, then, a multiplicity of routes and roots available to us, which can simultaneously open up the possibilities of connection, or a foreclosing on diversity through a search for stability to banish the ambiguity of the unfixed and the multiple. However, I contend that national identity, rather than standing as the opposite of these fluid modes of connection, is similarly heterogeneous, is constituted by innumerable pathways, connections and sources. In the contemporary network of identity formation, the national is found in a bewilderingly dense profusion of signifiers, objects, practices and spaces. Although globalisation has produced a complexification of flows and networks, there remains an abundance of nodes, events, and situations which foreground national identity. In a globalising world, national identity continually reconstitutes itself, becomes re-embedded, reterritorialises spaces, cultural forms and practices. Thus, like other identities, nationhood is 'constituted through powerful and intersecting temporal regimes and modes of dwelling and travelling' (Urry, 2000: 18). For instance, as national and local territories become increasingly permeable, so iconic representations are peddled across the world as markers of national identity. What may be useful as marketing shorthand for tourists, entrepreneurs and television audiences may also be re-enchanted back home, repatriated to serve national(ist) interests, as we will see when I discuss the Hollywood film, *Braveheart*, in Chapter 5. National identity has become decentred but has also been recentred, and is continually being redistributed in matrices which extend from the local to the global. And just as there is an infinite range of possibilities for the creation of alternative networks of identity, so there is an ever-expanding range of resources through which to construct national identity.

I do not want to deny the global potentialities for rhizomic movement, as Deleuze and Guattari have it, to acknowledge the ways in which people can make lines of flight out of normative cultural arrangements. But a matrix exists in conjunction with rhizomic connections; indeed, it facilitates the making of horizontal connections. Crucially, though, it allows us to identify the cultural constellations forged out of the huge catalogue of intertextual reference points concerned with national identity. I do not want to perpetuate the illusion of fixed identities, for all cultural elements contain elements of ambiguity, and yet by virtue of their relationality to other elements within a wider matrix of meaning and practice, certain meanings attach to them which are hard to disestablish. Nevertheless, the expansion of networks brings with it a potential for the destabilisation of meaning and for the possibilities for new connections to be made whereby objects become connected into other, different networks. Thus cultural elements may become increasingly fluid, contested and mobile. In everyday life, for instance, mundane technologies instantiate a sense of order by combining people, objects, places and discourses. But whilst they mediate and reflect everyday life, they may also produce disorder, may undermine habitual routines, because they are inevitably the site of ambiguities and disruptions. Because of this polysemy, new meanings and uses are apt to erupt out of everyday life, as elements intrude to interrogate long-held relationships. Previously unimaginable connections are made as global flows produce unexpected juxtapositions and assemblages of things, people and places.

Thus heterogeneous elements are distributed by different global flows, are variously ordered or disordered, fixed or fluid. New connections are made or remade, or elements become disconnected. Accordingly, constellations may exist in a state of flux or stability, may persist in 'freezing up' relations or be in a continual process of becoming. As Michael stresses (2000: 38), the metaphor of the network and the rhizome are not mutually incompatible. At certain points, identities territorialise and assume recognisable characteristics, can establish consistencies through time, become embodied in habit, and constellate in places. In other circumstances they are dynamic and fluid. Identity and 'common sense' results where things, processes and flows are domesticated and tamed, adopted and adapted through complex modes of 'integration through symbolic, social and practical reordering and routinisation' (ibid.: 10). This incorporation of otherness into everyday life generates an intersubjective understanding of the linkages between people, spaces and things, though not one that is always articulated through discourse and representation. It acts to epistemologically and ontologically install things and people in place.

Of course, here we must acknowledge the effect of power to consolidate and reify relationships, and, further, to argue that certain assemblages and linkages pertain more than others. In a matrix, power is unevenly distributed, and reflects a distinct global 'power-geometry' where certain locales and nations are attached to networks, generate flows, and are the centre of numerous constellations of power and effect within these global matrices. Thus economic success may be assisted by being situated in key nodal points of production, marketing, distribution and consumption networks which extend the operational reach of local and national economies. Large corporations institute a global McDonaldisation of provision to ensure predictability and control (Ritzer, 1993). Some institutions facilitate certain connections and points of intersection whilst curtailing other links. We must therefore interrogate who is able to tap into networks, get connected, and who is not.

However, whilst recognising that the ways in which certain networks establish modes of control are accessible only to particular groups, we must equally be aware that national identity doesn't necessarily require fixity for its survival. Indeed, over-reified culture may be inimical to its survival. For national identity relies more on condensation symbols, flexible ways of making sense of shared resources. Nations and national identity are protean and promiscuous in their form. For like all cultural forms, practices and expressions, they are invariably syncretic. As Crang asserts, cultures 'are not "holistic" ways of life – but instead are composed of people assembling and reassembling fragments from around them' (1998: 175). A contemporary national identity makes use of the proliferating cultural forms and practices and meanings that are available. Throughout this book I will attempt to highlight the range of intertextual, inter-practical connections between cultural resources which give sustenance to national identity, and in the final chapter will attempt to illustrate the density of such multiple interconnections.

Crucially, the historical weight of national identity means that it is hard to shift as the pre-eminent source of belonging, able to draw into its orbit other points of identification whether regional, ethnic, gendered or class-based. As Calhoun asserts, national identity acts as a 'trump card in the game of identity' (1997: 46), overriding more supposedly 'parochial' or particularistic identities even as it allows their diversity to persist (national identity is, of course, another form of parochialism and particularism). Whilst the historical formation of 'national' culture has been transformed, this legacy still exerts power on the ways in which contemporary formations of culture – much expanded and fragmented – are subsumed by a common-sense notion that the nation remains pre-eminent. The complexification of identity has entailed the expansion of cultural resources and repertoires, and yet constellations of interrelated cultural indices coagulate around national identity, not in any fixed or essentialist sense, but in the multiple ways in which they can be assembled and connected around key themes.

Finally, I want to return to the importance of identifying scaling processes in the constitution of national identity. The metaphor of the matrix enables us to identify connections between localities with nation, performances in parochial settings with a larger stage, the everyday domestic and the national quotidian, the mundane with the spectacular, the location of places within larger spatial frameworks, and representations and discursive fragments within larger texts and image banks. The forthcoming chapters will exemplify this in greater detail.

–2–

Geography and Landscape: National Places and Spaces

To conceive the nation in spatial terms is a complex matter that brings together a number of processes and theoretical approaches. For the relationship between space and national identity is variegated and multi-scaled, producing a complex geography that is constituted by borders, symbolic areas and sites, constellations, pathways, dwelling places and everyday fixtures. And the national is evident not only in widely recognised grand landscapes and famous sites, but also in the mundane spaces of everyday life. My approach here is to look at a range of different national forms of spatialisation which interweave with each other to consolidate a strong cognitive, sensual, habitual and affective sense of national identity, providing a common-sense spatial matrix which draws people and places together in spectacular and banal ways. Accordingly I will look at spatial boundaries, preferred ideological landscapes, iconic sites, sites of popular assembly, generic everyday landscape, and the notion of 'home'.

The Nation as Bounded Space

The nation continues to be the pre-eminent spatial construct in a world in which space is divided up into national portions. The nation is spatially distinguished as a bounded entity, possessing borders which mark it as separate from other nations. Borders enclose a definable population subject to a hegemonic administration in the form of a discrete political system holding sway over the whole of this space but which, in a world of nations, is expected to respect the sovereignty of other nations. These borders are also imagined to enclose a particular and separate culture, a notion which is articulated by hegemonic ways of differentiating and classifying cultural differences. It is not that different cultures cannot exist within any nation, but that they are subordinate to the nation, and conceived as part of national cultural variety.

Smith remarks that nations 'define a definite social space within which members must live and work, and demarcate an historic territory that locates a community in time and space' (Smith, 1991: 16). The nation masquerades as a historical entity, its borders giving it a common-sense existence. Yet despite the appearance of fixity, nations continually change. They dissemble, emerge, conjoin with each other, lose parts and expand as any glance at a sequence of political maps throughout the twentieth century will show. In fact there has been a proliferation of nation-states throughout the twentieth century. For instance, the United Nations had 51 founder-members in 1945; by the end of the century it had 192 member states. As a power-container, the nation is always under threat of being decentred as the 'obvious' space of sovereignty and identity. Perhaps this threat is presently greater than ever before. In order to contextualise the forthcoming discussion, I will briefly identify three ways in which this is so.

Firstly, the nation-state seems to be threatened by large, supra-national federations which organise around trade, social legislation and law (for instance, as with the European Community). Control over national economy and government is undoubtedly altered by such federations, and widespread fears about the demise of national political autonomy and culture arise. There is no room for a sustained analysis here, but I want to point out that it seems as if the spatial container of power here is expanding to transcend the national. In Europe, the fears in certain nations, especially the UK, to this supra-national extension of politics and culture have led to highly defensive reifications in which essentialised cultural markers have been utilised to denote a treasured uniqueness which is imperilled by foreign cultural infection. Thus fears about spatial transformation are accompanied by cultural responses which imply that culture is contained and bounded by national borders. Notably, a host of interest groups have mobilised rather archaic cultural symbols to protest about the erosion of sovereignty. These have focused on 'traditional' farming practices, the appearance of money (the desire to keep the monarch's head on coins) and, as we will shortly see, appeals to essentialist constructions of particular symbolic landscapes. Whether the development of the EC will lead to a decline in national identity is difficult to guess, but the defensive reactions which have challenged these federalist processes perhaps indicate that this might not be so, for the nation has been reasserted as the pre-eminent container of culture and identity, both amongst 'pro-Europeans' and their opponents.

The second spatial entity that jeopardises the 'integrity' of national space is that of the autonomy-seeking region or 'stateless nation' contained within its borders which mobilises opinion or arms against the larger entity. There are many such nationalist movements throughout the world which continually test national borders, sometimes forcing nations to divide into smaller parts. The success of such movements since 1945 testifies to the fluidity of the nation, despite its continual reification as a 'natural' space which contains a commonality of interests and culture amongst its inhabitants. What is interesting about such processes from a cultural perspective are attempts to delineate cultural identity within alternative (national) spaces which assert a cultural distinction from the larger entities which incorporate them. Strategies to resist secession likewise highlight the cultural integrity of the threatened nation, and point out the historical and cultural common denominators which outweigh any differences. I explore strategies to elicit cultural difference in Chapter 5, where I discuss the responses to the film *Braveheart* in Scotland and the contesting ways in which it is used to distinguish Scots from the English but also to assert common points of Britishness.

The third process endangering the bounded space of the nation is globalisation, which I have discussed in the previous chapter and will address in the following chapters. The global challenge to nation-states comes from many sources, ranging from the global flows which bring goods, information, images and people from elsewhere, to the creation of supra-national spaces such as the much-vaunted cyberspace, and the development of planetary consciousness or global awareness, prompted by greater knowledge of challenges and threats to the world as a whole. This identifies the commonalities which enjoin all people, such as the potential for environmental devastation and the importance of human rights and world peace, which are believed to take priority over the relatively parochial concerns of national self-interest.

Although we continue to live in world of nations Ascherson (2001) argues that 'self-creating, hardwalled, homogeneous cells' which assert defensive forms of national identity are increasingly obsolete, since nations now need to have more permeable borders to admit the financial, informational, commodity and cultural flows which circulate the globe. Indeed, he further argues that globalisation provides an 'ideal environment for microstates as long as their cell walls are porous' (ibid.), and we might further add that the proliferation of diasporic identities generate alternative, more tentacular forms of spatial organisation which are constituted by these flows. Despite these undoubtedly powerful processes, claims that the nation as space of primary belonging is in decline are exaggerated. For national identity can be reconstituted in diaspora, can forge new cultural constructions of difference out of the confrontation with otherness, and not only in a recursive fashion. But still, at a practical and imaginary level, national geographies continue to predominate over other forms of spatial entity, as the following sections will underline.

Ideological Rural National Landscapes

It is difficult to mention a nation without conjuring up a particular rural landscape (often with particular kinds of people carrying out certain actions). Ireland has become synonymous with its West Coast (see Nash, 1993). Argentina is inevitably linked with images of the pampas: gauchos riding across the grasslands. Morocco is associated with palm trees, oases and shapely dunescapes, and the Netherlands with a flat patchwork of polders and drainage ditches. Of course, the deserts, swamps and mountains of Argentina tend to be overlooked, as do the highlands of Morocco and Holland. These specific landscapes are selective shorthand for these nations, synedoches through which they are recognised globally. But they are also loaded with symbolic values and stand for national virtues, for the forging of the nation out of adversity, or the shaping of its geography out of nature whether conceived as beneficent, tamed or harnessed. Specific geographical features may provide symbolic and political boundaries, natural borders formed by seas, rivers and mountains, that forestall invasion and contain culture and history, sustaining mythical continuities. Out of the transformation of raw nature has emerged the most treasured national attributes, and the agricultural means by which the nation has been nourished. Moreover, landscapes come to stand as symbols of continuity, the product of land worked over and produced, etched with the past, so that 'history runs through geography' (Cubitt, 1998: 13). Nations possess, then, what Short has termed 'national landscape ideologies' (1991) charged with affective and symbolic meaning. So ideologically charged are they, that they are apt to act upon our sense of belonging so that to dwell within them, even if for a short time, can be to achieve a kind of national self-realisation, to return to 'our' roots where the self, freed from its inauthentic – usually urban – existence, is re-authenticated. These spatial ideologies are indelibly stamped with the modern construction of separate urban and rural realms, where the *gesellschaft* of the city is contrasted with a highly romanticised rural *gemeinschaft* (Kasinitz, 1995). European nations, whose emergence is in many cases coterminous with the development of modern romanticism, are clothed in this rhetoric of the rural, a rural which most frequently encapsulates the *genius loci* of the nation, the place from which we have sprung, where our essential national spirit resides. Moreover, they are the locale of a mythical (and commonly racialised) class of forebears, the peasants, yeoman or pioneers who battled against, tamed and were nurtured by these natural realms.

These iconic, privileged landscapes are continually recirculated through popular culture. They form the basis of tourist campaigns to foreign visitors, and frequently come under environmental pressure from large numbers of pilgrims who wish to experience their symbolic power, so that often preservation movements have ensured that they are conserved as national parks. They thus become conceived primarily as spectacular landscapes and hence become part of a different economy of identity, valued for their visual and romantic affordances rather than their fertility or agricultural productiveness. The conversion from productive to tourist landscapes is telling in terms of the marketing of national identity and the way that increased mobility has renewed such locales as pilgrimage sites. Yet myths about agricultural values persist, often as part of heritage interpretation. For instance, in France the rural is envisaged as the source of varied and distinct products, such as cheese and wine, is conceived as producing infinite geographic and gastronomic variety (Lowenthal, 1994: 19; Claval, 1994).

To exemplify the ideological power of such landscapes, I want to consider rural England as supreme marker of national identity. Lowenthal (1994) has identified four imagined attributes which epitomise the English countryside. Firstly, he cites 'insularity' – in the sense that the countryside had been wrought by the English alone. Free of the influence of invading forces, the island of Britain forms a natural barrier which means it is untainted by 'continental' influence. Secondly, the land has been carefully crafted and adorned, domesticated by the stewards who inhabit it, who have created the hedgerows, coppices, and drainage systems that testify to an *enhancing* of nature over centuries. This contrasts with those national landscapes which are celebrated for their primeval naturalness, the mountains, forests and deserts that have not been tamed and yet have induced a hardiness in their inhabitants. Thirdly, Lowenthal points to the imagined stability which rural Englishness is believed to embody, the continuities which responsible rural steward-ship has retained (in contrast to the ever-changing towns and cities), materialising a memory of historical England in space. Finally, there is the sense of order which is found in the rural realm, the product of a mythical era when stability apparently ensured an enduring sense of one's place in the world. This situatedness involved the acceptance of distinct paternal and peasant roles and responsibilities to produce a supposedly harmonious world. Such ideological currents run through much heritage industry in rural England; for instance, in the celebration of the country house by the National Trust (Hewison, 1987), not only evident in the historical accounts which surround such sites but also in the desire for 'tidiness' as a preferred aesthetic.

The rural scenes that are held to epitomise Englishness are highly selective. They are quite geographically specific, confined to the South, particularly the areas surrounding London known as the Home Counties, though sometimes extending to the Cotswolds and more western areas, and marked by history – rarely do modern buildings intrude into these scenes. Typically, the visually and verbally recorded elements comprise a rather fixed signifying system. Parish churches, lych-gates, haystacks, thatched or half-timbered cottages, rose-laden gardens, village greens, games of cricket, country pubs, rural customs, hedgerows, golden fields of grain, plough and horses, hunting scenes, and a host of characters including vicars, squires, farmers, gamekeepers, are part of a series of interlinked cues which are widely shared at home and abroad.

It is difficult to overstress the rigidity of this version of rural England, which has been the focus of many well-worn accounts which celebrate its qualities (see Middleton and Giles, 1995: 73–109). Accompanying the rise of romantic aesthetics, and perhaps culminating in the first half of the twentieth century, artists, photo-graphers, novelists and poets foregrounded these 'modern systems of visiting, telling and repeating' which have 'allowed England to be known in its imaginary and idealised aspect' (Taylor, 1994: 29). The sheer density of references to this rural realm have been updated by the more contemporary technologies of representation across popular culture, which endlessly recycle images in films, television programmes and tourist campaigns, not to mention more mundane artefacts such as postcards and chocolate boxes. And the widely available technology of photography enables such images to be sought out and (re)produced by visitors to the countryside.

Claiming to be Britain's best-selling quarterly magazine, the glossy *This England*, subtitled 'England's loveliest magazine', is one of the most remarkable expressions of a particular vision of English rurality and the ways in which it may be used ideologically to reinforce specific national(ist) values. This publication fortifies an exclusive geography by endlessly recycling photographs and sketches featuring a countryside that contains little or no signs of modernity (no 'modern' buildings, hardly any cars and even television aerials are strangely absent). No youths are present in any picture, certainly no non-white locals or visitors are depicted, and the urban is kept at bay. This England is located in the distant past, with little evidence of any post-war development. Typically, each issue commences with a picture essay, supported by nostalgic, patriotic poetry, which combines the rural images of country cottages, village greens, parish churches, pastoral and vernal scenery, with iconic photographs such as the White Cliffs of Dover, Royal personages and Big Ben, together with a range of more humble signifiers of Englishness including steam railways, windmills, war memorials and stately homes. All these elements constantly recur throughout the rest of the magazine. Although this obsessively selective approach carries a particularly powerful affective charge, it is in the combination of these images with a medley of other features that the full ideological power of *This England* becomes apparent. The historical suggestiveness of a pre-war era is bolstered by the numerous articles, poems and pictures of the Second World War (never the First) which is celebrated as a defining moment of Englishness (specifically foregrounding sacrifice, national bonding of classes, the closeness of the people to royalty, the repulsion of totalitarian powers). A strong emphasis on Christianity, old-fashioned methods of policing, country customs, archetypal rural characters, nostalgia for music and variety personalities, and hobbies further condenses this imaginary Englishness. Most tellingly, a section of the magazine is entitled 'Don't let Europe rule Britannia', including numerous polemics from readers and contributors about the dangers of a 'European superstate' to the British way of life, and featuring lampoons of European bureaucrats and essentialised portraits of 'sensible' British folk being betrayed by politicians. Other political issues such as the ordination of women Anglican priests, the decline of the 'traditional' family, and the demise of Christianity and 'authority' also feature. It is clear that the landscape here is utilised to enhance the appeal of a complex of other political issues. The suggestion is clear: as Britain changes, the fixity of rurality is a bulwark and a resource which can be mobilised in the contest over national identity. In rurality inhere timeless values which speak back to distasteful modern developments.

Despite the enormous changes that have taken place in rural England, or perhaps because of them, these dominant images retain an affective and cognitive power that serves exclusive variants of nationalism. The prevalence of agribusiness, housing estates and commuter communities, large fields without hedgerows, vast tracts of larch and spruce forest, leisure practices such as action sports, factory farming and rural unemployment, means that the elements which *This England* features are now rare. It is worth speculating about what photographs exclude through the selection of angles and frames, for there are no pylons, mobile phone masts, new buildings or telegraph poles to be seen. These more recent features of the countryside co-exist in the palimpsest of Englishness, but are edited out of the picture. This bespeaks of an extraordinary will to prove a purity which does not exist, and probably never has, but lodges somewhere in half-remembered trips to the countryside and is enhanced by the contemporary desire for nostalgia.

The effect of this ideological perpetration is to produce a 'purified space' (Sibley, 1988) in which anything 'out of place' stands out as un-English. This includes kinds of people, who thereby cannot be considered proper denizens of the country (and therefore are excluded from Englishness), as I will shortly discuss, but also signs of otherness in architectural features, garden styles, non-Christian places of worship, signs of modernity in non-traditional pubs and houses. This desire for rural purity is also manifest in responses to the perceived threat of change. One remarkable expression of this is in responses to changes in natural history, notably where 'invasive' and 'alien' flora and fauna 'colonise' the countryside. English ruralists have lamented the appearance of the muntjac deer, the collared dove and the coypu – indeed the latter has now been exterminated – and the spread of non-English plants like Himalayan balsam, rhododendron and eucalyptus trees, not only for environmental reasons but because they affront the 'natural' landscape. As Wolschke-Bulmahn details, 'the doctrinaire plea for "native" plants is often accompanied by the condemnation of "foreign" or "exotic plants" as alien invaders or aggressive intruders, thus suggesting that native plants would be peaceful and non-invasive' (1996: 65). He provides a spectacular example in the nationalistic desires of German Nazis to celebrate native plants, despite the paucity of species identified as German, culminating in the Reich Landscape Law which devised policies to exterminate botanical 'invaders'. With regard to the proposed extermination of one small forest plant, *impatiens parviflora*, he quotes the following declaration by Nazi botanists: "'As with the fight against Bolshevism, our entire occidental culture is at stake, so with the fight against this Mongolian invader, an essential element of this culture, namely, the beauty of our home forest is at stake'" (ibid.: 67).

Yet as a national landscape ideology, these images serve particular political agendas, as is evidenced by the rise in support for the Countryside Alliance in Britain – essentially a pro-hunting lobby – who have capitalised on popular myths about the countryside to foster notions of an urban–rural divide where a metro-politan elite are constructed as the antithesis to countryfolk and are immune to the 'traditional' needs of the countryside. The internet web pages of this organisation makes use of stereotypical rural imagery to generate patriotic sentiments, as does the homepage of the Conservative Party (www.conservatives.com) which at this moment (July 2001) presents an image of a large oak tree bearing the legend 'Under Threat', which alternates with an image of a blighted tree stump, a bulldozer and a row of new houses accompanied by the title 'Under Labour: Labour plan to build millions of homes on our green land. Is this what you voted for?' The party tends to position itself as the defender of patriotism and rural order and has recently campaigned against a ban on hunting with hounds. This association is persistently reproduced. During the 1998 party conference, the visual backdrops used during party leader William Hague's speech could have come straight out of the pages of *This England*.

The regimes of signification which construct this rural idyll as a manifestation of Englishness mask the underlying undecidability of the countryside and the nation, their ambivalence and multiplicity. This mythic England flies in the face of rural development, for while traces of its former hegemonic power remain, the vast transformations that have overtaken rural life have decentred its authority. Increasingly, the rural, as the opposite of the urban, is positioned as 'backward', the realm of recursive superstition, aberrant sexual behaviour and class subserv-ience, full of hidden poverty and the harmful effects of farming (see Bell, 1997). Several writers and groups have taken issue with these glorified representations. Rose (1993) has pointed out the gendered construction of representations of the rural landscape – typically represented in female terms, and protected by male guardians from invasion and 'rape'. The construction of English rurality also marginalises or demonises other 'out-of-place' groups such as gypsies (Sibley, 1988) New Age Travellers (Sibley, 1997), the rural poor (Cloke, 1997), and gay men and lesbians (Valentine, 1997). The urban–rural dichotomy also perpetrates the notion that the urban is black or ethnically mixed, whereas the countryside is imagined as a wholly white space, marking the invisibility of white ethnicity, and fostering a myth of the historical purity and immemorial presence of a (white) English racial stock (Agyeman and Spooner, 1997). The work of the Black Environment Network, and of photographers like Ingrid Pollard who place them-selves in the English rural landscape, has attempted to reclaim it as a multicultural space by physically and artistically putting themselves in the picture. The possibilities opened up by visual technologies of deconstructing the mythical English countryside are considered by Taylor, who includes a number of photo-graphic works which reveal environmental despoilage, the reign of private property, the presence of Indian Muslim and black people in the rural to jar expectations (1994: 240–283).

In the USA, alternative attempts to reinterpret landscape ideologies have also been recently undertaken. The great American ideological landscape is undoubtedly the West, and the prevalence of a masculinised, conquered landscape, a landscape in which rugged individuals could achieve their destiny and create a new Eden, has circulated through popular film and fiction, and been espoused by ideologues to evoke patriotic sentiment. Yet such a myth has gained prominence by effacing other stories and contrasting understandings of the West, the stories of the Mexicans and the Native Americans who formerly worked and lived on the land until their displacement, and the experiences of women as part of the westward adventure. Campbell and Keane detail how these marginalised voices are now putting themselves back into the story of the West, fracturing its hegemonic geographies and histories with their alternative iconographies (1997: 125–139). In the same way, particular spaces are marginalised within the nation, often on regional or 'racial' grounds. For instance, Westwood (in Westwood and Phizacklea, 2000: 46) suggests that the coastal area of Esmeraldas in Ecuador, a region primarily inhabited by black Ecuadorians, has been invisibilised by its neglect in official representations of national geography.

Iconic Sites

Besides his assertion that nations are distinguished by spatial demarcations, Smith also refers to how nations 'provide individuals with "sacred centres", objects of spiritual and historic pilgrimage, that reveal the uniqueness of their nation's "moral geography"' (1991: 16). As with the ideologically loaded landscapes discussed above, these iconic sites are highly selective, synedochal features which are held to embody specific kinds of characteristics. Typically these spatial symbols connote historical events, are either evidence of past cultures, providing evidence of a 'glorious' past of 'golden age' and antecedence (Stonehenge, the Great Pyramids, the Taj Mahal), or they are monuments erected – often within larger memoryscapes – to commemorate significant episodes in an often retrospectively reconstructed national history (Statue of Liberty, Arc de Triomphe, Nelson's Column). They also frequently celebrate the modernity of the nation, are symbols of its progress (Empire State Building, Petronas Towers, Sydney Opera House). As such, the destruction of the 'twin towers' of the World Trade Centre proved to be a potent attack on the idea of 'America'. In addition, there are a host of sites which symbolise official power: the royal palaces, halls of justice, military edifices, presidents' houses, parliamentary buildings, and so on, which provide the materialised spaces of national rule.

These spatial attractors often occur in an ensemble of related sites, to constitute ceremonial points of reference. As Johnson says, they are 'points of physical and ideological orientation' often around which 'circuits of memory' are organised

(1995: 63). For instance, a tourist trip to Paris involves gazing upon a number of emblematic places, including the Eiffel Tower, the Place de Concord, Notre Dame Cathedral, the Arc de Triomphe, the Champs Élysées and the Louvre. These are significant both as signifiers of France for outsiders and as ideological statements about Frenchness and the republic within France. Marina Warner (1993) has shown in her discussion of statuary along the Champs Élysées in Paris, how a post-revolutionary elite wanted to convey particular attributes and ideals which emerged out of the Revolution. Unfortunately, the classical allusions upon which such monoliths depends for their meaning are now no longer familiar to us and cannot be read in the hoped-for manner. The obsolescence of such inscriptions is also evident in recent times by large programmes to remove statues in Eastern Europe after the crumbling of communism and the Eastern bloc, and, often, their replacement by an earlier generation of national heroes sculpted in stone. This is a vital point for it illustrates that despite the desires of the powerful to imprint meaning upon the landscape so that it can be read by witnesses, such aims are often thwarted by the changing basis of knowledge and aesthetic convention. The projects of cultural nationalists to imprint meaning on space for all time, like other attempts to fix national meaning, are doomed to failure. In any case, such symbolic sites are usually claimed by competing groups, who invest them with meanings which are attuned to their political project or identity. This is particularly apparent in the old stone signifiers of national identity which unproblematically represent male military heroes, philanthropists and statesmen in ennobling poses in central locations, and tend to erect feminine statues as metaphors for abstract qualities such as 'Liberty', 'Victory' and signs of the nation (Edensor and Kothari, 1996). This hugely gendered process has now been revealed by feminists as having 'typically sprung from masculinised memory, masculinised humiliation and masculinised hope' (Enloe, 1989: 44).

I have previously carried out research at the Taj Mahal in Agra, Uttar Pradesh, India, one of the most widely recognised global tourist landmarks, and commonly understood as a synecdoche and symbol of India, by foreign tourists and Indians alike (Edensor, 1998a). The Taj is a tomb dedicated to Mumtaz Mahal, the wife of the seventeenth-century Moghul Emperor, Shah Jahan, set in a garden bounded with walls which contain sundry other buildings including a mosque. First and foremost then, the Taj, as a globally renowned icon of beauty, has become a symbol of India, yet the building is invested with differently symbolic attributes by different groups. For most foreign tourists, the building is the prime reason for their visit to India, for it has been constructed for the past 150 years as a signifier of the 'exotic East'. Descriptions of the Taj in contemporary guidebooks almost exactly match those in the accounts of British colonial tourists and administrators of empire who concocted travel stories recounting their visits, not to mention nineteenth-century guidebooks. Such themes focus on the unparalleled magnificence of the building, detail the (untrue) story of how the emperor cut off the hands of the workers who built the Taj, inevitably discuss at what time of day the building is best viewed (moonlight, mid-day, dawn, dusk), include some comment about the tomb's ethereality and frequently allude to some fantasy of 'Oriental' despotism or the pleasures of the flesh. For most Indian visitors, on the other hand, the site represents national pride, most particularly concerning the interweaving of the diverse ethnic, religious and cultural traditions which are believed to signify the Indian 'genius' for cultural synthesis; in addition, the Taj is commonly acknowledged as a place which brings visitors from all over the sub-continent and is a great place to meet fellow Indians. For many Muslim visitors, the presence of the mosque and the Koranic calligraphy carved into the walls and buildings mean that it is primarily conceived as a sacred site, where worship and religious contemplation is appropriate. Formerly free admission was available on Fridays, when the mosque was frequented by local worshippers. However, the introduction of prohibitive admission charges on all days to maximise revenue has made this unfeasible, stirring up controversy amongst Indian Muslims who claim their right to worship is being infringed. In addition to this religious function, the building also connotes a powerful sense of loss in that under Islamic (Moghul) rule, Indian Muslims were in a more advantageous position that today, especially now that India is ruled by an expressly Hindu government. Finally, for 'fundamentalist' Hindus, the Taj is another example of how the sacred Hindu sites of India were destroyed by the Moghuls, for it is alleged that it is the site of a former temple dedicated to Shiva. It is claimed that these apparently numerous wrongs ought to be righted, as in the notorious demolition of the Babri Masjid at Ayodyha in 1992. These contentions either express the belief that the Taj is actually a Hindu temple which has been appropriated by Muslims, and therefore reflects Hindu genius, or see no merit in the building at all because it is a symbol of Moghul disrespect for Hindus.

These widely varying interpretations of the site testify to the ways in which such places become freighted with different identities, and are the locations for competing identity claims which assert a specific relationship between site and narrator/ performer. Thus contestation over the Taj Mahal is an exemplary instance of the ways in which symbolic sites have a mythical function, in that they can be widely shared as a cultural resource, there is a consensus that they are of importance, and yet the values which inhere in this status can be contested.

The ongoing (re)interpretation of iconic national sites has particular resonances in those nations which were subject to European colonial rule. In a fascinating discussion which catalogues changes in the dominant meanings of a particularly symbolic space, Duncan focuses upon Kandy, in Sri Lanka (1989: 185–200). Firstly, he elaborates upon the cosmological design of pre-colonial, pre-national Kandy, the sacred ceremonies that took place there and the hierarchy of power enshrined in the temples and palace which sacralised the power of the rulers as of divine origin. Thus the power of the 'God-king' was deeply inscribed upon the landscape. But with the onset of colonial rule, by both co-opting and replacing the symbols of kingly power with their own, the British re-inscribed the symbolic import of this landscape. The government agent was installed in the palace, streets were renamed after British figures, and a huge pavilion which dwarfed the king's palace was erected. The central areas of symbolic power were colonised by a jail, a church, police courts, a Protestant school, statues and sports facilities. Other areas were left to decay. Moreover, the town was redesigned to resemble 'a romanticised image of pre-industrial England' (ibid.: 192). Thus was Kandy reshaped to facilitate British movement, cater to British tastes, and reflect British power. With Sri Lankan independence, the effaced symbols of Singhalese power became revitalised. Statues were removed, street names changed once more, and the palace was turned into a museum which celebrates the pre-colonial grandeur of Singhalese civilisation. What is more, as a place of national(ist) resistance that held out against colonial power long after most other areas had succumbed, Kandy was recharged as a site of national significance. Similarly, the site of Great Zimbabwe, formerly assessed by European colonisers as indisputable evidence of the existence of a European civilisation in Africa – since 'primitive' Africans were incapable of erecting such a sophisticated complex – has become symbolic of independent Zimbabwe. It was reconstructed as a site that testifies to a pre-colonial 'advanced' African society showing that (national) history predated colonial 'development'.

Sites of Popular Culture and Assembly

In addition to iconic sites are nationally popular sites of assembly and congregation, not tightly regulated and sanctioned by the state but places where large numbers of people gather to carry out communal endeavours such as festivals, demon-strations and informal gathering. Such sites, as at the Taj Mahal, can be places of proximity, where people go to look at and meet others. Certain spaces of assembly inevitably associated with national identity, such as Times Square in New York City, Trafalgar Square in London, the Djma-el-Fna in Marrakesh, India Gate in Bombay, and the Zocalo in Mexico City, are venues for seething motion and a multiplicity of activities, identities and sights. In contrast to the rather purified, single-purpose spaces of state power, they are more inclusive realms which allow for the play of cultural diversity. They provide an unfixed space in which tourists and inhabitants mingle, people picnic and protest, gaze and perform music or magic, sell goods and services, and simply 'hang out'. Amongst such symbolic spaces, we might also include sports stadia, popular parks, promenades, show grounds, bohemian quarters, religious sites and a host of well-patronised urban areas which are thick with diverse people and activities, and are well-known within the nation, and outside it, as popular centres.

Irrespective of the form of spatial regulation imposed upon these popular national spaces, they are invariably subject to contestation about what values they signify, and which activities are appropriate. Often, a historical perspective is mobilised which romanticises about how they used to be used. For instance, Game (1991) has shown how Bondi Beach, as a site of national significance, is subject to strategic claims which rhetorically attempt to specify the 'real' Bondi. An ideological trope has insisted upon the democracy of the beach – its equalising function – as all are reduced to bodies on the sand, and this is also partly reflected in the identification of the carnivalesque manners and activities which assert a version of the 'true' Australian character and undercut un-Australian attempts to refine or gentrify the scene. Moreover, Bondi serves to fuel the Australian myth of sporting prowess in the performance of surfers and swimmers. This energetic, outdoor co-existence with nature is also a key theme of Australian identity, and a primordial, dangerous nature, albeit within an urban context, is mapped onto Bondi by the threat of sharks and waves (but also by the more recent perils of sewage and drug abusers). The lurking danger inherent in the power of nature is contrasted with the danger posed to nature by humans – as polluters and despoilers. The beach as a venue in which resplendent equality amongst the unclothed masses persists is also feared to be threatened by it being turned into an over-commodified attraction, a money-spinner for tourist developers. Thus Bondi has become a focus for those who express concern about changes which are conceived as interrupting a historic, Australian tendency to celebrate unceremonious behaviour, sporting ability and the authentic encounter with nature. Game further asserts that the power of Bondi also emerges from a sensory apprehension of the beach. A way of being-in-place emerges from the kinaesthetic experience in a context in which bodies meet sand and sea and other bodies. She considers that this shared sensual experience escapes the fixings of representation, and strengthens its affective hold over Australians.

The beach is also germane to the spatial construction of Englishness, at turns nostalgic and ironic, which can encompass class-inflected stereotypes of English gentility and more carnivalesque 'sauciness'. Despite the changes to seaside holiday resorts over the twentieth century, the beach retains its affection for the English as a site of shared activity and sensation, and one which still looms large in popular films and children's and adult literature (Walton, 2000).

To show the ways in which national landscape ideologies and popular sites of assembly and activity can be merged, I want to explore a particularly pertinent essay by Eduardo Archetti about the relationship between symbolic Argentinian space and football. As I have described, landscape can be a particularly affective signifier of national identity because it can 'combine geographical belonging with complex narratives of human exploits, extraordinary characters and cultural-historical heroes' (Archetti, 1998: 189). The founding landscape in Argentina is the *pampa*, regarded as a rich ecosystem that is nostalgically imagined as an 'antidote to the poisons of modernity, capitalism and industrialism' (ibid.: 190). However, although the *pampa* became gradually domesticated by private estates, remnants of the original grasslands persist in the *portreros*. The *portrero* is the realm of the *gaucho*, a rebellious free spirit who roams across the grasslands on horseback watching over livestock, and is typically conceived as being neither Indian nor Spanish, but of mixed blood, appropriately moving beyond a purely European or 'native' ethnicity. These liminal figures and the spaces they inhabit have been transposed onto the topography of the city, in the shape of the *pibe* – a young boy, immune to the authority structures of school and police – and the *baldio* – an empty space in the city, akin to the unregulated rural *potreros*. The *pibe* is the archetypal symbol of the spontaneous, agile Argentinian footballer, a young boy playing on the *baldio*, unhindered by the discipline of teachers and football coaches, who has been 'placed in a mythical territory that inherently empowers those that belong to it' (ibid.: 197). This unfettered, improvisatory *pibe*, with his dribbling and ball-juggling skills, is contrasted with the disciplined, machine-like football teams and players who characterised the English originators of Argentinian football. The *pibe* is believed to be perfectly incarnated in Diego Maradona, the rebellious footballing genius who led Argentina to victory in the 1986 World Cup Final. Here we can see the magical potency of landscape, its power to endow national subjects with almost supernatural powers, a popular blending of masculinity, anti-colonialism, sport and space.

In contradistinction to idealised landscapes and iconic sites, the values associated with popular sites of assembly and pleasure tend to be non-exclusive in their celebrations of lower-class activities and social mixing. Such spaces are often described as authentic, where class and social distinction is levelled and national communality prevails. These values are not generally passed down by cultural authorities but emerge from familiar interaction with such spaces in conditions of co-presence with fellow nationals, and, again, they are represented in innumerable films, novels, tourist guidebooks and television programmes.

Familiar, Quotidian Landscapes

Most accounts of the relationship between space and national identity have focused on the kinds of grand symbolic landscapes and famous sites discussed above, concentrating on the textual meanings of these spaces. However, there have been few depictions which have explored the more mundane spatial features of everyday experience which are equally important in constructing and sustaining national identity. I now concentrate on these quotidian worlds, examining how they absorb localities into the nation.

Despite the effects of globalisation, and despite what some of the more excessive postmodernist accounts of contemporary space assert, most of us live in recognisable worlds, distinguished by distinct material structures, distribution of objects and institutional arrangements. Within these inhabited realms, surrounded by familiar things, routes and fixtures, we make our home by the accretion of habitual enactions, by our familiar engagement with the physical space in which we live. Whilst these spaces may be considered as the agglomeration of regional or ethnic synchronicity, shared understandings and collective enactions through which places are known and dwelt within, I want to consider the ways in which places are sewn together to constitute a powerful sense of *national* spatialisation.

First of all, the semiotic imprint of familiar features constitutes a sense of being in place in most locations within the nation. These fixtures are not only read as signs, though, but are also felt and sensed in unreflexive fashion. I am referring here to the plethora of everyday, mundane signifiers which are noticeably not present when we go abroad. These institutions, vernacular features and everyday fixtures are embedded in local contexts but recur throughout the nation as serial features. To return to the British landscape, irrespective of how symbolically important particular landscapes may be, they contain a host of unremarkable items. The institutional matrix of everyday life is signified by familiar commercial and bureaucratic notices which indicate where services can be procured or commodities purchased. Likewise, service provision is marked by (red) telephone boxes and postboxes, distinctly designed equipment for conveying flows of power and water, including grids, fire hydrants, street lighting, guttering, telegraph poles and pylons. Also prevalent are conspicuously identifiable signs and artefacts belonging to roadscapes, as will be discussed in Chapter 4. In terms of domestic architecture, styles of fencing, garden ornamentation and home décor generally fall within a recognisable vernacular range. Such elements do not generally confound expect-ations of what we will see and what kinds of space will feel like, and when they do, they stand out in relief against this normative spatial context.

The landscape is pervaded with familiarity by the distribution of numerous other elements: the style and materiality of suburban and working-class housing, the design of parks, the prevalence of leisure facilities such as football and rugby pitches, pubs and the mundane codes reinforced by street names. This regular pattern of spatial distribution means that little jars us out of our accustomed habituation of such landscapes. However, when familiar features are missing or threatened, or when new or foreign features encroach, they are immediately noticeable and can result in disorientation and discomfort. For instance, in the UK there was a minor campaign to retain the red telephone box as newly privatised utilities replaced them with a less distinguished transparent booth. In France, the plane trees which line roads in the south of the country have been described as 'anomalous lateral obstacles' by politicians, and local motoring groups campaigned for their wholesale removal because of their contribution to the high death toll in traffic accidents. For the many defenders of the trees, however, they are ancient features of the nation. According to a spokesperson, they are 'a fundamental, living part of our national heritage', a visual marker and a sensually cooling space that is part of everyday motoring (*The Guardian*, 6 July 2001).

These mundane signifiers are also accompanied by the recognisable forms of flora and fauna which recur throughout most environments. The circling black kites throughout India, and a plethora of other unspectacular animals and plants, are also part of these everyday landscapes, rarely commented upon except when they are no longer so common. For instance, in the UK there have been a number of articles in the national press which express alarm at the drastically reduced number of the common house sparrow, a formerly ubiquitous presence. In addition to these living moving elements, quotidian landscapes also produce distinct soundscapes, sonic geographies that provide a backdrop to everyday life. The distinctive sounds of traffic, muezzins or church bells, birdsong and music also install people in place (an evocation of English sounds was produced for the 'Self-Portrait' zone in the Millennium Dome in London, which I will discuss in the final chapter).

The comfort of spatial identity is partly provided by the thick intertextuality of these vernacular landscapes across the nation. For instance, English churches are a familiar feature of rural and urban landscapes, their steeples and towers inscribe a faithscape across the land, and the various styles of regional architecture and the historical forms of churches provide points of contrast which are assembled under the master category of English church. Not only do such features surround us in our domestic environments but they are part of familiar mediascapes, unheralded props in television dramas and documentaries. Besides the replication of ecclesiastical scenes in artistic, touristic and filmic productions, they also are settings for familiar kinds of characters. For instance, the figure of the harassed urban vicar or the eccentric, amiable rural cleric are stalwarts of film, television and literature, regular fictional actors within this familiar landscape. As Silverstone says in his discussion of English suburbia, television, especially in talk shows, sitcoms and soap operas, continually recycles the themes and anxieties of everyday suburban life. This is evident in the settings and the characters who populate these televisual forms but also by the discourses which guide the themes and topics of concern, which is 'grounded in suburban, bourgeois experience' and contained in 'the experiential structures of everyday life' (Silverstone, 1997: 10).

However, certain fixtures are occasionally more overtly celebrated as quotidian features of national identity. Billig provides an apt example of how these familiar settings are reinforced by media commentary, by highlighting the *Daily Mirror*'s 'British Pub Week' which celebrated pubs as national icons, as 'the bastion of British social life', including their products (beer), routines shaped around them and their geography (pub signs) (Billig, 1995: 114). This kind of campaign is devised to reproduce the idea of national readership and to consolidate the relationship between newspapers and their readers by referring to common denominators. It is also possible that a more reflexive awareness of the qualities of pubs has been stimulated by the recent proliferation of 'continental' style café bars in the UK which provide a competitive attraction.

As with the ideological landscapes discussed above, these more mundane spatial signifiers acquire a national significance. Again, certain well-known features become more ideologically charged than others, so that there is selectivity in the identification of distinctive spatial markers, which may become manifest in the national popularity of certain regional styles and their nationwide distribution. For instance, Meinig (1979) identifies 'New England villages', 'Main Street of Middle America' and 'California suburbs' as the pre-eminent symbolic landscapes of America. These idealised spaces resound through literature, cinema, magazines, advertisements, comic books, calendars and greetings cards and a host of other popular cultural forms, but they are also being built across the USA as preferred spaces in contexts beyond their geographic origins. In a related discussion, Rybczynski shows how Ralph Lauren fashions clothes that are based on 'recognisable home-grown images: the Western ranch, the prairie farm, the Newport mansion, the Ivy League college' (1988: 2), which are born out of a 'desire for custom and routine' (ibid.: 9), utilising these generic landscapes to reinforce the American-ness of the clothes and their prospective wearers by situating them in symbolic national space.

Whilst familiar spatial characteristic features provide anchors for spatial identity, they should not be imagined as testifying to a static landscape. As the production of space goes through dynamic cycles, inhabitants must also accommodate themselves to new generic developments. In an innovative account, Clay has attempted to distinguish a huge range of generic landscapes in the USA – not the easily identifiable tourist sights nor those areas subject to the designations of official, bureaucratic knowledge, but what he calls 'epitome districts' which are 'crammed with clues which trigger our awareness of the larger scene' (1994: xi). These generic places continually change and require that a flexible grammar is used to relabel them so that a shared geographical knowledge is retained which is relevant to lived experience. The awareness of change, and growing familiarity with the new, creates a complex spatial network. As people adapt to transformation they domesticate and narrativise changing space, identifying the growth of new particular landscapes such as 'gentrifying neighbourhoods', 'drug scenes' and 'cultural arts districts'.

The most important point about the generic landscapes described above is that they stitch the local and the national together through their serial reproduction across nations. These features are generally taken for granted, but they may become more expressly symbolic of the nation if they are perceived as being under threat.

Dwellingscapes

I now want to emphasise the routine experience of space, the ways in which particular actions recreate space and the modes of habituation which render it familiar, homely. After all, despite the geographical focus of space as text, as representation or as evidence of power (of capital), the most common spatial experience is that in everyday life, where familiar space forms an unquestioned backdrop to daily tasks, pleasures and routine movement. It is thus the terrain on which quotidian manoeuvres and modes of dwelling are unreflexively carried out, a habitat organised to enable continuity and stability, and which is recreated by these regular existential practices. As Charlesworth says, a place 'exists through the realisable projects and availabilities, patterns of use and users, all of which are practically negotiated daily'. This 'unnoticed framework of practices and concerns is something in which we dwell' as 'habituated body subjects' (2000: 90–91). Thus there exist spatial constraints and opportunities which inhere in the organisation and affordances of places and these mesh with the bodily dispositions emerging out of the routine practices of its inhabitants that become embedded over time. The semiotic meanings of space must be separated for analytical purposes, for space is not only understood and experienced cognitively. Rather it is approached with what Crouch (1999a) calls 'lay geographical knowledge', a participatory disposition in which the influences of representations and semiotics are melded with sensual, practical and unreflexive knowledge.

Time geographer Hagerstrand provided an influential reading of how time–space paths become marked upon familiar space. Collectively, places in which shared work and recreation are carried out link the individual time–space paths which Hagerstrand sketches out. Whatever the limitations of this kind of geography, it usefully identifies points of spatial and temporal intersection and alerts us to the routinisation of action in space (see Gren, 2001). As well as being signifiers of identity as discussed above, local shops, bars, cafés, garages and so forth are points of intersection where individual paths congregate; they become sedimented in the landscape and in the habit-body, providing a geography of communality and continuity. Linked by the roads down which people drive and the paths which they walk along, places which accumulate venues for shopping, services, relaxation and entertainment are particularly obvious examples of what Massey (1995) calls 'activity spaces', spaces of circulation in which people co-ordinate and synchronise activities. Such spaces stabilise social relations in time–space (Gren, 2001: 217). These are small-scale congregational sites, the 'crossroads, street corners and open squares where people meet, shop, chatter, tell stories, fight at night' (Kayser Nielsen, 1999: 282). Mapping enactions in everyday spaces would comprise the inscription of paths, constellations of co-presence, fixtures, meeting points and intersections.

To elaborate upon this skein of purposive and unreflexive action in unrepresented space, I want to draw on the notion of the 'taskscape' which foregrounds unreflexive modes of dwelling, of 'being-in-the-world, of mundanely organising and sensing the environment of familiar space. Ingold and Kurttila (2000) explore the ways in which the Sami people of northern Finland understand the weather they confront. Unlike the more abstract, quantifiable and scientific approach of climatologists who *record climate*, the Sami *experience weather*. As a sensuous form of knowing, weather is intimately related to patterns of work and important events, is recalled in cherished memories – and as such forms 'part of the ongoing construction of those familiar places, along with their surroundings, that people call "home"' (ibid.: 187). Weather is also part of the everyday experience of work and play and is part of a practical knowing of familiar space. Accordingly, some Sami develop great skill at reading and anticipating weather, daily and seasonally, although this changes along with perceptions generated by changing technology – for instance, new forms of transport such as the snowmobile and motorbikes require different forms of knowing weather, of *feeling* forms of snow and manoeuvring vehicles appropriately. The apprehension of weather is, for the Sami, a multi-sensory awareness which facilitates spatial orientation and co-ordinates activity, an immersed, space-making practice which embeds identity.

In drawing a distinction between their apparently modern way of knowing and the embodied, sensual, improvisational knowledge of the Sami, the bureaucrats and scientists label the latter as 'traditional', a notion which is conceptualised as having been handed down for generations, typically as a fixed set of ideas, and thus as a form of cognitive knowing. Instead, reiterating my points about tradition in the previous chapter, Ingold and Kurttila insist that this misunderstands tradition, which should be properly understood not as a reified set of endlessly repeated practices, passed on as cultural heritage, but as knowledge acquired through flexible practice. Tradition thus 'undergoes continual generation and regeneration within the contexts of people's practical engagement with significant components of the environment' (ibid.: 192).

This kind of tradition is not a matter of common descent, but is inseparable from a situated, sensuous engagement with the environment, and thus can be 'continuous without taking any fixed form' (ibid.). In conclusion, Ingold and Kurttila regard this knowing as a skill, understood as a quality inhering within the relations between people, and between people and things in a particular space, as an unfixed and improvisatory disposition, which is influenced by 'the presence and activities of predecessors' (ibid.: 193). Thus such knowledgeable practices make space, are part of the ways in which people inhabit space and come to belong in it.

The 'taskscape' is space to which inhabitants have an everyday practical orientation. The land does not determine action, but the materiality of the environment, its surfaces, contours and the elements in it, offer affordances that foster a range of actions, delimiting some and enabling others. This insistence on the practical use of inhabited space resounds in how people 'dwell' in place, sensuously adapting everyday practices and assumptions from the past. The relationship we have to places, rather than being conceived solely as representative and cognitive, is embodied, sensual, bound up in what we do in space, in how we co-ordinate our movements and organise routes and nodes around which we orientate ourselves, in how we feel and sense them, in what we focus on and ignore. This collective sense of inhabiting is also shaped around the technologies we employ, and how we contest their use and meaning with fellow inhabitants. This is emphatically, then, not a static spatial reification but an ongoing process through which space is (re)produced.

Primarily, these ways of inhabiting are unreflexive and constitute part of the 'common sense' of dwelling within space. Yet again, when they are subject to contestation from without, or when rapid change seems to threaten the continuity in ways of doing things, when enduring fixtures, familiar pathways, characteristic features and landscapes are removed or radically altered, a sense of disorientation can result. Suddenly, what was a taken-for-granted aspect of the object-world can symbolise resistance to change.

Space is produced by inhabitants through habit, through a constant engagement with the world which relies on familiar routines, which constructs an ongoing spatial mapping through the enaction of everyday mobilities: the daily commute to work, or the drive to the shop, or walking the dog in the local park – and the quotidian points of congregation, interaction, rest and relaxation. Out of this mobile mapping of space evolves an embodied rhythm which sews time and space together. As an immersed practice, the accumulation of repetitive events becomes sedimented in the body to condense an unreflexive sense of being in place. This sense of place is consolidated at an individual level, where the same rituals are enacted at a daily level, enactions which become part of a biographical career in traversing space–time constituted by following regular routes along which an accumulating sequence of distinct events are experienced. And this is further sustained by a collective sense of place which is grounded through a sharing of the spatial and temporal constellations where a host of individual paths and routines coincide. Meaning becomes sedimented in time as successive social and cultural contexts are materialised, remembered, projected and performed upon space. In this poetics of ordinary spatial life, bodies and places become intertwined, much as in Jacobs's (1961) depiction of the 'intricate sidewalk ballets' which local pedestrians perform to constitute regular choreographies on New York streets, weaving territory over and over again. The congruence of cognitive, affective, sensual and embodied effects which inhere in these dense relationships between people and space serves to strengthen the power of place.

Whilst the notion of taskscape is extremely rewarding in highlighting the unreflexive constitution of spatial belonging, it suggests a certain active engagement with the world which appositely renders the relationship between work and space but tends to downplay modes of inhabiting space which are not task-driven, such as relaxing, resting and dwelling in the world. Referring to the kinds of (southern) English landscapes cited above, Kayser Nielsen avers that they are not merely part of a symbolic realm but also involve a 'bodily action-dimension' in the 'bodily pleasure in partaking in a landscape together with other people' (1999: 281). Thus we might summon up the smell of freshly mown grass, the shade of a deciduous tree and the noises experienced whilst watching a match on a village cricket green. Perhaps the collective impact of the various ways in which people apprehend and understand familiar space is captured by Tuan's notion of 'topophilia' (1974). The acquisition of this topophilia can be facilitated by engaging with space, in the sense that Kayser Nielsen says that 'physical activity in the open air seems to be a way to acquire "Norway"' (1999: 286). Developing his remarks, he argues that to move physically in a landscape, to get out into the open air, to use the body, becomes a work of identity that we undertake with the national popular purpose of self-understanding' (ibid.). Such topophilia perhaps turns into 'topophobia' when transformations in agricultural production, for instance, render the landscape unfamiliar, such as the swathing of land with coniferous trees or the erasure of hedges as field size is increased.

Homely Space

I want to develop the above discussion by changing focus to explore the emotional notion of 'home', often synonymous with nation. 'Home' is a vitally important spatial concept which echoes in much of what I have described above. As Sopher has observed, home can equally refer to 'house, land, village, city, district, country, or, indeed, the world', transmitting the sentimental associations of one scale to others (1979: 130). As a way of making spatial sense of the nation then, home is able to link these spatial levels together, from the small-scale domestic to the large-scale space. 'Home' conjoins a myriad of affective realms and contains a wealth of transposable imagery. For instance, 'good housekeeping' can be applied to the family finances and to the policies of the state treasury, monarchs are often referred to as the head of the national family, the national football team plays 'at home' and 'away'. The centrality of home to constructions of identity partly testifies to the desire to achieve fixity amidst ceaseless flow, and metaphorically is used to proffer a unified, identifiable culture within a specified space, being 'drenched in the longing for wholeness, unity, integrity' (Morley and Robins, 1995: 6).

The construction of home, like the nation, is integral to the boundaries of space-making, specifying the enclosed realm of the 'private' in contradistinction to the 'public', and the national as distinct from the space of the 'other'. This notion of privacy is perhaps best expressed in the idea of home as a place of *comfort*: 'convenience, efficiency, leisure, ease, pleasure, domesticity, intimacy and privacy' (Rybczynski, 1988: 231), where the body is relaxed and unselfconscious – although such modes of bodily relaxation are not 'natural' but culturally variable, as I will discuss in Chapter 4. The term 'home-making' pinpoints the ways in which we 'make ourselves at home' in the world according to social and aesthetic conventions about conviviality, domesticity and furnishing and decorating space. There are recognised codes of décor and aesthetic regulation which are passed across generations and between locals and fellow nationals: the colour codes of interior domestic spaces, the styles of furniture, the range of artefacts and ornaments, the modes of demarcating domestic territorial boundaries.

Home-making includes the domestication of things and experiences from the external world, and of otherness, so that a kind of vernacular curation takes place whereby items are assigned to places in the home. The distribution of 'foreign-ness' within domesticity is usually contained, rarely takes over the home, and is contextualised as *style*. The importation of exotic and unfamiliar objects and aesthetics is thereby incorporated to mark out difference, and operates as a form of distinction. And such aesthetic codes gradually become normative and recognis-able as dimensions of national home-making. For example, English suburbia has experienced crazes whereby 'exotic' plants signify superior taste. The whole idea of English suburbia might be said to concern the domestication of a sentimental version of (English) rurality into the urban. Bringing things from the wider world into the home establishes connections with other places and times, but the home remains the hub of such relations.

Once more, it is important to remember that the home is the site of a wealth of unreflexive, habitual practice, where the norms of reproduction, housework and maintenance are entrenched. The competence of householders with regard to the often unspoken codes about household reproduction raises again the idea of the 'taskscape'. Home is where we know how the appliances work, and which tele-vision programmes will distract the children. These unreflexive dimensions are also inherent in the spatial organisation of home. As Young argues, the home is the arrangement of things in space 'in a way that supports the bodily habits and routines of those who dwell there' (1997: 136). Modes of communal dwelling are shaped by such knowledge regarding what particular activities should be carried out in which spaces – where we should eat, cook, watch television – and where the inhabitants of the house should be located in terms of bedrooms and so on. Such conventions are part of routine life and yet become glaringly apparent when we enter domestic spaces in which inhere different codes. For instance, I have already mentioned how in the Gujarati village I stayed in some years ago the grandmother from next door would enter the house in which I resided to relax on the couch or bed, seemingly possessing no notion that this transgressed any (British) idea about privacy.

To exemplify these distinct modes of space-making at home, Chevalier (1998) shows how for the French the kitchen is the most affective, symbolic space for the interaction with nature, for the transformation of natural products (foods) into cultural products. This necessitates an expertise in cooking and preparing food, as part of a particular (gendered) taskscape, which, she argues, has its parallel in the English passion for gardening. Both produce an intimate relationship with space, and generate particular modes of conviviality and routine which constitute distinct forms of domesticity. It is interesting that these domestic practices of gardening and cooking, together with ideas about DIY and interior decoration, have long been subject to the supervision of public 'experts' who mediate innovations, and the influence of commercial interests who capitalise on new trends. In fact, Chevalier argues that these spheres of activity are increasingly mediated and reflected upon by television programmes in both nations. This certainly acts to introduce new ideas which promiscuously borrow from other cultural traditions of home-making. But rather than being wholly influenced by this mediatised information, the domestic gardener negotiates with these contexts, accommodating and adapting elements within the context of his/her own garden. Moreover, a core of convention remains in the revalorisation of 'traditional' approaches and the recentring of national forms of domestic production in such media forms.

However, above all perhaps, home is most affectively charged through the way it is sensually apprehended, producing a kinaesthetic experience of place which is embedded in memory. Bachelard particularly focuses on the 'felicitous' and 'eulogised' areas within domestic space, such as bedrooms, attics and parlours, and the smaller spaces they contain, the dens, niches and favoured spots in which the sensual experience of texture and micro-atmosphere are absorbed through childhood imagination. Bachelard maintains that in this sense, memory is spatialised so that by remembering these special realms 'we learn to abide within ourselves' (1969: xxxiii), for these 'corners of our world' are the fundamental basis of 'home' and provide a lingering sense of place. In the house of remembered childhood, 'each one of its nooks and corners was a resting-place for daydreams' (ibid.: 15). The power of these reveries is revealed as 'our memories of former dwelling-places are relived as daydreams' and persist during our lifetime (ibid.: 5–6).

Besides the application of Bachelard's ideas to the house, we can extend them to explore a wider sense of the local felicitous spaces in the immediate locality. The nooks and crannies of derelict buildings, bus shelters, dens, benches and groves, the back streets, the forbidden zones, the routes of childish adventure, the fields and woods, places of gathering and parks are the sensual theatres of childhood performance and can likewise provide a rich source of memory. The adventurous child concocts a map of familiar routes and sites of play which constitute an imagined geography that precedes the more pragmatic adult spatial networks. But these later practical frameworks can be continually invaded by dreams and reveries stimulated by the earlier map. Passing or sighting the sites of childhood sport can disrupt the business-like progression towards a destination with the sensual memory of an indefinable childish experience. For instance, walking around the environs of childhood I am reminded of how I used to collect cocoons under the ledges of walls, and form loops out of privet stems and collect hundreds of spider webs from the garden hedges during the morning walk to school. I can identify where me and my friends would choose apt places from which to ask passers-by if they would give us a penny for the guy, and can remember the grassy slopes which were used to sledge down in the winter. I do not mean to be sentimental; rather, my intention is to raise the deep embeddedness of place and its links with biography and the wider world which constitute how we come to 'know' places, understanding their textures.

For familiar spaces are commonly the instigators of involuntary memories of earlier sensual experiences. As Lippard comments, 'If one has been raised in a place, its textures and sensations, its smells and sounds, are recalled as they felt to child's, adolescent's adult's body' (1997: 34). Margaret Morse writes that home may be conjured up by a 'fortuitous and fleeting smell, a spidery touch, a motion, a bitter taste . . . almost beyond our conscious ability to bid or concoct or recreate' (1999: 63). This sense of home is 'chanced upon, cached in secret places safe from language' (ibid.: 68). Thus the texture of the world, the feel of familiar spaces underfoot, the barely perceptible subtleties of climate, the vegetation of the everyday places: the feel of grass, crops in fields, woodlands, the grids and curbs familiar to roadside childhood games are all part of a sense of place which extends from home and garden to the wider locality and beyond. The structure of feeling of place is not simply a matter of subjective experience, for the affordances of fixtures, textures and climate link places together as knowable, sensual spaces, impressions that can be hinted at in fiction and film. Laurie Lee's novel about a Cotswold childhood, *Cider With Rosie*, draws on sensual experiences that also pertain to other areas of England, and Terence Davies's memorable film, *The Long Day Closes*, set in 1950s Liverpool, resonates with other historical experiences of British urban life in its brilliant reproduction of the sounds and textures of the director's childhood. The home and its hinterland is the realm for 'a specific *materialisation* of the body and the self; things and spaces become layered with meaning, value and memory' (Tacchi, 1998: 26). Here Tacchi is addressing the domestic soundscapes whereby 'radio sound creates a textured "soundscape" in the home, within which people move around and live their daily lives'. Thus the home is also a smellscape and soundscape, a space of tactile sensation which can be deeply embedded in everyday life and in memory.

The home, though, as I have emphasised, is not a static realm but is continually reproduced by domestic work and by social and cultural activities. A sense of home can be threatened by the presence of otherness and in this sense is linked to national constructions of 'us' and 'them'. It is, as I have argued, concerned with erecting boundaries between spheres of activity and exerts powerful conventions about what belongs in domestic space. There is always a lurking sense of the uncanny or the dangerous in contrast to the safety of the home: the stranger who comes too close, the wild beasts – pests and other people's pets – and invasive flora which can undo the domestic ordering of space. This can be illustrated by referring back to *The Long Day Closes*, where the sudden appearance of a black man at the family door generates a combination of panic and hostility to an unfamiliar face in this parochial context. Home is thus the subject of other kinds of exclusion, a purified space into which species of otherness must not enter, or at least not stay very long. For Rapport and Dawson, the notion of *heimat* is an 'attempt publicly and collectively to impose home as a social fact and a cultural norm to which some must belong and from which others must be excluded. Hence, "exiles" and "refugees"; and hence, too, "tramps" and "bag-people" expelled from the ranks of those felt deserving of combining house and home' (1998: 8–9). These defensive operations act to debar the unwelcome from entering the 'homeland' at an official level, and are also mobilised at a smaller scale where cultural, ethnic and 'racial' difference is subject to communal prejudices in housing markets and rented accommodation, in employment and in social services, and of course, by routine insults ensuring that 'outsiders' are 'not welcome'. Homely areas are thus protected against those who are unable to masquerade as national and often they are consigned to special areas by edict or to achieve safety in numbers. These 'places on the margin' (Shields, 1991), 'ethnic areas' or 'ghettos' are typically distinguished from other spaces within the nation as enclaves within which difference can be contained (and desired).

I have discussed the imaginary home as an idealised refuge but, as Watkins (2001) details, home is a multiple site, a place of both oppression and liberty, it can restore and stifle, it can be a place of nightmarish rigidity and regulation or a site for the transcendence of the mundane. This raises the highly gendered nature of most forms of domestic space, a division whereby gendered spaces and spheres of activity are arranged in diverse cultural ways. Regressive notions of *dasein* can persist wherein home is a fixed kind of being as opposed to a process of becoming. This is strikingly borne out in Clifford's announcement, 'to theorise, one leaves home' (1989: 177), which certainly recognises the unreflexive comfort of home but seems to propose a masculine pioneer, paying his adieus and setting off into unchartered territory. The home is a (feminised) place in which to dwell and must be left in order to engage with the wider world, after which it is returned to once more. This is certainly a well-worn trope in national myth, in masculinist and colonial fiction (Shurmer-Smith and Hannam, 1994: 17–28; also see Dawson, 1994; Low, 1993). It is to preserve and enrich home that men go out to confront monsters, raw nature and other perils. For the women to whom they return, home can be a prison rather than a refuge. By contrast, Young argues that the gendering of space may not be entirely negative, arguing that the 'feminine' domestic practices of 'arranging, ordering, protecting, cleaning and caring' (Young, 1997: 135) are important because they produce value and meaning in space, and provide a realm of sustenance and self-expression, since 'dwelling in the world means we are located among objects, artefacts, rituals and practices that configure who we are in our particularity' (ibid.: 153).

Increasingly, despite the apparent fixity of home, a sense of homeliness may not only be achieved by a situatedness in particular physical space but may also be reached via homely networks of people and information. By means of a phone call, an e-mail, by tuning into a radio or TV station which broadcasts national programmes, home can become a set of regular links and contacts. It is possible, indeed is increasingly common, for there to be several simultaneous senses of home as social and cultural networks become more complex. Yet familiar reference points are sought. This is nowhere clearer than in the kinds of homes-from-home that are established in expatriate communities. The attempts of the British in India to develop cantonments which were utterly distinguished from the 'native quarters' of cities is a useful example. Creating a landscape full of well-watered parks, gardens, sports grounds and even English flora which did not prosper in Indian climates, the colonial administrators and residents of these spaces tried to recreate an Englishness in the midst of unfamiliarity. Interior décor, forms of familiar architecture such as English churches, and the infrastructure of clubs and rituals reproduced an imaginary England around which routines and habits could be re-enacted. Similarly, Lippard refers to the ways in which Japanese migrants to the USA, identified as suspiciously 'other' and incarcerated during the Second World War, created 'memory landscapes in miniature, making small ponds, gardens, parks, vistas and dioramas in the arid wastes' as a form of identity sustenance and cultural resistance (1997: 68).

This making of home is also evident in more contemporary situations. Wilson describes how British expatriates working on a water supply scheme in Nigeria in the 1980s dwelt within a strictly demarcated, fenced-off compound. Attempts to recreate a homely Britishness in the realm of the unfamiliar extended to the establishment of several fixtures and practices. British styles and ornaments were imported to decorate homes, children were encouraged to join clubs such as the Brownies and attend Sunday School, English bank holidays and common festivals such as Shrove Tuesday and Bonfire Night were fastidiously observed, World service broadcasts (described by one inhabitant as a 'lifeline') and recorded sporting occasions were regularly listened to and viewed. The consolidation of identity was a deeply gendered process where men – usually the workers on the project – established sporting routines, whilst the women took up the replication of a form of British domesticity. Perhaps the most significant element of this home-making and the recreation of a taskscape was in the provision of food. One expatriate wife described the lengths she went to make sausage rolls, making pastry and mincing a side of pork into sausage meat. In Britain, such foods are available from bakers and in frozen form, yet the necessity of maintaining a specific diet and lifestyle was imperative. This was further reinforced by the propensity of women residents to greet new wives to the enclave with an array of pies and flans to establish a feminised British commonality and to prove that they could cope in the realm of otherness (A. Wilson, 1997). Another interesting, more ambivalent, account of a British expatriate community (in Spain) is provided by O'Reilly (2000), who shows how dense networks of associations and activities consolidate a shared Britishness in the space of otherness. Yet Spain is also articulated in more positive ways as a space which enables greater self-expression and a better lifestyle in marked contrast to Britain, where the weather and social conventions can be restrictive.

This reveals how one kind of home is re-established in a world of greater movement. Yet although such attempts to remake home may tend towards the recursive, writers such as Gilroy (1994) have described how a mobile sense of home is possible, where the focus is on 'routes' rather than 'roots' and where the nomadic home-from-home is a feasible counter-construction. The ways in which people increasingly set up home in different places over a lifetime does not necessarily mean that a sense of home becomes dissipated; rather, a form of domestic seriality is achieved, where familiar routines are reintegrated with place, familiar reference points are sought, and well-known networks are plugged into once more. In this more mobile context, home may become less rooted in a single place and be constituted by the connections between places, as memories, practical and decorative artefacts, and knowledge are serially recreated. Watkins, explaining her own experience of different domestic locations, maintains that the process does not 'represent a linear progression or hierarchy of periods that were lived and somehow "completed": this was not a succession whereby one home fully *replaced* another, but rather an *accumulation* of lifeworlds, or of space-times, with each addition reconfiguring the interconnections between the others' (2001: 10). Points of similarity between places are woven together, the spatialisation of habit ensures that recognisable pathways and fixtures are sought around which to orient practical action; the domestic sphere becomes enlarged in space and time but is no less effective as an emotional and cognitive constituent of identity, as common frames of reference are set up. For instance, in discussing her move from the UK to Vancouver, Watkins describes how she filled her new space with music and movement, establishing a soundscape and a rhythm that simultaneously consolidated a feeling of home and announced her arrival (ibid.: 13). In the networks established by such travelling, 'proximity is a relational effect constituted by similarity, or . . . familiarity, and "distance" becomes a case of contrast rather than kilometres' (ibid.: 11), and so identity and a sense of home can be simultaneously grounded and mobile. Emphatically then, home is not only a matter of place but exists 'in words, jokes, opinions, gestures, actions, even the way one wears a hat' as part of a life 'lived in movement' (Berger, 1984: 64).

So it is that nationals living abroad retain a sense of national identity, irrespective of the multiple sources of home they experience. This is nowhere more obvious than in the diasporic spaces inhabited by migrants who retain links with the homeland which can allow for a sense of identity which switches between the physical location dwelt in and one sustained virtually. For instance, Gillespie has showed how young Asians living in the South extend their viewing practices by watching British television programmes along with the products of satellite broadcasts, video and cable television produced for Asian diasporas (1995).

Conclusion

In recent years there have been several accounts that point to the increasing placelessness wrought by globalisation. Through global processes, it is asserted, the national, regional and local specificities of place are erased in the production of homogeneity and 'serial monotony' (Harvey, 1989). They become 'non-places' (Auge, 1995). Inhabitants who formerly possessed an easy understanding of what their homely spaces meant and what could be practised therein are now, it is claimed, faced with 'illegible landscapes' (Allon, 2000: 275). Whilst these descriptions appear to relate to certain spaces such as international airports and certain kinds of shopping centres, global processes are more typically context-ualised within a local setting. Rather than overwhelming local space, they are inserted into it through various codes of spatial ordering, where over time they become domesticated additions to a familiar spatial palimpsest. Responses to these processes have been described as defensive and essentialist rearticulations of national identity, and yet it would also seem that such developments foster the making of innumerable potential connections and opportunities for dialogue across space. At another level, the stability of spatial belonging is also threatened by other kinds of identifications. With an increase in the potential for mobility, particular kinds of identity are forged through a familiarity with otherness – for instance, in the creation of a 'cosmopolitan' as opposed to a 'local' identity (Hannerz, 1990). Moreover, there has been a proliferation of 'third spaces' or 'spaces on the margins' (Shields, 1991) where alternative identities are established (or to where outsiders are despatched). The nomad has been a popular metaphor to account for the growth in international migration and to describe the rhizomatic movements of those subversively undercutting the reifications imposed by spatial fixity. Such movement promulgates the possibility that spatial referents become stretched across space rather than being situated in local or national settings. It is my contention here, though, that whilst these are all pertinent descriptions of contemporary spatial processes and processes of identification, the nation remains the paramount space within which identity is located. At cognitive, affective and habitual levels, the national space provides a common-sense context for situating identity. Indeed, it is worth mentioning that diasporic communities are apt to constitute dense networks of association which are based upon national identity, as Nugent (2001) details in her study of diasporic Irish communities, producing an evermore dynamic and contested Irishness which is no longer located solely in Ireland.

I have tried to show that the ways in which the nation is spatialised are complex and fold into each other. The complicated geographies of national identity depend on a range of institutional and everyday practices, from the drawing of boundaries between countries and at home, to convivial collective celebrations at places of congregation to the habits of the home, from the representation and ideological use of particular landscapes to the inured enactions grounded in taskscapes. To engage with the deep ways in which the nation is embedded in notions of space, it is vital to conceive of space as multifaceted: as evidence of (political, capital) power, as symbolically and semiotically loaded, as aesthetically interpreted and fashioned, as sensually apprehended and part of embodied identity, and as a setting for reflexive and unreflexive practices.

For national space to retain its power, it must be domesticated, replicated in local contexts and be understood as part of everyday life. The diverse spaces I have discussed here are of different geographical scales and, as I have mentioned, the power of national geography gains its power from the linkages which pertain between these spaces. This spatial scaling of the nation operates at a variety of levels. It is present in the televisual space (in the space of the home) which is beamed to a (national) community of viewers, which transmits a host of spatial images, including national ideological landscapes, iconic sites and sites of popular congregation, everyday spatial fixtures and the mundane landscapes of quotidian life. It is facilitated by technologies of mobility which enable people to travel across the nation and experience national signs and the regional distinctions which are identified as being incorporated into the nation. It is present in the structure of feeling engendered by a complex of everyday living, personal and collective memory, common topics of shared discussion, shared and synchronic activities, and the affective and sensual experience of place. These spatial experiences are located in well-known habitats, in taskscapes and leisure spaces, and in institution-alised settings in which ordinary activity is pursued, at shared events in collective space, from watching the big football match in the pub to partaking in national ceremonies in local contexts. And the exclusions established at national level concerning who belongs where according to race and ethnicity and political belief can also be monitored at local levels. I have shown how the spatial metaphor of 'home' operates across a variety of spaces, and how the strength of its association with nation means that other, smaller-scale meanings can be absorbed or elided with the national.

An interesting dimension of this spatialisation is that each of the modes I suggest also conjures up forms of temporality which characterise national identity. The national landscape ideologies are imagined as enduring spaces, spaces forged over millennia through the sacrifice of blood and toil. They are in some cases tied to earlier eras of nation-formation, such as the Argentinian *pampa* or the American Rockies, or are believed to have been an essential part of national identity from time immemorial. Iconic sites and places of congregation are sites visited as part of biographical imperatives – worthy of a visit during a lifetime – or they are associated with commemorative occasions or special national events. They thus might annually mark rituals or form part of the national history. Quotidian landscapes and everyday spaces are associated with cyclical time, the ongoing reproduction of place-bound lives and local and national space (for a more developed discussion concerning the temporality of national identity, see Johnson, 2001). As Crang contends, temporal patterns 'can encompass the dialectic of life course and daily life with different scales of projects intersecting, and thus meshing longer-term power relations and positions within society with small-scale events' (2001: 193).

Modern nation-building has entailed the incorporation of all internal differences, so that whatever regional and ethnic differences may pre-date the nation's formation they all become subservient to, and part of, the greater national entity. Region, city, village all remain tied to the nation as a larger ontological and practical framework within which local activities take place. Local differences are absorbed into a 'code of larger significance' (Sopher, 1979: 158). Such differences are not erased; far from it. For the modern classifying imperatives which accompany the formation of national identity (re)construct regions and localities as integral constituents of national variety. Accordingly, distinct customs, dialects, costumes and diets, natural history, sites of interest, styles of architecture and historical episodes are all catalogued and disseminated as part of an imagined, internally complex national geography. Thus the English countryside has been intensively mapped, demarcated and described in the compilation of a national geographical treasury, as regional difference has been commuted into the national by an army of academic experts. These celebrations of regional diversity have been more widely propagated by the publication of popular books such as H.V. Morton's *In Search of England* and the more contemporary multitude of coffee table books, road guides and atlases which detail the ornithological, archaeological, historical and arch-itectural curiosities of regions. Thus the outpouring of popular volumes about

'England' is backed up by institutionalised modes of knowing the nation. They accompany and fuel the imperative, since the early years of motoring, to tour the nation. As Crang reports of the champions of motor touring in Sweden: 'to really know Sweden meant to get out there amongst it' (2000: 91). Through these classificatory programmes, Lowenthal (1994) points out how the 'traditional objectivism' of geography ignores the complexity of lived spaces, for the bounded realms containing these local particularities were formerly not apparent. The continuities of experience which characterised pre-modern travel between areas meant that such distinctions were far more ambivalent and geographically indeterminate than they are now believed to be. For instance, Billig describes the distinct, pre-national regions of France, where accents, food, produce and language were not properties of identifiable regions but changed incrementally through space, according to the testimony of contemporary travellers (1995: 30–31).

Yet the compendium of regional distinction is commonly organised in hierarchical fashion. As is apparent in my discussion of national landscape ideologies, certain landscapes and regions are assigned heightened status as markers of national identity than others. Taylor (1994: 22) discusses the prevalence of the southern 'Home Counties' in the English geographic imagination. He shows how the nineteenth-century British Association for the Advancement of Science aimed to investigate – through photography – the distinct regional, 'racial' characteristics that existed throughout the United Kingdom. Yet these were defined against the norm, namely those inhabitants imagined as 'Anglo-Saxon' or 'Teuton' who lived in the Home Counties and London. This early example of the hierarchical coding of regions is part of a selective approach to the varied spaces within a nation which has generated the association of specific regions with national identity, so that Southern rurality serves as the prime exemplar of Englishness. This partiality persists in television, film, advertising and tourist marketing and is evident in the popular books about the English countryside which I have mentioned, where there is a preponderance of Southern scenes, histories and attractions. Crang describes how the particular Swedish vision of 'the folk' becomes particularised around the key region of Dalarna (Crang, 2000).

The elements of national space are linked together to constitute practical and symbolic imaginary geographies which confirm the nation as the pre-eminent spatial entity. At the level of representation and in their semiotic design, places – links in this chain of national signifiers – reproduce meanings because they are intertextual: 'various texts and discursive practices based on previous texts are deeply inscribed in their landscapes and institutions' (Barnes and Duncan, 1992: 8). And at many levels – in the embodied experience of space, the affective responses to familiar and spectacular sites, and the consumption of familiar spatial representations – our experience is apt to carry echoes of other places which are part of a national geographic knowledge. This is well exemplified by the article by Archetti cited above where urban and rural symbolic spaces (the *pampa*, *potrero* and *baldío*), symbolic national activities (horse-rearing and football), and symbolic characters (gauchos and Diego Maradona) are combined to produce a (masculinised) geography. This linking of spaces occurs in various ways. For instance, in the same way that visitors link the famous landmarks that are visible from the top of the Eiffel Tower in an attempt to categorise what they see (Barthes, 1984: 9), tourist organisers and tourists link together spaces of national significance in itineraries, and also search for samples and signs of everyday national identity.

This geographical matrix is further associated with symbolic institutions, performances and practices, objects, people, times and other cultural elements of national identity. Imagined communities are solidified and naturalised by the density of such bonds. These chains of national signifiers frame identity and tend to delimit other ways of conceiving and feeling, and making connections between places. Constituting a shared set of symbolic geographical resources, they make possible the continual reassembly of the nation. The nation as space, like a force field, supersedes other forms of identity and incorporates them, adding to an ontological and epistemological weight which is difficult to shift.

Massey's notion of a progressive sense of place does much to decentre essentialist notions of place. Places can be considered as 'knots in networks of meaning' (Shurmer-Smith and Hannam, 1994: 15) through which a host of cultural, economic, social and material flows ceaselessly occur. Places are becoming increasingly stretched out to include points of origination and destination from further afield. However, despite the vast increase in international flows, most journeys at daily, monthly, annual levels, and over the life-course, are most densely accumulated at local and national level. While people increasingly choose foreign holidays, their weekend jaunts are within the nation. They largely shop, work and travel in national contexts, linking up symbolic and familiar features and places through their family networks and television-viewing habits over time. Constellations of symbolic, practical and everyday space primarily continue to be organised in national contexts. To illustrate this, Lippard writes of the 'dialectic between centre and movement, home and restlessness, that every American understands – even if s/he has never budged, has only watched road movies, read the novels of restlessness, listened to the plaintive ballads of loss [in country music]' (1997: 41).

−3−

Performing National Identity

In this chapter, I focus on the ways in which national identities are (re)produced by using the metaphor of performance in order to explore how forms of national dramas are organised and enacted, and how the nation – and selective qualities associated with it – are staged and broadcast. I will look at both 'official' and popular dramas, but also will examine the ways in which people act in national contexts by performing everyday routines, habits and duties. This allows me to further explore the differently scaled ways in which the nation is (re)produced, from state-sanctioned ceremony and popular spectacle, to the quotidian, unreflexive acts by which people inscribe themselves in place.

Performance is a useful metaphor since it allows us to look at the ways in which identities are enacted and reproduced, informing and (re)constructing a sense of collectivity. The notion of performance also foregrounds identity as dynamic; as always in the process of production. Performance continually reconstitutes identity by rehearsing and transmitting meanings. To fix an exact meaning of identity through enaction is almost impossible for action always takes place in different spatio-temporal contexts, yet it is necessary to transmit a sense of continuity and coherence. By extending the analysis to other theatrical concepts we can further explore the meaningful contexts within which such action takes place. Extending the spatial analysis from the previous chapter, by conceiving of symbolic sites as *stages*, we can explore *where* identity is dramatised, broadcast, shared and reproduced, how these spaces are shaped to permit particular performances, and how contesting performances orient around both spectacular and everyday sites. Moreover, by looking further at ideas about scripts and roles, stage management, choreography, directing, improvisation and reflexivity, we can investigate the parameters of performing national identity.

The previous chapter has identified some of the symbolic stages upon which national identities are played out. To reiterate, these spaces include national landscapes, particular symbolic sites (monuments, historic centres and institutions), points of assembly, and the everyday landscapes of domestic and routine life. Symbolic spaces are (re)produced by performers as sites of importance, even though they may reproduce diverse meanings about them and follow different ideas about the kinds of activities that should take place. And enaction in places frequently expresses people's relationship to space, dramatising themselves and place, often mapping out identities which are situated in wider symbolic, imagined geographies of which the particular stage may be part.

Different performances are carried out on beaches and mountains, in cities, heritage sites, museums and theme parks. These settings are distinguished by boundedness, whether physical or symbolic, and are often organised – or stage-managed – to provide and sustain common-sense understandings about what kinds of activities should take place within them. Indeed, the coherence of such performances depends on their being performed in specific 'theatres'. Following the continuities suggested by performative conventions, enactions are carried out that reinscribe who belongs to place and, crucially, who does not. For particular performances – and particular actors – might seem out of place, revealing the operations of exclusive identities. Whilst the organisation of space cannot always determine the kinds of performance which occur, normative performative conventions that persist through processes of commodification, regulation and representation ensure that regular kinds of performance can be identified at most sites. Nevertheless, competing ideas about what particular sites symbolise may generate contrasting performances, as we will see.

Performances are socially and spatially regulated to varying extents. Stages might be carefully managed, and the enactions of performers can be tightly choreographed or closely directed. Moreover, performances might be scrutinised by fellow performers to minimise any diversions from the usual performative code. Alternatively, the stage's boundary might be blurred, be cluttered with other actors playing different roles, be full of shifting scenes and random events or juxtapositions, and able to be crossed from a range of angles, facilitating improvisatory performances. However, whilst the organisation, materiality and aesthetic and sensual qualities of stages may influence actors, they rarely *determine* the kinds of performances undertaken. For there is a two-way relationship between performers and stage, for the nature of the stage is equally dependent on the kinds of performance enacted upon it. A space that may seem carefully stage-managed may be transformed by the presence of actors who adhere to different norms. Again, this emphasises how stages can change continually, can expand and contract, and how different performances can undermine attempts to fix meaning and action.

Probably the most influential theorist of performance – 'performativity' as she likes to distinguish it – is Judith Butler. Butler has most famously used the metaphor of performativity to identify how *gender* categories are reproduced by actions which are imagined to be pre-discursive, 'natural' effects of *sex*. By playing with dolls, wearing gendered clothes, and generally adopting the gamut of attributes assigned as 'feminine', girls and women continually 'perform' gender. Through this repetitive iteration, performativity materialises gendered bodies as unambiguously fixed and bounded (Butler, 1993: 9). Interestingly, Weber (1998) has considered the nation-state as a performative body, particularly in its institutional effects, and moreover has conceived of this corpus as one that is sexed and gendered.

Butler's discussion is particularly enlightening in discrediting essentialist ideas about gender and, by implication, wider processes of identity formation. It is also valuable that she highlights identity as an ongoing performance, continually in process – and that it is this reiteration which gives it its ontological power, naturalising categories of gender and sex. Butler also considers enactions which use the selfsame normative codes of performativity to challenge and subvert the endless cycle of iteration. However, I am not convinced of the separation Butler makes between *performance* and *performativity*, where performance is characterised as self-conscious and deliberate whereas performativity is understood as reiterative, citational and unreflexive. This unfortunate dualism does not reflect the blurred boundaries between purposive and unreflexive actions. For instance, apparently reflexive performances may become unreflexive 'second nature' to the habituated actor, and unfamiliar surroundings may provoke acute self-awareness of iterative performances where none had previously been experienced. Moreover, it is a misconception to describe habitual acts as unreflexive, for the habitus is formed by a *practical* reflexivity in which embodied know-how modulates unforeseen events.

Addressing the division between reflexivity and non-reflection, Merleau-Ponty argues that intellectual faculties are secondary attributes which are 'rooted in practical and pre-reflective habits and skills' (Crossley, 2001: 62). To illustrate this argument, Crossley describes how Merleau-Ponty used the metaphor of football to explain that much action is practical and engaged rather than contemplative (ibid.: 74–79). Such performance depends on a knowledge of the game, a contextual awareness which for the player incorporates 'the schemas, skills and know-how which dispose her to read and play the game' (ibid.: 76) within the relational space of the player's interactions. This common-sense knowledge utilised whilst playing is not a self-aware consciousness, which would surely minimise one's effectiveness as player, but nevertheless the player's shared assumptions, skill and use of space epitomises a practical reflexive performance. This, of course, is akin to Bourdieu's notion of habitus, which functions below consciousness and 'produces individual and collective practices, and hence history, in accordance with the schemas engendered by history' (1977: 82). Such dispositions are incomprehensible to outsiders who cannot immediately immerse themselves in an unfamiliar field. Throughout this chapter I will be pointing out the different modes of reflexivity which inhere in particular kinds of performance, ranging from the overt rituals of grand national ceremony to everyday habits.

The above discussion also emphasises the relevance of thinking about the body when considering performance, and the need to move away from archaic mind–body dualisms so that we may conceive of 'the *lived*, experiential body – an active, expressive, "mindful" form of *embodiment* that serves not only as the existential basis of culture and self, but also of society and institutions more generally' (Williams and Bendelow, 1998: 208; italics in original). Consciousness is embedded in the body, not separate from it. Thus the body is a carrier of culture and identity, not merely as embodied representation but through performance – what it does, how it moves, speaks, stands and sits. This notion is developed by Thrift, who includes performance in a category of what he describes a 'non-representational theory'; that is, theory that is concerned not with representation and meaning but 'presentations' and 'manifestations' of everyday life (Thrift, 1997). Performance in this sense, is concerned with *becoming* a subject through embodied, affective and relational (to other people, to spaces and to objects) practices in a world-in-process (Nash, 2000: 655). Yet the body image which people have of themselves also reflexively acts back to shape the ways in which they 'locate themselves in space, how they carry themselves, how they experience bodily sensations, how they conceive of identity' (Lupton, 1998: 85). For instance, in some cultural contexts, modes of disporting the body are considered grotesque whereas in others they may be acceptable modes of relaxation. This complex relationship between the body and performance, in which reflexivity vanishes and reappears, is particularly evident when we start to consider the ways in which identity is performed. There are roles which we are conscious of at certain times and not others, and we undertake actions which are not governed by consciousness but which might give rise to intense self-awareness in unfamiliar contexts. Certainly, particular kinds of performance are intended to draw attention to the self, are a vehicle for transmitting identity, and others are decoded by others as denoting identity irrespective of the actor's intentions.

These themes of spatial specificity, regulation and reflexivity re-emerge in the following attempt to distinguish the kinds of performance which express and transmit national identity, and the ways in which the enaction of national identity might be changing. I look at grand formal rituals, popular rituals, touristic staging of the nation, and everyday performances. Whilst these are identifiable modes of performance and distinguishable settings and events, there is considerable overlap, especially with regard to the everyday, mundane performances discussed in the final section.

Formal Rituals and Invented Ceremonies

Still the most obvious and recognisable ways in which national identity is performed are at those national(ist) ceremonies with which we are familiar, the grand, often stately occasions when the nation and its symbolic attributes are elevated in public display. In highly specified, disciplinary performances, the cast of actors during these events – the soldiers, police, marching bands, commanders of horses, government ministers, honorary officials, members of royalty and functionaries carry out specified, pre-ordained manoeuvres, which have often been rehearsed and minutely detailed to ensure the effective conveyance of efficiency and majesty. Such ceremonies are played out to legitimate the power, historical grandeur, military might, legal process, and institutional apparatus of the nation-state.

Most of these rituals have been devised to appear time-honoured but they are, as Hobsbawm and Ranger (1983) have pointed out, 'invented traditions', primarily emerging during the era of nineteenth-century Romantic nationalism – especially between 1870 and 1914 – along with the erection of national monuments, the establishment of museums, the devising of 'scientific' schemes for classifying cultures and races, collections of folklore and canons of national literature, and the instalment of public holidays. Despite their recent origins, claims about their immemoriality are usually an integral part of their appeal for they are normally 'governed by overtly or tacitly accepted rules and of a ritual or symbolic nature, which seek to inculcate certain values and norms of behaviour by repetition, which automatically implies continuity with the past' (ibid.: 1). By circumscribing the use of specific costumes, imposing a rigid order of events, including pseudo-antique carriages and artefacts to form a pageantry that is saturated with the gravitas commonly accorded to ancient rituals, such events perform timelessness, grounding nation in history, symbolising community and legitimising authority. These invented ceremonies, aptly exemplified in the volumes edited by Hobsbawm and Ranger (1983) and Gillis (1994b), seem to have been devised by almost all nations. Across the world, independence day celebrations, presidential inaugurations, flag-raisings, anthem singing, religious occasions, funerals of important figures, military parades and 'archaic customs' tend to follow the same format year upon year, inscribing history on space. Yet these rituals often ape the trappings of antiquity even if of contemporary origin. For instance, as Crang (1998: 166) explains, the Investiture of the Prince of Wales in 1969, a ceremony which was widely celebrated across the British national media, was played out through 'antiquated' rituals specifically designed for the event.

I have discussed elsewhere that certain modes of social performance are subject to a control which minimises the potential for improvisation and attempts to erad-icate ambiguity (Edensor, 2000a, 2001). Thus the key personnel in the organisation of large-scale national rituals – the stage-managers, choreographers and directors of the event, along with the costume designers and stage-hands – co-ordinate the sequence of events and train the participants in how to perform appropriately. They manage the stage upon which these actors will perform, providing cues and advice to facilitate, guide and organise performances in accordance with normative conventions, which are, of course, the 'goals, constraints, resources, conventions and technologies of particular culture-producing groups and their audiences'

(Spillman, 1997: 8). The 'correct' enaction of these rituals often achieves the illusion of fixity and common purpose, although the participants are not necessarily homogeneous but may represent various interest groups. Nevertheless, the imperative to accomplish the proper performance affects them all. Failure to carry out the necessary manoeuvres, or to adopt the correct disposition or attire, can result in harsh censure. In 1982, Michael Foot, the then leader of the British Labour Party, attended the Ceremony of Remembrance at the Cenotaph in Whitehall, Central London, for those killed fighting for the nation. Much media coverage of the event focused on Foot's dress, which was said to resemble a 'donkey jacket', and, as such, showed how little the politician respected the seriousness of the occasion, bringing into question his patriotism and his competence as a potential future Prime Minister. The issue was gleefully capitalised upon by the ruling Conservative Party and their right-wing media allies.

According to Geertz (1993), communal rituals often articulate a 'meta-social commentary' which celebrates and reproduces social ideals and conventions – or at least provides a context for discussions around shared performative conventions and values. The transmission of national identity and ideology is typically achieved through these grandiloquent pageants which through their solemn and precise formations of movement are laden with high production values. But besides offering spectacle, these nationalist ceremonial dramas also inculcate specifiable forms of bodily conduct and comportment, constituting what Connerton (1989) describes as 'incorporating rituals' (contrasted to 'inscriptive' rituals, such as photography and writing) by which groups transmit ideals and reproduce memory through disciplined performance. According to Connerton, by demanding stylised and repetitive performances from the participants, memory and identity become inscribed into the body. Since there is no scope for interpretation or improvisation in these enactions, they become part of 'social habit memory'. This mnemonic effect, embodied within the (national) subject, bestows an affective yet disciplined sense of belonging, a sense that one can successfully perform, that one possesses a competence to enact the ritual and may be called upon to ensure its continued specificity in the future. Memory and identity are thus incorporated into the performer. Moreover, such rituals specify the relationship between performers, and between the performers and the symbolic site (and the wider national symbolic space into which it is incorporated). Such rituals thus constitute powerful pro- grammes for the enaction of collective remembering (and systematic forgetting) (Chaney, 1993: 20). Connerton argues that they require no further questioning, providing 'insurance against the process of cumulative questioning entailed in all discursive practices' (1989: 102). This suggests that contra Geertz, such rituals are performed in an unreflexive manner, and do not create an intersubjective arena for mutual purposive acts to maintain solidarity, for such rituals are not discursively (re)constituted but performed through embodied memory.

A recent example of a small invented ceremony devised (in 1982) to imprint a relationship between site and group, and broadcast this nexus by promoting the event as a tourist attraction, is the ritual of the Knights Templar at Bannockburn Heritage Centre, near Stirling. This occurs on the morning of the anniversary of the Battle of Bannockburn of 1314, where a Scottish army under the leadership of Robert Bruce defeated a larger English force and paved the way for political independence. The group's disciplined and stately manoeuvres around the site, and the militaristic specifications of its ordered enaction, are characterised by dramatic costumes, specified movements and script, and rigorous timing (Edensor, 1997). Although of recent vintage, the play derives its coherence from the willingness of the audience to respectfully record the proceedings and consent to the masculinist, military ideals being presented. The claim for a part in the national story, and the inscription of the participants as Scots and as Templars, depends upon the efficacy of the show to persuade the audience of its ancient character.

Tellingly, in the era of national commemoration that Hobsbawm and Ranger describe, the lack of any existing national ceremonies led cultural nationalists to search for scraps of local rituals to adopt and rebrand as national ceremonies. Thus selective local cultural repertoires became reconceptualised as national (Spillman, 1997: 5). Of course, as discussed before, this leads to the privileging of certain rituals as 'national' and the consignment of the majority of other rituals to the sphere of the 'local'. And yet this latter move is also an integral part of the nation-building project, as the diverse cultures of regions become incorporated within the nation, the container of diversity. Another way of conceptualising these incorporating rituals is to consider them as part of a systematic attempt to channel the energies of popular carnivalesque customs into a more 'civilised' form. The adherence people felt to carnival could be transferred to allegiance to the state. Through creating spectacular rituals, where reason and morality triumph over sensuality, the state could project 'the paradigm of an ethical citizenry' (Lloyd and Thomas, 1998: 53). The effects of these attempts can be to reduce meaning, as Guss argues, for situating carnival and selective local rituals in a national frame 'has required that the hallmark of festive behaviour, its superabundance of symbols and meanings, be shrunk as much as possible to a handful of quickly and easily understood ideas . . . a borrowed image of difference made to stand for the nation as a whole' (2000: 13). Of course, such stagings, in aestheticising and regulating performances, are likely to erase any reference to conflict and oppression, masking the issues of power and domination which may inhere in their local performance and participation. But they are imprinted with different traces of power. The inscription of national identity by disciplined bodily performance has not only been limited to ceremonial events but has been a part of the inculcation of military values onto conscripts, and has also been a feature of national schooling systems, where forms of physical exercise and drill have aimed to create 'correct' comportment. There is thus a continuum between grand national spectacle and the everyday enaction of disciplined movement in national institutions.

In imposing disciplined ritual, stage managers' and directors' attempts to fix meaning by organising the stage and the framework for performance are generally sufficiently rigid to minimise the deconstruction of such acts by questioning, contestation and mockery. However, such subversions must be continually held at bay by the enaction of precise and repetitive movements. Thus the retention of meaning is an ongoing struggle which requires re-enaction to keep at bay alternative interpretations and the claims of contesting identities.

In contemporary times, many of the large-scale commemorations that celebrate national identity are increasingly being performed on a global stage. Large sporting exhibitions such as the Olympic Games provide an opportunity for national stagings in the opening ceremony, and recent bicentennial commemorations of the USA and Australia were projected across the world. In an interesting discussion, Spillman draws a contrast between the American and Australian celebrations. While both events were 'culturally dense and relatively inclusive' (1997: 9), they were also both highly contested. This highlights a general point about how large-scale rituals and ceremonies are less shaped by a cultural elite who delimit the partic- ipation of others, and have been opened up by the clamour for inclusion from those not previously represented. In other ways, however, the priorities of the commemorations differed. Australia was more concerned with projecting its image externally, to the rest of the world, whereas American organisers were more concerned with symbolising internal integration – perhaps, because of the persistence of sharp class, racial and ethnic cleavages in the USA, this was not surprising (Spillman, 1997: 13–14). Also, the search for common cultural denominators and shared symbols around which (most) groups could mobilise were different. For Americans, much focus was directed towards the 'founding fathers', who are acknowledged as key figures in American history by many groups but whose value is contested across political lines. Moreover, shared political values and institutions loomed large in America around condensation symbols such as 'Freedom' and 'Democracy' – which again are concepts which can be interpreted in multiple ways. Australia, by contrast, placed great emphasis on the importance of the land, while in both nations the importance of cultural diversity was contin- ually alluded to. Both nations arranged large and precisely organised showpiece events during these celebrations.

These global stagings also testify to the increasing mediatisation of grand national ceremonies (Thompson, 1995: 179–206). Commentators refer to the tele- vised broadcast of the Coronation of Queen Elizabeth II in 1953 as an event that heralded a national communion via the media. Likewise, the monarch's Christmas speech, instituted in 1932, was a way for the monarch to reach her subjects over the airwaves, firstly by radio and latterly by television. The Royal Tournament, the Trooping of the Colour, and Royal weddings and funerals have been a staple of the British television diet in the latter half of the twentieth century. Becoming merely part of the annual television timetable has removed much of the mystique and gravity of such events, which join the sequence of numerous television spectaculars. While the screening of these rituals has not necessarily led to any diminution in the rigidity of performance, such televised events are also accompanied by other, looser, more informal spectacular dramas, ranging from international sporting events to Royal Command Performance and charity telethons. Such events offer more affective and convivial shared theatricals.

This mediatisation has also been accompanied by the commodification of identity, often through the tourist industry (discussed on pp. 133–140), and also the ways in which these grand rituals have promoted the selling of nostalgia. The flow of global images of selfhood and otherness partially engenders the need to 'record, preserve and collect' (Gillis, 1994a: 14) as the pace of change seems to speed up. For within global culture there has been a proliferation of memories on offer, including global events such as the assassination of American president J.F. Kennedy, the moon landings and events such as Live Aid. This abundance of memories decentres official, national forms of remembrance and 'challenges the status of memory as knowable object' (ibid.: 16). We can choose from an ever-expanding range of memories according to the diverse contexts of identification in which we find ourselves. This possibly indicates the increasing externalisation of memory, as it becomes commodified and enmeshed in mediascapes.

Although Connerton has insisted on the effectiveness of formal ceremony in transmitting and consolidating memory and identity by virtue of the incorporating functions of such performances, recent developments in staging the nation show that there is no need to privilege such events. Indeed, Gillis argues that such performances are less likely to promote memory, for 'traditional memory sites actually discourage engagement with the past and induce forgetting rather than remembering' (ibid.). Especially in an era of detraditionalisation and informal-isation, remembering is an engaged process which does not merely involve the passing down of 'official' knowledge but also the creative, sensual, expressive arts of narrating and staging improvisations. This is well exemplified in the case of the Welsh Eisteddfod, which, in its modern incarnation, was devised as a spectacular display of Welshness primarily for English people. Having been repatriated as an occasion of Welsh national belonging, it was initially circum-scribed by formal poetry reading and musical performance. More recently, however, it has become an event containing many more performances, ranging from pop concerts and raves to political demonstrations and displays of politically informed art. This process whereby 'official' and 'high' culture becomes decentred is furthered by the television transmission of these contested and heterogeneous enactions (Davies, 1998).

Gillis maintains that by 'the end of the 1960s, the era of national commemoration was clearly drawing to a close, but not before bequeathing to later generations a plethora of monuments, holidays, cemeteries, museums and archives' (1994a: 14). Thus, these rituals retain some of their power but are merely part of a wider range of ceremonies which are devised to express identity. Modes, places and occasions for remembering are proliferating and we are now as likely to remember at times and places which we choose ourselves.

Popular Rituals: Sport and Carnival

What is useful about Connerton's account of disciplined, incorporating ritual is that it draws attention to somatic involvement, but such embodied action is also apparent during more convivial, pleasurable and playful ceremonies which may be equally memorable and significant for participants. Moreover, the topophilia engendered by collective engagement in popular symbolic spaces is not only found in official and sober performances but is also evident in a host of popular sites where less formal, directed rituals occur, places of public congregation such as sports stadia, parks and civic squares. I am also referring to more quotidian, homely spaces where national festivities are carried out, including independence day celebrations involving family feasts, and communal rituals, such as Bonfire Night, Burns Night and Thanksgiving (see Susskind, 1992). I suggest that the power of disciplinary incorporating rituals is matched by the affective qualities of these more carnivalesque celebrations, where looser, more improvisatory performances are enacted. In this section, I will look at sport and popular carnivals to explore occasions where bodily expression and emotional participation manifest highly charged expressions of national identity.

Probably the most currently powerful form of popular national performance is that found in sport, progressively more a global spectacle: 'an embodied practice in which meanings are generated and whose representation and interpretation are open to negotiation and contest' (MacClancy, 1996: 4). Sport is increasingly situated in the mediatised matrix of national life, is institutionalised in schools, widely represented in a host of cultural forms and is an everyday practice for millions of national subjects. These everyday and spectacular contexts provide one of the most popular ways in which national identity is grounded.

Famously, shortly after its inception as an organised pursuit, sport was used in the English public schools to train pupils to reinforce national superiority and develop the characteristics of moral manliness deemed necessary to rule in the colonies. Prepared to endure pain stoically, concerned with 'fair play' and team spirit, these middle-class schoolboy exemplars were mythicised as future heroic colonialists, and their deeds were interwoven with imperial conquest and war in poetic and ideological accounts which mapped sport onto empire (Mangan, 1996).

Likewise the idealised English batsman in the game of cricket was utilised to transmit ideas about class and nation. Such characters were exemplary 'gentlemen', where as 'noble and leisured amateurs, they were 'elevated into a new civic idea of vigour, integrity and flair' (Holt, 1996: 53) through their conduct on the field, their immaculate white garb. Later, they were iconic *suburban* paragons, 'modest, reserved and thoroughly respectable' (ibid.: 68) in another form of idealised Englishness.

These performances of national identity on the sporting field are no less persistent today, for national sporting styles are commonly recognisable in sports as varied as tennis, rugby, cricket and football. In football, French, German, Italian, Brazilian, English and Cameroonian national teams are easily identifiable by fans and journalists. These performances of 'traditional' national style are expected, even demanded, often irrespective of success on the field, and express particular national qualities that extend far beyond the sporting arena. Such national attributes are not usually open to question: they form a common global understanding of where particular sports stars and teams originate, and they are, of course, well suited to propagating stereotypes about self-identity and otherness. Whilst these identifiable styles certainly nourish such preconceptions, they also emerge from cultural contexts – ideas about training regimes, the respective values accorded to hard work, teamwork and individual skill, and flamboyance. (For the origins and historical development of national styles, see Lanfranchi and Taylor, 2001: 191–211.) They are therefore part of a habitus, expressing shared dispositions to bodily endeavour, and so conventions of play are shaped by unreflexive perform-ance and habits echoing Merleau-Ponty's notion concerning a 'feel for the game' discussed above. Where these 'natural' approaches to sport seem to be threatened, trainers and fans may protest if the national style is not evident. For instance, Kuper (1996) writes about the reign of Bobby Robson, the former manager of the England national team, as manager of Dutch side, PSV Eindhoven. Despite the team's success, winning the Dutch league in consecutive seasons, he was disliked by the fans for altering the style in which the team played, apparently introducing the less artful 'English style' instead of the elegant 'total football' for which Dutch football is renowned.

National stereotypes of sporting styles circulate amongst fans, and are prop-agated in the media. Besides the routine deixis whereby readers are assumed to share in support for ('our') teams which Billig (1995) discusses, newspapers and television commentators seek recourse in fairly repetitive stereotypes. In the case of Boris Becker and Michael Stich, successful German tennis players in the 1980s and 1990s, English tabloid sports pages were full of comments about their German 'efficiency' and their likeness to 'ruthless' German 'machines'. Descriptions abounded about their 'armoury', for instance – their 'howitzer' serves. These comments are widely understood in a post-war English context in which German economic performance outperformed the British economy. Similarly, Swedish tennis champion Bjorn Borg was routinely referred to as 'Ice-Borg', denoting a mythical Nordic coolness, even lack of humanity (Blain and O'Donnell, 1994). Press coverage of international football tournaments has similarly abounded with such stereotypical comments about national identity (McGuire and Poulton, 1999).

Sport is frequently used in a metaphorical sense, where sporting performance expresses particular forms of embodied capital valued by particular groups. Showing how sport embodies forms of cultural values and social knowledge, Stokes discusses the symbolic importance of wrestling in Turkey as a hegemonic assertion of masculine values. Grounded in Turkish history as a 'theatrical enactment of the struggles and contests of everyday life' (1996: 24), wrestling also allows for a subversive acknowledgement that craftiness and deceit, rather than merely brute force, are also part of the constitution of keeping face and maintaining a masculine status. Tellingly, Stokes compares enthusiasm for wrestling with that for football. Whereas wrestling is seen as definitively and traditionally Turkish, football is conceived of as progressive, modern and European, again highlighting the janus-faced nature of national identity which both asserts tradition and modernity.

These metaphorical codes are most pertinent where representatives of different nations meet in sporting competition. Rauch (1996) shows how for the supporters of French boxer Georges Carpentier, his bout with the American World Heavy-weight Champion Jack Dempsey theatricalised the supposed qualities of each nation, the brutish American against the skilful, cultivated French boxer. The French fighter was endowed with various attributes, epitomising family values, rurality, honour and sophistication, and this was conceived as being embodied in his distinctive boxing style which was distinguished from the purely brutal style of Dempsey. Such metaphorical contests are particularly dramatic when they involve teams or individuals representing previously colonised nations in contest with opponents from the previously colonising powers. The cricketing competitions between India or the West Indies and England have particular resonances as symbolic re-enactments of colonial struggles.

Despite the facility of sport to provide an occasion for the parading of nation-al(ist) antagonisms, it is important to acknowledge how it can stoke up rivalries between groups within the nation, whether ethnic or regional. I have argued (in Edensor and Augustin, 2001) that club football in Mauritius has been a potent vehicle for the parading of ethnic identity, whereas the victories and defeats of the Mauritian national team are of little interest to fans. Here sport seems to undercut any attempt to establish a national identity, foregrounding ethnic rivalries which continue to be more affective sources of identity than the Mauritian nation. The enmity which emerged in Mauritian club football released violent communal conflict, and accordingly those clubs which were traditionally owned, played for and supported by particular ethnic groups have been disbanded in favour of new clubs which are regionally, rather than ethnically, based. Such rivalries within nations are far from unusual, as Armstrong and Guilianotti (2001) catalogue.

There are other threats to the nation from sporting participants who do not perform 'properly' as national representatives. In international sporting endeavour, national identity is *sine qua non*, the uppermost identity on display. This is graphically illustrated by an event during the 1968 Olympic Games in Mexico. Two Black American athletes, Tommie Smith and John Carlos, after winning the gold and bronze medals respectively in the 200 metres athletics final, performed a protest against American racism: in support of the radical Black Power movement they raised black-gloved fists as the US flag was raised and the anthem played. This astonishing performance was televised across the world, interjecting racial protest 'into a ceremonial system that quite literally had no place for representing non-national collective identities such as race, class, religion or ethnicity' (Hartmann, 1996: 550–551). So far beyond the pale was the act believed to be, that it resulted in harsh censure from the American media and effectively ended the athletic careers of the two protesters who were debarred from future contests in the USA.

In the same way as sports journalists and commentators 'present the style of the German or Brazilian football teams as "evidence" of their respective national character' and 'Wimbledon is promoted as "proof" of the historical continuities of British life' (MacClancy, 1996: 13), sports fans are equally labelled as manifestations of national character. The performances in stadia of fans, their use of song and music, the clothes they wear and the flags they wave, their responses to sporting action, defeat and victory, and their propensity to fight all signify what are believed to be identifiable national characteristics. For instance, MacClancy shows how the 'public theatrical antics' of few drunken British football fans in a provincial Spanish city supporting their team in a European competition provided an 'easy symbol for the decline of British society' (ibid.: 14) for Spanish onlookers and press.

Like sport, dance is a form of popular embodied performance where particular styles are believed to embody national characteristics. Through dance, Desmond suggests that social identities are 'signalled, formed and negotiated through bodily movement' (1994: 34). Grounded in located ways of using the body, dance is akin to a language in that 'every dance exists in a complex network of relationships to other dances and other non-dance ways of using the body' (ibid.: 36). Through modes of participation on the dance floor, the collective creation of distinctive atmospheres, the kinds of bodily movements linked to specific styles of music, the acquisition of status through skilled performance, and the combining of individual and collective identity and pleasure, dancing is invariably culturally located as a specific affective expression of identity. These normative embodied performances are evident in the ways in which boundaries around identity may be drawn by identifying national styles – for instance, through the articulation of the Anglo-American conception that Latin dance styles evince a primitive and dangerous sexuality in contrast to the refined movement of European dances (ibid.: 47–50). And despite the promiscuity of dance styles in a global context, where they are exported and adapted, certain symbolic dances are performed to reinstate a sense of identity, varying from the continuous re-domestication of the tango by Argentinians (Savigliana, 1995), to the weekend performance of the Sardana in Catalonian towns and cities as a marker of Catalan identity. In a similar vein, Matless describes the ways in which morris dancing was used to ideologically enchant English rurality with the timeless values of stability and organicism whilst performing a particular kind of English masculinity (Matless, 1998).

These dancing performances are especially evident during carnivals where bodies are displayed in expressive ceremonies that tend to be more fluid and concerned with a politics of pleasure than the stately manoeuvres described in the first section. Festivals range from local pageants to larger-scale national gatherings, and are increasingly likely to be penetrated by other forms of popular culture, promiscuously borrowing from film, popular song and fashion. Thus familiar cultural points of reference are recycled through these performances in an informal, carnivalesque atmosphere. Above I have discussed the stolid ceremony of the Knights Templar at Bannockburn Heritage Centre. On the same day, Nationalist Scots descend in their hundreds at the culmination of a procession from Stirling, including pipe bands, banners, and more recently, participants clothed in the kind of designer-Celt garb that featured in the movie *Braveheart*. Whilst the rituals of wreath-laying and the speeches of politicians observe the formalities, the occasion is permeated by a party atmosphere where old friends meet up, kids play on the grass, literature is sold and people drink alcohol. The chance for participants to imprint their identities on the site in more emotional, convivial fashion contrasts with the sober playlet performed earlier in the day (see Edensor, 1997).

Rather than fixing identity through rigorous stage management and disciplined acting, these popular festivals are more protean, adaptable and contested, can be the site of divergent performances and change from year to year. David Guss's marvellous study of popular festivals in Venezuela highlights the multiple ways in which festivals may be interpreted and contested, varying from global, nationalistic, religious, ethnic and local celebrations. Since the 1950s, many Venezuelan festivals have been drastically transformed by their adoption by the state, which has resituated local traditions in national contexts, through the setting up of a state-funded infrastructure central to the project of establishing a shared national identity. These desires to record and curate performative rituals highlight a nostalgic disposition towards the elsewhere of tradition which becomes manifest in their incorporation into national(ist) projects. No longer merely expressed in local contexts, they are 'suspended between the worlds of ritual obligation and national spectacle' (Guss, 2000: 20).

Most strikingly, Guss points to the continuing role of Cigarrera Bigott, the Venezuelan subsidiary of the multinational company British American Tobacco, in promoting popular culture, notably at a time when the corporation was being integrated into popular consciousness and state policy. The corporation has set up a foundation, producing publications, providing grants to cultural groups, funding workshops and organising TV programmes devoted to Venezuelan popular culture, especially musical and dance forms. The autonomy claimed by artists sponsored by the Bigott Foundation has been compromised by greater company control to ensure that the avowedly populist, leftist ideas they broadcast on TV and in work-shops did not jeopardise the commercial aims of the company. The company has established greater control over the elements and the selection of cultural forms, and the cultural campaigns have been evermore closely allied with the Foundation through more overt sponsorship. This has promoted their goal of attaching the image of their products to national culture and thus inculcating a patriotic desire to purchase amongst consumers, to make the company synonymous with the nation (ibid.: 90–128).

As Guss argues, 'anthropologists and folklorists have ignored the pluralistic nature of cultural forms, preferring to characterise them as the uniform expression of a collective consciousness' (ibid.: 3). Functionally described as rites devised to maintain social solidarity or articulate shared cultural norms, such views proffer static conception of culture and erase agency. There has been little sense, then, of the reappropriation or resignification of such popular festivals by various actors, their linkages in networks of identity which vary from the local to the global, and an expansion of festive forms which are increasingly mobile as they physically and virtually move across space. Yet Guss convincingly shows that the development of Venezuelan festivals has placed them within wider matrices of signification. Now, they are contested by 'local factions, political parties, commercial interests, government, church, media and tourism all tearing at the meaning of these events' (ibid.: 21), not to mention ethnic groups of pre-colonial Venezuelans and Black groups. In a similar fashion, Nurse (1999) shows how the Trinidad carnival has been exported, being variously adapted within a range of cultural contexts. The carnival has always been contested, most typically around the lines of ethnicity and in terms of how cross-class participation has been manifest and represented, but increasingly issues surrounding the commercial content of the carnival, between tourist agencies and other Trinidadians, and between diverse political groups, have emerged. These controversies result out of the globalisation of the carnival, surfacing outside Trinidad, and in the domestication by Trinidadians of themes derived from elsewhere.

There is clearly a global process whereby festivals are increasingly used as a means to advertise commodities through sponsorship. For instance, the Notting Hill Carnival in London – originally an occasion for the celebration of diasporic Caribbean identity – became the Lilt Notting Carnival in 1995 (Nurse, 1999: 677). In addition, there seems to be a further trend to discipline the more carnivalesque elements of such rituals. Handelman (1997: 396) argues that many festivals have been 're-taxonomised, reorganised and disciplined through bureaucratic logic', generated by opponents of 'bacchanalian' aspects. Even at the world famous Rio carnival – signifier of Brazilian national identity – 'rhythm, spontaneity and satire are being controlled and constricted' by bureaucratic power (ibid.: 395). Although the carnival remains an occasion at which normally concealed social tensions are revealed and dramatised, and utopian displays of equality and the body are celebrated, Handelman discusses the forms of regulation that are imposed upon the participating 'samba schools' in the climactic great parade, in accordance with the political imperatives of unity and order. The themes chosen by the dancers must not be satirical or critical of national government, and marks are deducted by the judges if strict conventions of time allotment, and musical and disciplined rhythmic performance are flouted. Seemingly, highly synchronised, spectacular mass dances are replacing improvisational and innovatory forms in an increasingly controlled carnival, which is organised as a spectacle for visual consumption as opposed to an occasion for physical experimentation and immersion. Like the performances discussed in the following section, carnivals are being tamed for tourist markets and to ensure that a 'positive' spectacle of the nation is transmitted.

Yet the mediatisation and spectacularisation of such events may also contribute to increasing contestation over participation and meaning. Guss gives the example of the St Patrick's Day Parade in New York, an occasion for the parading and celebration of American-Irish identity. Yet the festival has been accused of welcoming only certain kinds of Irish-American due to the widely reported protracted legal battle about the right of the organisers to debar a gay and lesbian contingent from marching (2000: 10–11). The drama of such contestations is potentially expanded by their widespread transmission and the politics of exclusion which concerns them. Yet the example also serves to highlight the impossibility of fixing meaning through commercialisation, regulation and incorporation, and it foregrounds the politics of inclusion and exclusion which continue to surround these mutable, open-ended forms of collective performance.

Staging the Nation

In theatrical terms, tourism encourages the production of distinct kinds of stage and is an activity which sustains a host of competing performative norms (see Edensor, 2000a, 2001). As tourism becomes the world's largest industry, national tourism strategies increasingly seek to compete in this global market by advertising their distinct charms; trying to carve out a unique niche that might attract the 'golden hordes'. This depends on both advertising generic landscapes and attract-ions, and promoting particular symbolic sites and events. Part of this imperative to entice tourists and to reward their choice of destination with memorable experiences involves the staging of the nation.

The staging of the nation for education and entertainment is a long-standing feature of national culture, but it has primarily been devised to appeal to and instruct domestic visitors. For instance, large showpieces such as the Great Exhibition in 1851 were designed to inspire a patriotic pride about the British Empire from the mainly domestic audience that witnessed this spectacle. Here, the world was staged for British consumption. Other, more formal attractions, such as the museum, were equally contrived to convey particular attributes and inculcate a specific kind of regulated performance from the museum's visitors. Bennett demonstrates how the organisation of these spaces of knowledge were devised to attain 'new norms of public conduct' (1995: 24). Performative conventions and normative choreographies were co-ordinated by attendants and spatially guided by the layout of display cases, information boards and room plans. Thus visitors performed a unidirectional passage along devised routes 'to comply with a programme of organised walking which transformed any tendency to gaze into a highly directed and sequentialised practice of looking' (ibid.: 186–187). Thus the stagings of officially sanctioned forms of knowledge demanded a particular kind of audience participation.

The stage management of symbolic national spaces and events is now principally directed to less didactic forms of instruction, where affective, sensual and mediat-ised stagings combine with a culture of instruction to produce a synthetic form often termed 'edutainment'. In particular tourist settings, and indeed across the urban spaces of the West, there is an ongoing proliferation of what Gottdiener (1997) calls 'themed' spaces in specialised tourist enclaves and in more quotidian spaces. Highly encoded shopping malls, festival marketplaces, heritage sites, cultural quarters and waterfront attractions comprise an expanding sector of tourist space. The extension of these themed spaces into shopping centres and high streets include such institutionalised theatrical settings as themed pubs and restaurants. The most (economically) successful form of the over-coded pub is, of course, the Irish theme pub, which has been exported to many areas of the world. The staging here involves the creation of a dramatic space in which Irishness is constructed by the inclusion of actual and simulated artefacts and designs which accord with media represent-ations. Such productions have been accused of manufacturing an 'inauthentic' Irishness. Nevertheless different kinds of 'Irishness' are produced. The Celtic Dragon Pub Company offer three 'Irish' themed design packages; namely, an 'Irish country look', the 'city pub' and the upmarket 'castle and manor house' theme where 'all guests will feel like lords and ladies' (http://www.celticdragonpubco.com).

The 'English' pub is also a fixture of many European and American cities, as are Indian and Chinese restaurants replete with many signifiers and symbols of Indianness and Chineseness. These shorthand signs proliferate across cities and so expressions of national identity becomes more promiscuous, colonising spaces beyond the nation from which they originate.

In such encoded spaces, stage managers attempt to 'create and control a cultural as well as a physical environment' (Freitag, 1994: 541), where strict environmental and aesthetic monitoring produces a landscape abounding with clear visual and sonic cues. Through the use of such 'sceneography' (Gottdiener, 1997: 73), the gaze is directed to particular attractions and commodities and away from 'extraneous chaotic elements', reducing 'visual and functional forms to a few key images' (Rojek, 1995: 62). These stagings often feature a limited range of mediatised motifs, or else a few key exoticisms which, like many commodity landscapes, promise infinite variety and 'unconstrained social differences', whilst delivering a controlled, stereotyped 'otherness' (Mitchell, 1995: 119). Here, the imagery and ambience of the carnival – the exotic, erotic and chaotic – are used to commodify selective differences, based on ethnicity and national identity.

These new technologies of entertainment are a feature of everyday, mundane settings as well as touristic 'honeypots', as selling culture becomes part of growth strategies. Very often, the sheer intertextuality of these themed spaces, the innumerable links with other commodities, media and other spaces, consolidates a string of associations that solidify their affective and epistemological power. However, it is important to avoid overdetermining the effect of such powerful commercial strategies on visitors to, and inhabitants of, such themed spaces. In a sense, the very regulated nature of such spaces, their carefully rendered surfaces and removal of clutter might act against the 'otherness' that is aimed for, for there is, as David Harvey (1989) has remarked, the production of a 'serial monotony' in the design strategies such stagings purvey. In other words, the aim of selling the 'exotic' is contradicted by the homogeneous ways in which it is fashioned.

Nevertheless, although Chaney exaggerates in claiming that as tourists 'we are above all else performers in our own dramas on stages the industry has provided' (1993: 64), at the more information-saturated and carefully themed tourist sites, where national identity is on display, it can be difficult to avoid being drawn to information boards, staged spectacles and evident pathways. In addition to these signs in space, guidebooks are also replete with cues about what to look at, what information to consider. As condensed suggestions to familiarise visitors with cultures and spaces – and as shorthand cues for performance – such directions inevitably omit infinite other ways of looking at and understanding sites. Thus there is a discursive and regulatory order in place to sustain practical norms, supporting common-sense understandings about how to behave, what to look at, where to go and what to hear. For instance, visual performances may be cued by the instructions of guides or by notices which recommend that photographs be taken at particular spots. As Chaney remarks, 'framed by implicit theatrical conventions . . . within a particular dramaturgical landscape' (ibid.: 86), we photographically compose different stagings of selves, places and groups.

In addition to these spectacular and mundane themed spaces of national identity, the tourist industry more overtly stages identity in the production of 'indigenous', 'folkloric' customs where tourists may collect signs of local or national distinctiveness. Typically, tours and hotels organise displays of 'native' dancing and music, selecting, for instance, which aspects of ritual are likely to be accessible to tourists and which should be edited out. By charting a course between 'exoticism' and comprehensibility, performances are typically devised to titillate tourists without alienating them by sticking too closely to complicated cultural meanings. In non-Western locations where such dramas are produced for Western tourists, the colonial origins of much tourism become acutely highlighted as, for instance, smiling dancing girls posture for the camera. This cultural staging inevitably raises problems about the reproduction of stereotypes associated with primitivism, exoticism and eroticism

To discuss how these performances can be fraught with controversy, I want to focus on the display of *sega* dancing for tourists staying in large hotels in Mauritius. The 'traditional' dance of the Creole population of the island, *sega* dancing accompanies a folk percussive music which has recently developed to embrace an electronic pop musical form. The dance is widely performed on beaches by Creole groups during holidays and at weekends, and is understood as a symbolic form of resistance to the brutalities of the slave plantation system which their antecedents suffered, through which East African and Madagascan people were enslaved and imported to work on Mauritian sugar plantations. Since the 1980s, a large and lucrative tourist industry has generated enormous economic development in Mauritius. Aiming at the exclusive end of the market, large 'international standard' hotels cater for wealthy Western tourists, forming enclaves that minimise contact with Mauritian people and non-tourist space. Because of the dearth of evident Mauritian culture in these self-contained holiday venues, music and dance shows have been imported into hotels to provide a 'taste of Mauritius'. Inevitably, tourist managers have alighted on *sega* as filling this gap in the tourist experience.

According to many Mauritians, the erotic nature of the dance has been adapted so that instead of a celebration of virility and vitality the performance of *sega* has become a spectacle designed to titillate. Compressed into floor shows, glamorously aestheticised and accompanied by Westernised versions of *sega* music, locals complain that the meaning of the dance has become cheapened and diluted for tourists, so that Mauritians are now sexualised objects rather than convivial participants in their own dance. In addition, it has been necessary for *sega* musicians to be flexible and learn a range of Western 'standards' to induce a sense of semi-domestic comfort for hotel guests. Thus they have become skilled in shifting between *sega* and Western pop performances. Whilst concerns about the lack of authenticity are widely shared by Mauritians, the employment and skilling of musicians has regenerated *sega*. Supplementing the folk performances which concentrate on the traditional music – based solely on percussion – the musical form has developed with the integration of Western instruments such as guitars and keyboards, and has become popular amongst Mauritian youth. Various forms blend *sega* with African, jazz and reggae musical styles, serving as contemporary expressions of Mauritian and Creole identity.

Although the staging of forms of 'traditional' or 'folk' national culture for tourists may be presented in 'inauthentic' and spectacular fashion, 'reconstructing' ethnicity and national identity, it also has the potential to replenish moribund traditions and thus feed into new expressions of identity (Wood, 1998). For there is frequently a tension between the effects of staged national identity for outsiders – for tourists, business travellers or audiences consuming a media product far away – and the reception and performance of the same festive elements amongst participants and national consumers. Again this provides evidence of the complex ways in which commodified culture can be reappropriated in dynamic ways by national subjects.

Everyday Performances: Popular Competencies, Embodied Habits and Synchronised Enactions

Having discussed the consciously collective, official, popular, commodified and touristic forms of national theatricality, I now turn to the ways in which national identity depends for its power upon the habitual performances of everyday life. For unlike these more evident displays, national identity 'flavours everyday life in familiar ways, and a commonsense rhetoric of nationalist talk makes an unnoticed backdrop to public life' (Spillman, 1997: 2). Accordingly, a focus on quotidian enactions can develop Billig's point that much national identity inheres in the 'banal' and the everyday. And it is also apparent that Anderson's notion of 'imagined communities' is insufficiently grounded in the details of everyday life, those shared practices, notions and convenient resources which Herzfeld terms 'cultural intimacy' (1997: 6). The continuity and reliability of familiar enactions contribute to a sense of security 'grounded in our experiences of predictable routines in time and space' (Silverstone, 1994: 7). Mundane continuities generally persist despite the changes and disruptions. Perhaps if they did not, shared forms of identity would break down more easily

Such performances are shaped by unreflexive assumptions and dispositions as often as they display calculated intentionality, revealing kinds of habitus that evolve within a national field. Usually, discussions about culturally coded patterns of behaviour focus upon dispositions that evolve around class, gender, ethnicity and sexuality, for instance. These distinctive forms of praxis are grounded in our specific habitus, distinct, 'common-sense' ways of being (Bourdieu, 1984), the 'second nature' which enables us to perform unreflexive and conscious actions in everyday life. In a national context, Billig usefully refers to these customary performances as 'enhabitation' where 'thoughts, reactions and symbols become turned into routine habits' (1995: 42). Yet notions of national forms of habitus have barely been discussed. I certainly do not want to minimise the centrality of class, ethnic and gendered forms of habitus, but rather to argue that they intersect with national dispositions. For instance, there are distinctive forms of playing and watching sport, drinking alcohol, cooking, child-rearing and home-making that are inflected by class, ethnicity and gender as well as by national identity.

In the introduction to this chapter I argued that rather than distinguishing between a self-aware performance and an iterative performativity as Butler does, it is better to conceive the two modes as imbricated in each other. This is especially pertinent with regard to the unreflexive performances I will discuss here. For instance, a theatrical performer may be so used to playing out the same role that it becomes 'second nature' – so sedimented in the habitual bodily enactions required that reflexivity and self-monitoring is no longer necessary. Equally, habitual performances which have been performed unreflexively for a lifetime may suddenly be revealed to those performing them as social constructions. A confrontation with different cultural codes – perhaps by being misunderstood in unfamiliar contexts or being challenged by those from outside one's everyday community – can reveal that others act differently, inducing a heightened sense of awareness towards what seemed common-sense enactions. Reflexivity and unreflexivity are not properties that are associated with particular kinds of enaction, but depend upon contexts and the conditions which shape the frequency of performance.

When discussing the everyday as a realm of performance, it is necessary to cite Erving Goffman, who insists that social life is inherently dramatic, and that we invariably play particular roles. Goffman (1959) contends that such roles are particularly evident in 'front-stage' situations where, driven by an urge for 'impression management', we strategically enact performances which are devised to achieve particular goals. However, we are apt to remove our mask only in informal, domestic 'backstage' regions. The suggestion that there is a backstage region infers that this is more concerned with reproductive functions of everyday life, and is therefore typical of the realms I am exploring in this section. The dichotomy is not helpful, however, for self-consciousness is a state moved in and out of according to far more varied and complicated contexts than the simple division suggests. In order that such performances are convincing – that they transmit the meanings we intend – Goffman usefully suggests that we acquire competence; that we reproduce performative conventions which are recognisable.

However, this insistence on the instrumentality of role-playing – especially on the front stage – conjures up a continually self-reflexive individual, intentionally communicating values to an audience. This captures some modes of performance but does not consider the host of unreflexive, habitual, unintentional enactions which occur in both 'public' and 'private' situations.

Everyday, habitual performances are constituted by an array of techniques and technologies, practical, embodied codes which guide what to do in particular settings. Where these are communally shared, they help to achieve a working consensus about what are appropriate and inappropriate enactions. Here then, performance is a 'discrete concretisation of cultural assumptions' (Carlson 1996: 16). Culturally bound procedures are enmeshed in diverse embodied dispositions, organised, for instance, around which clothes, styles of movement, modes of looking, photographing and recording, expressing delight, communicating meaning, and sharing experiences are 'proper' in particular contexts. As Goffman suggests, all enactions need to be learnt so as to achieve a degree of competence. The efficacy of the impression made may depend upon the level of rehearsal and practice. Moreover, in particular social contexts, actors monitor their performances and they are also subject to the disciplinary gaze of co-participants and onlookers, who read the meaning the actor hopes to transmit, and must share the values transmitted if the performance is to be successful. This internal and external surveillance restricts the scope of performances and underscores communal conventions about 'appropriate' ways of behaving. Such shared norms thus instantiate a way of being a national subject. But while they need to be learnt, often in youth, they typically become unreflexive, habitual, second nature. This is why it is so difficult for those unfamiliar with national cultures to simply learn them and 'pass' as national subjects unproblematically.

The everyday can partly be captured by habit, unreflexive, inscribed on the body, a normative unquestioned way of being in the world: 'from the embodiment of habit a consistency is given to the self which allows for the end of doubt' (Harrison, 2000: 503). The repetition of daily, weekly and annual routines, how and when to eat, wash, move, work and play, constitutes a realm of 'common sense', offering a deep understanding of the link between culture and identity. Thus 'interspersed with cultural quotations and imitations of other people' (Frykman and Löfgren, 1996: 9), habit is internalised, ingrained through interaction with others. Habits organise life for individuals, linking them to groups so that 'cultural community is often established by people together tackling the world around them with familiar manoeuvres' (ibid.: 10–11). These shared habits strengthen affective and cognitive links, consolidate a sense of shared action and doxa to constitute a habitus, including acquired skills which minimise unnecessary reflection every time a decision is required. Habits are 'a way to economise on life' (ibid.: 10).

There is then a synchronicity between participants' actions and a shared range of practical enactions and assumptions which constitute mundane choreographies, everyday knowledge and embodied approaches to quotidian problems. These are forged by doing things rather than thinking about them. Although focusing on distinctions afforded by class, Bourdieu refers to the routine social performances, including 'automatic gestures or the apparently insignificant techniques of the body – ways of walking or blowing one's nose, ways of eating or talking', which 'engage the most fundamental principles of construction and evaluation of the social world' (1984: 466). Crucially though, these and other habits are not static. The habitus is the practical basis for action, but consists of 'forms of competence, skill and multi-track dispositions' rather than 'fixed and mechanical blueprints' (Crossley, 2001: 110). Nevertheless, the popular saying, 'old habits die hard', is also partly accurate, since the familiar social world consists of enduring contexts and habits which depend upon each other. These contexts, or 'fields' as Bourdieu describes them, are replete with rules and conventions, and are complemented by the ways in which their *habitués* practically mobilise and draw upon knowledge which has emerged out of their sensual, embodied interaction with the world. Habits are therefore full of flexible skills which can operate in an improvisatory fashion within a known field but may flounder outside it.

Whilst the shared norms of actors help to consolidate norms of everyday performance, so does the regulatory framework of the state. Through its modes of surveillance, laws, broadcasting policies and economic management through measures such as taxation, the state provides a regulatory apparatus which informs many quotidian actions. The nation is thus partly sustained by the mundane machinery of the state. And yet while this is a powerful ingredient in shaping the 'way we are', daily routines and habits may be at variance to governmental preferences; indeed, there may be a tension between codes of conduct preferred by the state. Herzfeld illustrates this by citing the example of smashing plates in Greece, a practice which was banned by the military dictatorship and is still deemed demeaning by certain national authorities. However, it is regarded by participants as a 'performance of high spirits and unconstrained independence' which articulates a disregard for authority (1997: 1–2). This exemplifies the tension which exists between popular practices within a group and the way in which such performances are used to portray the nation from without, often by the state. It is also significant that the state, or certain reform-oriented sections of the middle class, are apt to identify 'bad habits' that are degrading the 'fabric' of the nation. For instance, late nineteenth- and early twentieth-century bourgeois campaigns tried to prevent the enfeeblement of 'racial' populations through promoting manly endeavour (such as the boy scout movement), anti-drink campaigns and a widespread concern to inculcate improving activities – especially to create 'respectable' pursuits amongst working-class populations who threatened national order by following 'bad' habits of gambling, drinking, brawling and so on. Contemporary government campaigns, shaped around health concerns, parenting skills, hygiene, diet, financial management and driving may also attempt to champion 'good habits' amongst citizens (see Frykman and Löfgren, 1996: 7–9). Widespread conceptions articulated in the media and amongst citizens about 'workshy' youth, drug abuse and single-parenting are similarly inflected with surveillant impulses to maintain national order via the monitoring of habit. These processes of 'self-observation, moderation and style' – for instance, through the enforcement of table manners (Nordström, 1996: 83) – constitute a form of 'civilising process' (Elias, 1978) which (re)constructs national subjectivisation.

Yet it is significant that the contesting practices cited by Herzfeld are also labelled *Greek*, indicating the ways in which everyday practices, grounded in what we might call a 'local' or 'domestic' habitus (Nugent, 2001), ranging from expressive pursuits – such as plate-smashing – to the performance of mundane tasks and duties, are identified in common-sense understandings as national. This highlights how the ontological force of the national persistently absorbs or contextualises local action and meaning, testifying to the abstract power of national identity. In order to claim a sense of belonging to this large and vague entity, it must be domesticated, localised and personalised. For as cultural nationalists have asserted, an impersonal allegiance to the state is severely limited in cultural appeal. Thus, people use 'the familiar building blocks of body, family and kinship in order to make sense of larger entities' (Herzfeld, 1997: 5).

It is likely that friends and family share this practical knowledge, so that it may rarely be challenged, but everyday ways of doing things are also conveyed through popular representations of everyday life, in soap operas, magazines and other forms of popular fiction. These familiar worlds – often informed by conventions of realist representation – entrench such rituals and routines in national worlds. So dense are these intertextual references to habitual, everyday performances in the fictional worlds of television and media, and so repetitive are their enactions by one's intimates, that they acquire a force which mitigates against deconstruction.

In order to convey the entrenched nature of such performances, I want to discuss three forms of quotidian, habitual performances which consolidate a sense of national identity.

First of all, I want to refer to what might be described as *popular competencies*, everyday practical knowledge which enables people to accomplish mundane tasks. In a sense, the ability of citizens to carry out the formal requirements necessary to get things done is part of the everyday bureaucratisation imposed by local and national governments to ensure a smooth running of the state, or what Habermas refers to as the 'colonisation of the lifeworld'. Therefore, this form of national knowledge is partly inculcated by the infrastructural requirements of the modern state, which simultaneously imposes conditions on how citizenship should be performed and provides people with the skills necessary to negotiate these conditions. For instance, as I will discuss in the next chapter, the state requires that people learn how to drive, and determines the range of specific skills required of drivers and car owners: what side of the road to drive on, how to license, tax and service the car, where to park (and avoid fines), how fast one can drive and where particular speed limits pertain. Likewise, the citizen must learn how to pay bills to the appropriate agencies, know how and where to post letters, vote, dump rubbish, apply for welfare benefits and register with the health services.

In addition, there are a host of other popular competencies that facilitate the running of one's life. For instance, it is necessary to know where to take public transport from and how the driver or conductor is paid. It is a part of popular (gendered) competence to know where to buy certain things, where to seek particular bargains, how to buy theatre tickets, where to enrol at local libraries, where to go to and how to worship. As well as demanding intimate geographical knowledge, these tasks also require a practical ability to carry out these tasks with a minimum of fuss. Such competence embraces a knowledge of locality, a geography of practical action which suggests the 'taskscapes' discussed in the previous chapter. But as well as constituting part of local knowledge such competencies tend to be duplicated across the nation since an infrastructure of recognisable venues and institutionalised settings provides shared sites in which to perform familiar actions. These everyday forms of practical knowledge are rarely the subject of any reflection, for they constitute part of the normal competencies required to sustain a livelihood and a social life. So instilled are many of these habits that they form part of a national habitus. Whilst it is assumed that we know how to carry out these things by our co-nationals, we generally know where to seek advice from others if we are thwarted in the accomplishment of tasks. This is not only limited to practical tasks but also inheres in leisure pursuits, as in the case of the Finns. In their leisure activities, 'such as sauna bathing, hunting or fishing they express Finnishness, not as an idea but as a competence acquired through activity and outdoor life' (Kayser Nielsen, 1999: 286).

The extent to which this is grounded in a national habitus becomes clear when we move to another country and are dumbfounded by the range of everyday competencies which we do not possess, where we come across a culture full of people who do not do things the way we do them, who draw on different practical resources to accomplish everyday tasks. Our limitations as practically competent human beings in these settings require a rapid retraining in how to get things done, how to understand the new practical codes. The effect can be similar when we meet visitors from other nations and try to explain how to accomplish missions when such explanation has rarely been required before. We might struggle for terms to explain the 'obvious', for this is a non-discursive form of popular understanding that we 'just know'. As Guibernau comments, 'individuals do not enter a foreign culture merely by learning the language of that culture. They have the necessary tools, but it takes a long time before they are able to capture the meaning implicit in words, expressions or rituals' (1996: 79). To acquire the second nature embodied in practical habit is difficult to achieve purely by cognitive application but instead requires a sustained immersion in everyday life so that common-sense enactions become ingrained and unreflexive. Habitual security is akin to what Ruth Holliday has called the 'comfort of identity' (1999), generated by the ease with which familiar actions are competently and unreflexively performed.

The second kind of everyday performance I want to discuss are ***embodied habits***. These are the forms of bodily hexis and social interaction, often criss-crossed with class, gender, ethnicity and age, which are closest to Bourdieu's notion of habitus as practical, embodied knowledge. I am referring here to normative kinds of manners or etiquette which instantiate what forms of conduct are appropriate in particular contexts, but also the embodied habits evident in ways of walking, sitting, conversing with friends and other modes of conviviality which constitute shared worlds of meaning and action. As I have discussed above, it is significant that states have used the education system to instil shared – and often highly gendered – ways of bodily enaction and demeanour through training children to march, carry out drills and specific exercises. In the early years of the twentieth century, it might be suggested that these regimes aimed to mark the national body with disciplined collectivity, since fears about 'racial' degeneration and the enfeeblement of the nation, with the rise of urbanism and industrialism were perceived as grave threats. Accordingly, a kind of moral embodiment was signified, conjoining national pride and self-respect.

Such embodied habits have become secularised, but, nevertheless, ways of walking, carrying one's body and sitting continue to be infused with resonances about appropriate comportment. Craib (1998: 173) points out the (enormously culturally varied) forms of unconscious emotional communication – gestures, smiles and body language – which are often ignored by cultural and social theorists. Integral to the unconscious ways in which identity is performed, these culturally located unreflexive enactions help to constitute a sense of belonging. Again, an unfamiliarity with cultural contexts can reveal the situated nature of such forms of embodied knowledge. We can identify 'the small differences in style, of speech or behaviour, of someone who has learned our ways yet but was not bred in them' (Williams, 1961: 42). In unfamiliar settings, ways of talking to other people may seem too loud or direct, too self-effacing or timid. Alsmark observes how conflicts around everyday habits arise in ethnically mixed Swedish housing estates around 'how green space should be used, how peace and quiet at night should be observed, how rubbish should be disposed of, how stairs should be cleaned' (1996: 90). Likewise, modes of walking might appear inappropriate. For instance, I recall feeling large and ungainly as I walked through a small Indian town where local pedestrians appeared to me to move across the terrain with a great deal more grace than I could manage, a self-aware state that was induced by the contrast in performing walking. The same applies to ways of wearing clothes, the kind of small talk to engage in, how loud to laugh, the gestures one uses to convey irritation, welcome or a host of other intentions, and all the small gestures within a repertoire of what we might describe as *expressive competence*. As Spillman considers, in unfamiliar contexts, inhabitants' 'easy way of dealing with shop assistants may be a puzzle', or 'the proper tone of debate amongst friends' may be baffling and difficult to achieve, so that a sense of being apart is difficult to ameliorate (1997: 6). Again, the influence of official forms of embodiment continue to linger – for instance in the much-vaunted English 'stiff-upper lip'. And yet such codes of habitual embodiment intermingle with more informal modes of comportment and verbal encounter, and are also distributed by codes embraced by other social formations – for instance by youth cultures and members of sports clubs.

These forms of habitus are invariably inflected with a range of power relations. In an interesting discussion concerning the *diasporic* habitus of British Chinese, Parker (2000) analyses the contrasting dispositions between young, male British customers at Chinese takeaways and those of the workers, who need to adopt habitual strategies to minimise conflict and limit the potential for racist insult and attack. Mobilising what he calls the endowment of 'imperial capital', Parker describes the forms of comportment and deployment through which customers brusquely order food, lounge on the counter, scrutinise workers and so forth. Here we have the enactment of a habitus grounded in history which often subconsciously reiterates a racialised form of national belonging.

Furthermore, there are a host of everyday practices that are concerned with the (re)production of social spaces in the kinds of spectacular, generic and domestic landscapes to which I referred in the previous chapter. These kinds of space-making practices merge with the popular competencies discussed above and include ways of gardening, cooking, eating, drinking, dancing, courting, having sex. Thus there are proper ways to behave in public spaces such as cafés, gardens, parks and bars, and domestic spaces like kitchens, meeting rooms and bedrooms. There are, of course, national stereotypes which are formed around these spaces and activities – Italians are 'good lovers', French are 'excellent cooks' and English have a skill in gardening. This not only testifies to the easy constructions of others as a means of drawing ethnic and national boundaries but also identifies how certain activities are valued more highly than others. Such cultural codes not only reconstruct these sites as theatres for specified forms of behaviour but also train bodies to adopt dispositions and actions 'in keeping' with such venues. The proper forms of conduct are also exported where expatriate communities are established and where groups of foreign tourists congregate, and do not necessarily confront the embodied habits and competencies of others, instead asserting a defensive articulation of what is 'proper'.

To illustrate this I want to refer to an account I have discussed elsewhere (1998a), where I argue that rather than being an exceptional and spectacular activity, tourist practice is frequently imbricated with quotidian assumptions and is replete with its own forms of habitus and convention. Tourist sites are thus locations at which different embodied habits clash, or are carried out synonymously by different groups. A young British tourist at the Taj Mahal had wandered around the site, stopping every now and then to take a photograph, or make a jotting in her notebook, and now spellbound in silent contemplation she sat on a bench gazing upon the monument. After joining her and after a brief chat, she became suddenly agitated by the behaviour of a group of nearby domestic tourists. With exasperation she exclaimed to me, 'I think Indians are really crap tourists. They just don't know how to be tourists, rushing around, talking all the time and never stopping to look at anything – even here at the Taj Mahal!'

Finally I want to discuss quotidian rituals and routines, the **synchronised enactions** of everyday life. I have already mentioned that the complicated construction of national time includes the important element of cyclical time, the enduring repetition of daily, weekly and annual routines, and entrenched notions about *when* particular actions should be carried out. More broadly, repetition is essential to a sense of identity, for without recurrent experiences and unreflexive habits there would be no consistency given to experience, no temporal framework within which to make sense of the world. Daily experience comprises simultaneous performances in the pursuit of work, leisure and reproduction, which compose distinct kinds of cultural rhythm or social pulse. At an institutional level, this takes the form of attending school between particular hours, shopping and drinking at certain times, and working according to a schedule. Thus state regulation ensures that there are conventions about when a whole variety of activities are carried out. And this is supplemented by an assortment of other popular practices not subject to official regulation but which follow conventions about when and where specific performances should occur, during circadian, weekly, monthly, annual and life cycles, constructing forms of collective temporality. For instance, in Morocco and in certain other Mediterranean countries, large numbers of people congregate on the streets between 5 and 7 p.m. to shop, socialise and walk. This time of public sociability is far removed from a British context when these hours tend to be filled with travelling home from work and the carrying out of home-centred tasks.

In the sphere of leisure there are many allotments of routinised time when, for instance, sporting or theatrical occasions can form part of weekly or monthly timetables: football matches are apt to take place at particular times, as are bull-fights, and likewise, a multitude of political and social meetings are stitched into collective schedules. These rhythms vary enormously according to different national customs. Times to work, eat and drink are very different in Spain and Britain, for instance. Typically the urban Spanish worker will commence work at

8 a.m. and have a long break in the middle of the day for a siesta and to enable lunch to remain a communal affair, restart work at 4 p.m. and finish at 8 p.m. The typical evening hours of leisure are accordingly stretched out well beyond midnight, when, in large Spanish cities, central streets containing restaurants and bars are still busy. In the UK, 9 a.m. is a more typical starting time for work, lunch usually lasts no more than an hour, and the working day generally ends between 5 and 5.30 p.m. The curtailment of the evening's leisure time is usually heralded by 'closing time', after which bars are not permitted to serve alcohol to customers.

This choreography of banal and familiar movements is part of the afore-mentioned 'time-geographies', the ways in which people's trajectories separate and intersect in regular ways. There is no doubt that, to a great extent, the fixity of diurnal social patterns has become detraditionalised, with the fragmentation of time and the decentring of timetables controlled by state and capital. The rise of night-time economies and the diversification of work schedules means that identifiable national routines are less obvious than they were. Yet these develop-ments can be rather overstressed, ignoring the temporal regularities of experience which persist.

Anderson's emphasis on the rise of printing and the subsequent distribution of national newspapers in the construction of the 'imagined community' identifies the extent to which national routines are enmeshed in the media. Daily newspapers are consumed by large sections of most national populations, and, even more, the synchronicity of television-viewing habits ensures that particular schedules are followed by vast numbers. Moores has described this mediatised timetabling as the 'domestication of national standard time' (1988: 67), and Barker considers that 'television sustains routines which are significant aspects of the reproduction of social life . . . [it] organises and co-ordinates a national public social world' (1999: 66). Silverstone elaborates by pointing to the ways in which television schedules reproduce the structure of the household's day, how the temporal shape of narrative patterns offered by television programmes acts to reconfirm the essential narrativity of subjective experience, focusing on the ways in which calendrical events are televisually reported, and how we organise our routines around technologies of information and entertainment (1994: 20). Importantly, it is primarily through daily routines that time 'is felt, lived and secured', and so the repetitive enactions of viewing are experiences which are 'themselves embedded in the times of biography and the life-cycle, and in the times of institutions and societies themselves' (ibid.). Television is, therefore, a means by which viewers in local contexts can feel part of a shared national experience which chimes with their own routines. It links 'the national public into the private lives of its citizens, through the creation of both sacred and quotidian moments of national communion' (Morley, 2000: 107). Martin-Barbero has pointed out that amongst Latin American nations, a sense of national identity was developed by the translation of the abstract idea of the nation 'into lived experience, into sentiment and into the quotidian' via television (1988: 455).

This temporal structure is divided up into daily routines, annual events and special events. And despite the advance of satellite and cable television, most television schedules remain organised on a national basis, and the most popular programmes are still those which are shared by huge numbers of the national viewing public. This is especially the case with soap operas, typically the most popular programmes scheduled by national broadcasting systems, which consolidate synchronised viewing habits. But there are numerous other regular television events which form an everyday topic of conversation amongst viewers and shape their timetables. Where certain programmes may derive from is often irrelevant in constituting these shared synchronised experiences. In India, currently the most popular programme is *Crorepati*, hosted by movie icon Amita Bachan, which is an Indian version of the successful British quiz show, *Who Wants to be a Millionaire?* Despite its origins, the programme has been domesticated to form an essential part of many Indians' viewing schedules, an occasion for shared domestic participation, and a prominent topic of conversation. Löfgren (1996: 107) ironically – but faithfully – describes the 'very Swedish Christmas tradition' of singing along to the televised Swedish voice-over of Jiminy Cricket's "When You Wish Upon a Star", from the Disney film *Pinocchio*. Likewise, the immense popularity of watching English Premier League football matches broadcast on Mauritian national television constitutes a shared experience irrespective of the games' location.

These examples are not intended to imply that such cultural forms are consumed and experienced by audiences in a homogeneous way. Instead the diversity of viewing contexts and kinds of decoding work utilise the polysemy of the product. Nevertheless, participation in familiar broadcast schedules informs an understanding of what it is to be a member of the nation, and those unfamiliar with such experiential, shared routines can experience an outsidedness that excludes them from national belonging. Linking this once more with personal biography, the density of shared television references over a viewing career can be identified in currently popular nostalgic quiz shows in the UK, such as *Telly Addicts*, *It's Only TV . . . But I Like It*, and *I Love TV*, which test contestants' detailed knowledge of the retrospectively kitsch and low-grade programmes of yesteryear. Of course, such programmes depend for their success on the shared knowledge of the viewers and their nostalgia for television experiences that formed a part of their personal history. The potency of the ways in which television and other media forms shape space and order time is evident when familiar schedules and rituals are disrupted – for instance, when programmes are cancelled or the daily newspaper is not delivered.

Conclusion

In order to retain their power, performative norms need to be continually enacted, whether these are the spectacular disciplinary performances of national identity or the unreflexive habits of everyday life. And prescriptive conventions and common-sense values are rarely disrupted if they are performed unreflexively and uncritically. The continuance of normative performances reveals the ways in which power can define and inscribe meaning and action on bodies. Yet the world is increasingly full of diverse performances which spark competing notions about what actions are 'appropriate', 'competent' and 'normal', and also may produce a reflexive awareness of the habitual performances which are so integral to individual and group identities.

This continual re-enaction means that rather than being fixed, performance is an interactive and contingent process which succeeds according to the skill of the actors, the context within which it is performed and the way in which it is interpreted by an audience. Even the most delineated social performance must be re-enacted in (even slightly) different conditions and its reception may be unpredictable. Thus each performance can never be exactly reproduced and fixity of meaning must be continually strived for (Schieffelin, 1998: 196–199). Moreover, Schutz maintains that whilst social performance does have its codes, 'clear and distinct experiences are intermingled with vague conjectures; suppositions and prejudices cross well-proven evidences; motives, means and ends, as well as causes and effects, are strung together without clear understanding of their real connections. There are everywhere, gaps, intermissions, discontinuities' (1964: 72–73). In addition, despite the prevalence of codes and norms, conventions can be destabilised by rebellious performances, or by multiple, simultaneous enactions on the same stage. As Schutz declares, 'social performances may bypass or negotiate with normative rituals, by organising a patchwork or bricolage of meanings and actions to generate new dramatic configurations' (ibid.). Judith Butler has pointed out that knowing the codes of performance via 'forced reiteration of norms' (1993: 94), besides fixing meaning, also provides a template from which to deviate and offers an opportunity to mark subjectivity by rebelling against these conventions. There are a range of performative deviations which arise out of a reflexive awareness that these norms exist. In the UK, there was a widespread response of this sort to the collective ritual grieving which accompanied the death and subsequent funeral of Princess Diana, a response which did not protest against the outpouring of communal patriotic emotion which quickly asserted itself as an 'appropriate' performance, but quietly and cynically ignored the roles expected by a temporary hegemonic code of action. Also we might consider cynical performances – akin to what Feifer (1985) calls 'post-tourism' – which stop short of rebellion, and are typified by a 'role-distance' engendered by an awareness of the constructed nature of a role but an unwillingness to confront it directly. Rather than enacting an overt challenge, enjoyment is gained from a knowing participation in the artifice of identity.

During popular festivals, whilst certain norms may pertain, the imperative to entrench meaning is weaker, for where performances are more amorphous and open-ended, and scripts and actions are not tightly managed, 'there is scope for lying, creative ambiguity, deliberate misdirection . . . improvised codings of subversive messages' (Palmer and Jankowiak, 1996: 236). The remnants of a carnivalesque spirit which permeate such occasions permit a certain licence in behaviour which includes critical enactions. Nevertheless, there are collective understandings that it is precisely these occasions which permit wider licence for subversion, that these are shared national spaces and events where such enactions can take place.

The prevalence of anchoring performative norms becomes clearer when habituated actors are plunged into unfamiliar settings. While there may be pleasure in the challenge of constant mental and physical disruption, a sensory and social overload means that reflexive performances may be denied by the immanence of experience, and, in any case, rehearsed roles have little coherence in these settings. This situation evokes the 'vertigo' described by Caillois (1961: 13) wherein perception is temporarily destabilised by a 'foregrounding of physical sensation, an awareness of the body set free from the normal structures of control and meaning', and entry into an unregulated and indefinable space. This is also akin to what Schechner calls 'dark play', full of 'unsteadiness, slipperiness, porosity, unreliability and ontological riskiness' (1993: 39). There are opportunities for people to escape the constraints of national identity inherent in identifiable, embodied roles, for everyday performances can be easily read back home but are not easily translated by those who are not fellow nationals. However, more likely is a recourse to the known, to the acting out of familiar routines to encompass otherness, or an escape from such *terra incognito*. Thus, as I have described, expatriate communities frequently recreate familiar stages which reinstate a sense of belonging, both participating in spectacular communal events and performing everyday routines to tether national identity in unfamiliar surroundings.

The everyday appears to be a realm of repetition, in which cultural norms get played out and common sense provides a bulwark against questioning conventions. Yet this is not all it is. Writings on everyday life have argued that it is paradoxically constraining and potentially liberating; that it is not merely full of rigid praxes but contains a multitude of other possibilities. The everyday is 'polydimensional: fluid, ambivalent and labile', according to Gardiner (2000: 6). Using the works of writers such as Lefebvre, Bakhtin and de Certeau, and the actions and manifestos of surrealists and situationists, he shows that the everyday contains 'redemptive moments that point towards transfigured and liberated social existence', and it possesses 'transgressive, sensual and incandescent qualities' (ibid.: 208). Likewise,

Harrison says that 'in the everyday enactment of the world there is always immanent potential for new possibilities of life' (2000: 498). This emergent quotidian process is open-ended, fluid and generative, concerns becoming rather than being, is a sensual form of experiencing and understanding that is 'constantly attaching, weaving and disconnecting; constantly mutating and creating' (ibid.: 502). Thus the immanent experience of the everyday – the daydreams, disruptions and sensual intrusions – constantly threatens to undermine the structure laid down by habit.

In an increasingly informalised world, previously tenacious traditions, rituals and everyday routines can be contested, as Frykman demonstrates in a comparison of the practices and attitudes of the generations of the 1920s and 1960s towards Swedish festivities and quotidian routines. The younger generation challenged the rigidities of their seniors, placing new emphases on corporeal expressiveness, affect and the erasure of boundaries between private and public realms, to construct a 'different country in which to live' (Frykman, 1996: 34). As disciplined ceremonies are becoming less sustainable and more heterogeneous expressions of (national) identity are emerging, so it becomes increasingly difficult to extend the life of formal behaviour and supposedly 'good' habits. Indeed, where such codes of enaction are over-prescriptive they are potentially subject to challenge. Frykman and Löfgren declare that 'regulation calls incessantly for freedom' (1996: 12). And habits provide an identifiable code against which younger generations can react. Again, however, these generational conflicts usually take place in a national frame, where, for instance, the old are pilloried for their fixed moralities and codes of conduct, whilst the elders rebuke the young for failing to consider the sacrifices they have made for the country. Indeed, these situated 'structures of feeling' become apparent 'when we notice the contrasts between generations, who never talk quite the same "language"' (Williams, 1961: 42).

In contemporary times, in addition to these generational conflicts, global processes increasingly penetrate everyday life 'through the objects we use, the activities and routines we enact, the places we inhabit, the relations we have and/ or seek'. Accordingly, as Frykman and Löfgren assert,

> in a mobile culture where people constantly meet otherness, habits are brought to the surface, becoming manifest and thereby challenged. It is precisely because people in their everyday lives meet different habits that they are forced to verbalise and make conscious the things that are otherwise taken for granted and thus invisible. Once a habit has been described, it has also become something on which one must take up a stance, whether to kick the habit or to stick tenaciously to it (1996: 14).

The prevalence of global 'mediascapes', 'ideoscapes' and 'ethnoscapes' (Appadurai, 1990) engenders a reflexivity fostered by confronting difference, by coming across people who carry out practices, from the ostensibly spectacular to everyday habits, which contradict and challenge cherished, embodied and unreflexive ways of doing things. Clifford has written of how people increasingly produce creolised practices through their use of an expanded range of cultural resources. They 'improvise local performances from (re)collected pasts, drawing on foreign media, symbols and languages' (1988: 15), yet these improvisations take place in local and national contexts. Nevertheless, patterns of performance are undoubtedly becoming more 'varied, differentiated and de-differentiated' (Rojek, 2000: 9) and 'performative and counter performative cultures abound' (ibid.: 17) and stages multiply, including 'mundane' sites.

Theorists of the performative tend to either stress 'reinforcing cultural givens' or consider performance to be 'potentially subversive' (Tulloch, 1999: 3). However, performance can be conceived in more ambivalent and contradictory terms, can be understood as intentional and unintentional, can be concerned with both being and becoming, can be strategic and unreflexively embodied. As Jackson says, performance 'encompasses both the rage for order and the impulses that drive us to confound the fixed order of things' (cited in Carlson, 1996: 192). Thus performance can both renew the conventions of the existing order and also provide an opportunity to challenge established meanings and practices. Thus, modish theories about the 'transience or replaceability of cultural identity' (Frykman and Löfgren, 1996: 11) can be rather hyperbolic. It is true that a more flexible (national) habitus may be called for, but, as Crossley argues, 'the past is always carried into the present by the body in the form of habitus (2001: 130). Although forms of performance may be increasingly diverse, and ambiguities always exist, I have tried to show that there are identifiable ways of performing national identity. These range from the old disciplinary (usually invented) 'traditional' rituals which marked the birth of modern nations, to looser, more popular events such as sport and carnival; and from carefully constructed enactions and staging of the nation in the tourist industry, to the innumerable habits and unreflexive rituals of everyday life which secure us in place and provide a temporal structure for (imagined) collectivities and individuals. And because so many of the performative elements I have discussed are outside the channels of consciousness, they constitute doxic beliefs, being sedimented in embodied dispositions, manifest in everyday and spectacular actions, giving a temporal and affective order to life. The totality of these performances of national identity still sustains a common-sense understanding that the nation is important and central to belonging, and provides a practical orientation to the nation as the contextualising field which bounds these actions.

-4-

Material Culture and National Identity

Like space, the material worlds of objects seem to provide evidence of the common-sense obviousness of the everyday. By their ubiquitous presence, things provide material proof of shared ways of living and common habits. By their physical presence in the world, and in specific times and places, things sustain identity by constituting part of a matrix of relational cultural elements including practices, representations, and spaces which gather around objects and minimise the potential for interrogation.

In this chapter, I want to follow on from the previous two chapters by exploring the ways in which things are organised and distributed in familiar and symbolic object worlds to constitute cultural, spatial and performative contexts. A focus on *national* material culture is not meant to occlude the numerous ways which we might use to identify distinctive object worlds (by gender, ethnicity, class, region, etc.) but to suggest again that epistemologically and ontologically, things are partly understood as belonging to nations.

There is no doubt that in sociology until recently, objects have been relegated to a position of insignificance. Despite the fact that all human societies surround themselves with instrumental, decorative, religious and symbolic objects, dominant sociological theories have tended to conceive them as either associated with their relation to labour – in Marxist readings – or as vehicles for status (Knorr Cetina, 1997: 11). Yet people grow up relating to things – some more familiar than others – in changing but identifiable object worlds. The sheer extent of the material world ranges from the distribution of things at home, work and in public space. An introduction will address the multiple cultural dimensions of things insofar as they relate to the expression and experience of national identity, before moving on to look at how cars, those most symbolic modern objects, materialise national identity.

Social Relations and Object Worlds

Human societies are invariably supported by a material infrastructure. Social interaction is partly enabled and characterised by the things which pass between people in the mundane material transactions of their everyday lives. People collect-ively come to (temporary) arrangements about the value of particular things, what they symbolically mean, how they should be used, and about who should own them and why. Rarely subject to reflexive assessment, familiar objects endure in everyday lifeworlds, are part of *the way things are*, discreetly contributing to forms of shared solidarity. Situated in familiar spaces, they provide orientations for movement and action. Although they may appear to be innocent bystanders, 'the things that we relate to have embodied within them the social relations that gave rise to them through their design, the work of producing them, their prior use, the intention to communicate through them and their place within an existing cultural system of objects' (Dant, 1999: 2). Thus things emerge out of and mediate social relationships. Human interactions with things are integral to cultures: the complex and varied specificities of the ways in which things are used, understood, made, shared, owned, domesticated, recycled, given as gifts, utilised in ritual, altered, discarded, talked about, used to transmit particular values, curated and represented.

One of the most profitable avenues for exploring the meanings and uses of objects has been via *actor network theory*, important because it identifies the relational nature of objects. They carry meaning because of their contextual emplacement in a network with other elements. They are produced, sold, bought and used and shared in ways which ensure that they interrelate with other people and non-humans within the network. The networks within which objects are situated may include places, technologies, industries, retail outlets and services, and representations of things. The metaphor of the network is useful in that it identifies an enduring set of connections within which the relationality of the elements is institutionalised. Of course, the symbolic meanings of objects – as well as the unreflexive uses to which they are put – can be fixed by the maintenance of such networks. The desires of cultural nationalists and sellers of nostalgia to fix the meanings of symbolic things can be assisted by the assignment of stable meanings by virtue of a network's longevity. Yet as I have already mentioned, the metaphor of the network has been criticised because it suggests a somewhat inflexible structure which cannot account for the multiple and contested uses and meanings which surround objects, and their inherent ambivalence. It downplays the changing uses and meanings of things over time and across space.

Although silent, things have communicative potentialities; they are associated with a host of meanings: 'things are often the topic of talk or the focus of action and they often facilitate interaction or mediate by providing a form of interaction rather like language' (Dant, 1999: 2). For the historical and geographical location of objects, the conventions of their usage, the aesthetic evaluations which they attract, means that they can embody particular values, promote certain activities and chime with forms of identification. For instance, particular forms of jewellery serve as statements of status, whether signifying marital status or wealth. Conventions about what items are worth keeping, restoring and displaying are part of collective histories.

The ways in which familiar objects are manufactured emerge out of historic systems of production and expertise, and although things – notably in the form of commodities – increasingly extend across the world, certain forms of object-centred expertise persist as practices passed down over time so that particular skills are sedimented in particular cultures. These include the production of everyday domestic objects, especially food, garments, crafts and other objects for the home (and garden). The intimate relationships between people and the things which they make (or used to make) become important signifiers of identity for national communities, and also for tourists and consumers who seek out and collect symbolic items. Besides items of everyday domestic production, mass manufactured commodities are associated with particular nations, also often carrying mythic associations that connote particular qualities and forms of expertise. For instance, the virtues of inventiveness and engineering skills are connected with certain British cars, as we will see.

We live with things in the home, and part of living with objects requires that we domesticate, customise and situate them. Objects then are included in numerous routine, everyday practices. Everyday action is facilitated by the organisation of things into systematic, habitual procedures. The organisation of mundane housework tasks, for example, involves the collection of particular cleaning materials and implements, and the subsequent re-enactment of a cleaning schedule which sequentially focuses on the restoration and upkeep of particular objects and spaces. The ways in which these tools are used will be passed on, usually to girls, so that *our ways of doing things* persist. It is the habitual relationships between things and people, and the ways in which objects are installed in familiar space and organise the relationships between people, that structure distinct material cultures. In the UK, where an uncarpeted floor needs to be swept an upright broom with a long handle is likely to be used, whereas in India the implement is likely to be a *jaru*, a much shorter tool, which requires a horizontally sweeping action across the floor. Of course, labour-saving tools may replace these implements, but these in turn will become domesticated within the household, for things are continually appropriated, incorporated and converted so that they are adapted and accommodated into the value system and routines of households. Objects tend to be gradually domesticated, for a sense of home must be maintained, and thus an element of familiarity. Ingold (2000) uses the metaphor of 'weaving' to account for the ways in which people interact with the object world in an ongoing fashion, maybe adopting handed-down techniques for making things, but inevitably adapting through an interaction with the contingent affordances of the material at hand. The development of a skill in making something involves a dextrous, careful engagement rather than a repetitive, mechanical technique.

The ways in which things are used is characteristic of the performances I have referred to as 'popular competencies'. Training to ensure the correct use of objects occurs in early childhood where children are taught how to use things 'properly', in accordance with social norms. They are taught how to use a knife and fork, or chopsticks, or eat food off an Indian *thali*, so that the feel of objects and the practices they facilitate become embodied in 'second nature' (Williams and Costall, 2000: 98). The mystery of objects in unfamiliar settings is evident when we try to use electrical appliances abroad and must confront different plugs. It is this habitual aptitude with things which fuses object and person so that they seem as if they are one. Particular objects often feel as if they are extensions of the body – for instance, the human-spade 'hybrid', the photographer, the sweeper and the car-driver (Sheller and Urry, 2000). They make thought possible and doable (Thrift, 2000: 38). This notion of the *hybrid* is another useful aspect of actor-network theory. In the insistence on the social ubiquity of human–object relationships, it is argued that part of what it is to be human is to interact with things in distinct object worlds. It is further maintained that objects have a certain agency, by virtue of their physical and technical properties and by their 'role' in a network. Accordingly, to remove humans from their central relationship with objects is to suggest an illusory independence which they do not possess. Thus humans and objects combine to constitute hybrids. To talk of a car driver as an autonomous human makes little sense, and I will shortly consider how this hybrid is situated within different networks which can be partly characterised as national.

In order to accomplish most tasks, objects which have been delegated an intermediary status within networks are utilised in ways that are limited by their qualities, or *affordances*, in the same way that the spaces referred to in Chapter 2 afford a range of opportunities and constraints. The competencies to which I have referred, the commonplace abilities to manipulate and operate objects and tools, are accompanied by the *bodily, sensual experience* of using particular things. This experiential history of interacting with things is shaped by the physical qualities of objects and the ways in which they are sensually apprehended. The everyday circulation of things between people, the ways in which they are handled, and the experiences of their form and texture sensualise the world. As I have emphasised, there are different ways of knowing besides the cognitive and it is important to acknowledge the embodied, habitual, unreflexive way of knowing one's place and the things which belong within it.

Objects structure sense and sensuality, since they are situated in relationships with environments and bodies. Their properties do not determine how they are used and experienced by the humans who interact with them but they afford particular possibilities and constraints through their technical and tactile attributes. Accordingly, being-in-the-world is experienced, and places are constituted by the kinaesthetic experience of things and the ways in which they facilitate and extend action (see Macnaghten and Urry, 1998). And such affordances are sustained by the conventions and iterations that are carried out by those co-present, to render things in place and comprehensible. Things have 'a physical presence in the world which has material consequences' (Dant, 1999: 2) in that they possess qualities which are smelled, felt, weighed, heard and looked at, although such sensory mediation is always culturally specific, located in traditions of sensual apprehension (Claessen, 1993) but also constituted by enduring interaction with familiar things which the body remembers. There is, then, a grounded and habitual non-cognitive understanding of familiar objects. They have particular properties and potentialities, can be used in competing ways, but their weight, shape and mechanical aptitudes define the range of contexts in which they are used. The ways in which objects enable and extend action and thought, for instance, about how to eat, make things and travel, are part of a milieu which literally makes sense of the world, cognitively, sensually, affectively and instinctively.

Anticipation of what ought to be and can be done with things (Thrift, 2000: 37) through continuous interaction with objects engages the senses and makes the body remember. This sensual and practical interaction thus constitutes part of the quotidian realm, so that ways of eating, bathing, playing and moving engage the body with particular things. An interesting example is the uniquely designed Berlin key described by Latour (2000), which he situates in a local network comprising other objects, technologies, dwellings and people. The presence of the key and the everyday ability to use it reproduces distinctive local social practices, such as approaches to home security, and habituates bodies to a particular way of opening doors, whereas non-residents are nonplussed by the operation required. Ethnic, gendered, regional and local competencies of interacting with material are evident, and so are nationally constituted experiences of dealing with things. The overlap between national identity and gender is particularly pertinent here, notably the ways in which familiarity and competence with certain objects (re)produces specifically national expressions of gendered identity. This is clear in Kirkham's edited collection, *The Gendered Object* (1996), where mundane, everyday items including bicycles, guns, dolls and other toys, and clothing, such as ties and trousers and suits, are assigned importance in common-sense forms of gender performance. Each of these human–object relationships is set in a specific cultural context – central amongst these is the national context – and produce specific sensual experiences which relate to the affordances of things. As Kirkham and Attfield point out, objects (in this case, children's clothes) cannot be considered without exploring 'parenting, grandparenting, conspicuous consumption, disposable income, social class, fashion merchandising, wider representations of femininities and masculinities' and the whole matrix into which objects are situated (1996: 5).

It is important that not only *tools* are considered as species of objects which engender familiar practical and sensual capacities. The everyday things which surround us convey familiar kinds of comfort. Comfort is not a 'natural' experience but can be understood as the accommodation of the body to particular settings over time, comprising habituation and bodily disposition to respond to the affordances which inhere in the object. For objects coerce bodies into particular physical performances. For instance, particular ways of relaxing rely on specific forms of furniture which accommodate bodies and produce familiar sensations. In most Western nations it has become commonplace to relax on a *sofa* or *armchair* within the home, whereas rural Indians prefer to disport their bodies on *charpoys* (rope beds) or *hitchkas* (communal swings) which are situated both inside and outside the house, and North Africans lounge on *banquettes*, wooden benches adjacent to the four walls of a room or courtyard. The ability to be comfortable on specific people-containing things is grounded in the habitual experience of the everyday.

When we consider the ways in which things contribute to our comfort, shape our competencies and produce familiar sensations, it becomes apparent that every-day life is replete with such objects; things which facilitate eating, cooking, cultivating, moving, packing, holding other things, decorating and adorning bodies and spaces, worshipping and grooming ourselves (Schiffer and Miller, 1999: 3). And clearly these objects are associated with and circulate within particular nations – which is not to imply that they are unfamiliar in other contexts. Nevertheless, the density of familiar object worlds, the everyday ways in which objects relate to each other and to their users, and the ways in which they produce habituated bodies and forms of unreflexive knowledge, are densely grounded in everyday national experience, divided as it is by region, class and ethnicity.

The most obvious material form in this regard, and that most closely associated with national identity, is clothing. Clothing is, of course, highly symbolic as an expression of national identity. In ceremonies, folk dancing, tourist displays and official engagements, clothing becomes an important marker of national identity. It is important also to note how frequently gendered is this nationalisation of bodies. The male suit, with its jacket, trousers, collared shirt and tie, has become a ubiquitous marker of global business and officialdom, connoting modernity and progress. Yet despite the universality of this outfit, it is very often the responsibility of women to carry national culture on their bodies by wearing national or 'traditional' clothing. As repositories of culture, and as transmitters of modes of cooking, dressing, dressmaking and child-rearing, women's responsibilities frequently reside in the home. The domestic sphere is frequently construed as national, whilst men go out into the world to do (universal) business. A further symbolic function occurs in the world of fashion where *haute couture* and design is a badge of innovative modernity and national prestige – and often retains a specifically national character where 'traditional' elements are fused with modern designs. Here national identity is expressed as *style*, most obviously by the dominance of French and Italian fashion houses throughout the twentieth century so that both Frenchness and Italianness have become associated with 'stylishness' and 'sophistication' (as also in food and film). Design here is a badge of becoming 'modern', and yet 'traditional' clothing is also nationally emblematic and fosters a sense of historical identity. Certain items of clothing also signify a more ideo-logical national belonging, such as Chinese Zhongshan uniforms (often referred to as Chairman Mao suits, which were popular between 1948 and 1978 and which expressed Chinese collectivity), Indian Nehru jackets (Indian anti-colonialism) and American jeans (the democracy of informality and freedom). Yet these iconic, traditional and fashionable items are also apt to be combined through vernacular and subcultural styles. For instance, Teddy boys recycled British Edwardian styles, and punks and Britpop bands have made ironic and celebratory use of older fashions.

Irrespective of fashion, there remain widespread assumptions about which clothes are appropriate to particular contexts and which seem out of place, although global fashions can displace a sense of national identity. For these meanings to be transmitted convincingly, clothes have to be worn in a specific fashion and clothed bodies must perform according to particular conventions. In addition to their symbolic purpose, clothes are, along with jewellery and medical prostheses, those items which are most evidently *inhabited*. They are next to the body and enclose (parts of) it. This enhabitation is performed not only through self-conscious enactions – it also depends on the affordances of clothes. For clothes produce sensual experiences, ways of moving and feeling, sitting and fiddling, by their 'textility' (Attfield, 2000). More functionally, they are appropriate garb for carrying out particular tasks or actions and afford specific ways of protecting the body. Moreover, clothes implicate the body clothed in them, facilitating the comfort of identity. They bear the imprint of use, and similarly our bodies bear the imprint of wearing them. This sensual relationship between clothes and their wearers exemplifies 'how we make sense of shapes, colours, textures, strengths and channelling of energy and so determines how we make use of and live with things' (Dant, 1999: 13). In a shared biographical sense, clothes may also signify particular times, 'putting people in touch with their age, peer group, generation, with rites of passage, badges of office and countless other significant life experiences' (Attfield, 2000: 83–84).

Commodities and National Identity

Consumption has proved a vexed terrain for academics, where it has stood as both the materialisation of false consciousness – buying goods we don't need – and the tactical appropriation of power so as to constitute a rebellious self-expression in the face of the overarching power of capital (Fiske, 1989). It should be clear that neither of these perspectives has much relevance to the approach adopted here, which is to consider consumption as part of everyday life, located in particular contexts and concerned with social relationships with particular kinds of things:

commodities. The problem with discussing commodities is that they tend to assume a reified form which depends on their exchange value as goods which are bought and sold. However, as Appadurai (1986) has commented, things may only pass through a stage where they are assigned commodity status, for frequently they change their meanings and cannot be solely understood as materialising exchange value. Neither are commodities empty signifiers in some postmodern sci-fi world. This is not to minimise questions of power and control, and the limits which consumption can impose on commodity-things, but I want to recast this in a national context. For the meanings of commodities are partly shaped by the criteria through which they are assigned (monetary) value, and these notions of value vary enormously between cultural contexts, notably between and within countries (ibid.: 57). Distinct modes of transmitting different expressions of status are perpetrated through the possession and display of commodities and other things; they are class-coded, regionally and nationally variable, and shaped by different gender relations, and these social distinctions feed into the determination of value.

Shopping for things is most frequently a familiar, mundane activity, necessary for the reproduction of self and household, as well as a means of experiencing pleasure, marking status, and expressing identity. In most parts of the world, the world of commodities is becoming increasingly diverse. Nevertheless, the most commonly purchased items are the 'necessities' bought during the weekly or daily shop: cleaning materials, basic foodstuffs, newspapers, lottery tickets, cigarettes and snacks. Decisions to buy these items are rarely the subject of great reflection or planning but are enabled by the consistent act of purchase over time, so that locating them on shop or supermarket shelves is second nature. The routine consumption of these regular goods may be interrupted by shortages or decisions to experiment with apparently more 'exotic' or 'new' products, but they give a consistency to the material world which is not only individually experienced but is echoed in the shopping patterns of neighbours and friends. Even if the shopping baskets of intimates are markedly different in content, they tend to be knowable, being bought from familiar retail outlets. There is thus a familiar retail geography around which consumption is organised. For instance, if I desire to buy a particular bar of chocolate in the UK, I can enter a variety of shops and I will know how to locate it, whereas if I am abroad, the item is usually either not stocked or difficult to find. Irrespective of their origins then, such commodities are part of everyday, nationwide retail and household worlds, and again are consumed through a popular competence in shopping.

These familiar goods are the subject of everyday knowledge, and persist over time. The anxiety that results from their disappearance testifies to this reproduction of everyday life. Similarly, any rebranding of particular well-known commodities is subject to close inspection by consumers, as manufacturers are well aware. For instance, the wrapper of the most popular British chocolate bar, KitKat, has recently been redesigned, yet the designers have been careful to only slightly modify the 'traditional' design lest customers become alienated, for as a marketing director admitted, 'we know *KitKat* is a much-loved brand, part of the fabric of daily life in this country' (Hilton, 2001: 2). Echoing my points about familiar affordances, the decision to retain a 'tear-off strip' between two of the fingers of the KitKat confection means that the 'tactile joy of opening a packet – running a fingernail along between the wafers and snapping off the foil clad chocolate' will be retained in modified form (ibid.). This also illustrates the continual balancing act between tradition and modernity where updating a product's image may require a complete makeover so as to appear contemporary, or may be only slight so as not to alienate consumers. However, for economic reasons, advertising and marketing campaigns increasingly feel the need to establish globally homogeneous advertising and packaging.

Certain commodities are altogether more symbolic of national identity, and buying or using them might constitute a patriotic duty. The rebranding of British Airways planes to convey a more global image so as to attract more overseas customers depended upon replacing the Union Jack motif of the aeroplane tail fins with a series of globally derived designs. They had not, however, bargained with the response of Margaret Thatcher, former British Prime Minister, who upon seeing the new designs, disdainfully draped a handkerchief over a model tail fin in protest at what she regarded as the erasure of British identity (Hilton, 2001: 2).

Foster argues that national material culture has been subsumed under a movement from political ritual to commercial ritual, where the market rather than the state has become the key reference point for national identity. He predicts that the result will be that 'nationality will live on as an idiom for some weak form of collective identity, one identity amongst others available in the global marketplace' (Foster, 1999: 279). This overstates the all-encompassing power of the market to generate meanings, but nevertheless highlights how citizenship has been complemented by the rights of people as consumers. A politics inspired by free market ideology has raised the profile of the rights of the consumer (notably in the UK since the 1980s when various services have been turned into commodities, and clients are now routinely referred to as customers). The realm of choice has been politically elevated and often articulated in national economic policies whereby owning things is foregrounded as a noble ideal. For instance, the American individual 'right' to possess cars has been postulated as sacrosanct, must not be threatened by 'green' high fuel prices and transcends other rights (to a clean environment, to the preservation of fuel reserves).

The circulation of commodities is increasingly dense, ever-changing and generated by a global speed-up of production and consumption, though this is highly uneven. Certain cities and nations are centres of an ever-complex flow of goods circulating within an increasing diversity of retail spaces. It is commonly assumed that these globalising processes are diminishing a sense of national identity, and that commodities are increasingly free-floating, detached from any geographical context and divorced from the conditions of their production. Particular products, which seem to have achieved global hegemony and saturate nearly all parts of the world, are held up as exemplars of Capitalism, Imperialism or Americanisation. However, as Miller (1998b) brilliantly shows in his exploration of the complex meanings of Coca-Cola in Trinidad, such generalised assumptions ignore the manifold specificities of the ways in which commodities acquire symbolic significance. Miller illustrates how Coca-Cola is part of a complex array of soft drink products, and their production and consumption. The identity of the drink has been conceptualised in various ways; for instance, as indicative of an exploitative relationship between US forces and Trinidadians, but also as a signifier of the more egalitarian, informal dispositions of American servicemen in contra-distinction to the stiff formality of British colonial administrators. In addition, Coca-Cola and its competitor beverages – known as 'black sweet drinks' and red sweet drinks' – are symbolically associated with different ethnicities ('White', 'African' and 'Indian'), both in terms of the ethnicity of the highly competitive companies who produce and bottle them and in terms of how they are consumed and by whom. Moreover, Coca-Cola is partly conceived of as modern, but this is often articulated as *nostalgia* for the earlier era of economic and social modern-isation in Trinidad. And its inclusion in what is regarded as Trinidad's national drink, rum and Coke, shows how it has been adapted. It is thus absurd to extract Coca-Cola as some sort of meta-product from this situational, dynamic context, for Miller shows that the production and consumption of such products in complex cultural circumstances is far from predictable. This does not deny the potency of the global but insists that 'globality is itself a localised image, held within a larger frame of spatialised identity' (ibid.: 184).

Another pertinent example of the complexities typifying the meaning and uses of commodities from abroad is provided by Rausing (1998) who explores the rearticulation of national identity in recently independent Estonia following the demise of the Soviet Union. He shows how newly available Western goods, though more expensive than local products, were purchased as if they were 'normal' because they were believed to be more reliable than similar Russian commodities, but, more importantly, because they expressed the *always-already* Western nature of Estonia which had been interrupted and denied during the years of Soviet control. Yet certain handmade Estonian crafts were esteemed above all. At the same time, goods donated charitably to Estonians by Swedes were accommodated with discomfort since there were few opportunities for reciprocation, engendering a sense of national shame.

These two examples highlight how global commodities are domesticated but that they also compete with local goods. People's engagement with the world of commodities utilises shifting frames of reference. For instance, consumers may be drawn to 'exotic' foreign commodities but also choose certain exemplary national products. However, this overt choice-making is also accompanied by habitual consumption where an awareness of the origins of everyday goods may not be so evident but is nevertheless grounded in quotidian experience. The ensemble of these diverse relationships between people and goods, insofar as they can be identified as a pattern of conventions and shared forms of knowledge and practice, can be partly considered as an element of the ongoing, increasingly complex, production of national identity.

Material Culture and Semiotics

Until now I have not discussed the semiotic facility for objects to convey particular meanings like a language. In national terms, this is most evident in those obvious material markers such as stamps, coins, flags, coats of arms, costumes, car stickers, maces and crowns, official documents which circulate between the everyday and the established fixtures of the nation. These are complemented by the array of souvenirs and popular artefacts which are collected as symbols of the identity of other nations by tourists. Thus bullfighting accoutrements signify Spain, models of the Eiffel Tower symbolise France, and tartan objects represent Scotland. Another manifestation of the condensation of these symbolic objects is their arrangement in collections, where the world of nations becomes reaffirmed in stamp albums, coin displays or cabinets of dolls. These projections of meanings onto objects overdetermine their significance, so that, for instance, national currency becomes 'the symbolic bearer of a distinctive national history and fund of national achievement' (Cubitt, 1998: 14).

Again, however, it must be stressed that although these fixings of symbolic value consolidate forms of common sense, the meaning of things can never be fixed. Particularly where objects are invested with symbolic import, the dominant meanings which centre upon them are apt to be challenged, not because the objects are insignificant, but in terms of what they signify, because such artefacts are likely to become shared condensation symbols. I have already provided an example of this in my discussion of the appropriation of the Union Jack flag in Chapter 1.

Nevertheless, certain artefacts are able to contribute to the stability of identity, and an excellent example of the enduring symbolic meaning of objects is illustrated in Jarman's work on the centrality of Protestant–Unionist banners in Northern Ireland, which have become the 'visual and material repository of the Orange tradition' (1998: 121). The continued importance of ritual and the way in which it entrenches and reproduces the importance of tradition and history to this community is furthered by the presence of 'traditional' banners during Orange parades. The subjects of the banners seemingly portray a rendering of historical events, complemented by more contemporary episodes of 'Loyalist heroism'. Here, objects reaffirm through materialising the intense focus on (a highly particular) history which is so central to this British Irish identity. This significance is furthered since the banners are made of cloth, highly symbolic to this Protestant community by virtue of its centrality to their nineteenth-century economic prosperity. This attachment to a rather static conception of history and tradition, a set of endlessly recycled symbols, modes of ritual, and the material culture which support these enactions, seems somewhat atavistic, harking back to earlier expressions of national identity in its refusal to engage with the modernity of becoming.

Things in Place and Out of Place

Things can be considered to be 'out of place' in the same ways that people are. Thus objects have to be conceived of in terms of their spatial contexts, for the ways in which things are used and understood depend on geographical knowledge about where they belong. This placing of objects is apparent in the most intimate material contexts, principally which centre upon notions about 'home'. As Dant says, the 'house is a locus for material culture, a meeting point for people and things, in which social relationships and material relationships are almost indistinguishable because both are bound together in the routine practices of everyday life' (1999: 61).

Domestic space is continually reproduced by what Attfield (2000) calls 'containment' whereby things are ordered and framed within existing materially and spatially regulated contexts. Housework includes the upkeep of things, ensuring that they stay in their assigned positions. And objects are arranged in domestic spaces in familiar ways to facilitate practical action; for instance, 'the arrangement of furniture in space provides pathways for habits' (Young, 1997: 136). Modes of decorating the home, the placing of ornaments and pictures, the siting of appliances and tools in areas of work tend to follow conventions about how domestic space is divided up.

Home-making also includes the domestication of new objects. Thus when souvenirs or other signifiers of otherness are positioned they are domesticated by their inclusion in a normative system of arrangement. This recontextualisation is a way of dealing with the strangeness and ephemerality produced out of the global flows of things. On the other hand, it is often only when familiar objects appear in unfamiliar contexts, or are absent, that we acknowledge their important role in facilitating everyday routines. For surrounding us in our homes, we spend energy on interacting with them, maintaining them, and when they are moved, restoring them to their assigned position. Where relocation of home is involved, there are usually attempts to recreate familiar domestic materialities. For instance, McCarthy (2000) demonstrates how migrants to the USA who work in spatial contexts in which they service the public, place television sets within an assortment of other objects, some connoting 'home', some relating to other experiences. These assemblages of objects, with the TV typically the central artefact, reveal the geographical and historical traces evident in mobile forms of home-making which incorporate transnational and national objects.

Diverse ideas about placing things may clash, particularly where established habits of situating objects confront 'foreign' ideas about the arrangement of things, which are often discredited as inappropriate – for instance, because there are too many things crammed into space, or because objects are imported into settings which are not deemed to be 'fitting'. In Sweden, according to Pripp (cited in Alsmark, 1996: 93), the arrangement of household furniture in the houses of migrant Turks is at variance to the distribution of the very same articles in Swedish homes, and they appear to Swedes to thwart the forms of social interaction and ordering that they are used to.

Such 'odd' arrangements of objects are apparent when we travel abroad, but may also confront us when we come across communities where migrants or non-residents dwell. For instance, as a boy I remember being driven past the housing quarters for the US naval servicemen, and their families, who manned the nuclear submarine base at Holy Loch near Dunoon on the Clyde estuary. I was captivated by the sheer unfamiliarity of the large barbecues that seemed to be situated on every lawn, and the colossal garbage bins that lay at the sides of the houses. These objects appeared to be glaringly un-British, and had presumably been imported as familiar domestic fixtures, perhaps partly to ameliorate a sense of being away from home, in their spatial enclave.

Although national forms of common sense instil notions about the placedness of things, it is vital to refrain from reproducing spatial and material essentialisms about localities and nations. Using the example of food, Cook and Crang (1996) refute the idea that particular cuisines are indigenous to places. Instead, utilising Massey's 'progressive sense of place' (1993), they show how this depends upon the connections that are made between places, noting that tea, supposedly intrinsically English, emerges out of the imperial links between Britain and its former colonies. Although things are used in particular spaces of identity they cannot be claimed as pure and authentic articles belonging to particular nations, for they originate, are traded, sourced, manufactured, represented and circulated in various locales, and increasingly exist in particular local nodes in complex global networks.

The Biographies of Objects

Individual and collective narratives are often organised around objects. A shared national history of consuming and using things comprises a resource which fuels the contemporary nostalgia boom. In the face of globalisation, commonly shared things anchor people to place. Spooner argues that people use commodities 'to express themselves and fix points of security and order' to enable them to deal with increasing complexity (1986: 226). Objects are signs of their own historical and geographical context. Old snapshots, instruments, clothing, certificates, pictures, gramophone players, modish ornaments and scrapbooks become keepsakes. Commercially, the heritage industry sells old-fashioned products in shops like 'Past Times' in the UK (Attfield, 2000: 230), and 'ordinary' objects are increasingly stored and catalogued in museums.

The ability of things to connote shared histories is potent. For instance, hula hoops, bobby sox and Chevrolets signify an America of the 1950s. A recent BBC television series, entitled *I Love the 1970s*, focuses on a melange of TV programmes, films, pop music, sports news and artefacts (http://www.bbc.co.uk./cult/ilove/years). For instance, the programme *I Love 1973* features the Austin Allegro car, the Raleigh Chopper bike, the board game Mastermind, and the popular fashions of the 'snorkel' parka, platform boots, flowing dresses and 'big hair'. These images of objects are accompanied by contemporary pop music, sitcoms and movie stars to provide a dense set of related items which conjure up a particular time. And the artefacts featured are contextualised by an ensemble of mnemonic props which organises a mediatised nostalgia for a part of the past that, it is assumed, will be shared by large numbers of viewers. By the interweaving of these quotidian artefacts and other media products, as objects which we domesticated and consumed, the era can be dramatised and narrated as part of national biography. Yet the memories of objects inspired by the programme also leave room for the personal memories that accompany recollections of, for instance, wearing particular garments. Thus collective memories mesh with personal memories to effect another means by which national identity draws upon various contexts of identification.

Commodities and keepsakes can be used to deflect a sense of disorientation generated by continual transformation and by the speed at which fashion changes to produce the always already new. Accordingly, certain objects commonly labelled 'classic', 'enduring', 'traditional', help to establish stability in the face of material ephemerality. National nostalgia for things is also apparent in the desire for 'craft' products, as distinguished from mass-produced, 'homogeneous' artefacts. Wooden toys, for instance, hark back to the prevalence of artesanal skills which were located locally rather than the contemporary disembedding mechanisms which remove production from locality. Such products are believed to emerge from a craft aesthetic which links product with place. A particularly pertinent version of this is found in the lingering appeal for handmade cloth (*khadi*) in India. Ghandi used *khadi* as a symbol of a distinctly Indian system of manufacture, part of an emerging industrial economy which was destroyed and replaced by British manufactured cotton items. It was accordingly a nationalist duty for Indians to produce *khadi* on handlooms as resistance to this form of colonial oppression (the symbol of the Congress Party remains a handloom) (Bayly, 1986). *Khadi* thus became a national symbol in the struggle for independence, and still possesses national(ist) resonance, though it must compete with nylon manufactures which connote modernity. Again, the symbolic properties of things invoke the familiar tension between modernity and tradition within expressions of national identity, the simultaneous desire for historical embeddedness and continuity, and the surge towards modernity and becoming.

The desire for fixity leads a host of items to be associated with 'authenticity', a particularly contested quality insofar as it is applied to material culture. 'Authenticity', Attfield claims, 'assures provenance and assumes origins' (2000: 79), investing objects with temporal and spatial fixity, and providing material evidence of roots. Yet she shows how objects may be considered as 'authentic' in contradictory ways: because they are traditional, because they are wrought through traditional craftsmanship, because they are modern, because they are made out of 'authentic' materials such as wood as opposed to plastic, because they are thought to be unique or designed by unique artists/craftworkers (ibid.: 99–120).

To return to collecting, there are distinctly popular, vernacular modes of remembering which may be far from recent. For instance, Kwint cites the huge popularity of commemorative plates, mugs and jugs commemorating national events in seventeenth-century England (1999: 5), and souvenirs and commemorative artefacts continue to be utilised to express affective remembrance for national events and customs. Official forms of remembering, however, have become rather more contentious. Part of the imperative of modernist nationalism is to record and classify, but issues about selection and interpretation have become extremely fraught in recent years, and are struggled over by curators. It is apparent that certain official modes of organising things according to national significance have become somewhat decentred, and are complemented by more individual, affective, sensual forms of relating with objects to sustain memories. For instance, photographs are objects which are used to exchange stories, are props through which communal bonds are re-woven by narrative. However, as E. Edwards points out, photographs are not merely encoded with visual information but 'demand a physical engagement' in that they are 'handled, touched, caressed' as sensual objects (1999: 227). Thus memory is also a sensual and embodied affair, not only that which is deliberately recorded and inscribed by authoritative experts. The evocation of objects through the sensory apprehension of their particular qualities continually reasserts the feelings of the everyday world, or captures past sensations of the material world in intimate settings. As Susan Stewart says, 'we may apprehend the world by means of our senses, but the senses themselves are shaped and modified by experience and the body bears a somatic memory of its encounters with what is outside it' (1999: 19).

Automobiles and National Car Cultures

In order to develop an investigation into the relations between material culture and national identity, I want to explore the national dimensions of what is probably the most richly symbolic artefact of the twentieth century, the automobile. For Sheller and Urry, the status and glamour of the car make it 'the quintessential manufactured object' (2000: 738; also see Sørensen, 1993), but, besides its iconic status, it has transformed societies in introducing new forms of mobility. Its emplacement in national cultures has also meant that the geographies it has produced, the ways in which it is represented, the various affordances of particular models, the ways in which it is inhabited and driven, the forms of governance which regulate its use, and the role of motor manufacturing companies have claimed a similarly iconic role in national(ist) imaginaries. In sociology, the key phrases 'Fordism' and 'Post-Fordism' indicate the centrality of the car to contemporary society. The sheer variety of qualities associated with (different kinds of) cars and the range of identities and practices associated with automobiles infest popular culture. Notions of desire and sexuality, mobility, status, family-related activity, independence, sport, adventure, freedom and rebellion play across films, advertisements and fiction. Moreover, for many the car has become part of our 'second nature', 'the habituated extension of ourselves that feels like nature in requiring no conscious mediation in their daily employment', whereby 'driving, roads and traffic are simply integral to who we are and what we presume to do each day' (Miller, 2001: 3). Nevertheless, the glamorous and romantic image of the car has often coincided with a view of it as dangerous and alienating. It has been seen as both advancing modernity and heralding decline. The romance of the automobile is under threat as never before as it becomes identified as a harbinger of ecological damage and social alienation.

As several recent writers have pointed out (Miller, 2001; Sheller and Urry, 2000), the car has been surprisingly neglected by social scientists and cultural theorists, who seem to be stuck with a conception of social life as static and place-bound, whereas transport technologies, notably the car, have brought about a tremendous revolution in mobility. Yet mobility is constitutive of modernity, is an integral part of the way in which people dwell in the world. I want to explore how different modes through which the car is inhabited, symbolised and utilised correspond to particular *national* car cultures. Rather than generalising about the cultural significance of cars, it is useful, as the contributors to *Car Cultures* (Miller, 2001) show, to explore the ways in which symbolic objects such as cars become embedded in distinct cultural contexts, or as Sørensen and Sørgaard (1993), Østby (1993) and Hagman (1993) point out, become 'domesticated' by owners, bureaucrats and artists, irrespective of the origins of manufacture. For instance, Miller (1994) contrasts the 'inward-looking' concern with embellishing the car's interior and the 'outward-directed', expressive use of decoration by car-owners in Trinidad, and maps it onto ethnicity. The first strategy, more typical of male Indian Trinidadians, negotiates the desire to express status whilst retaining the domestic values associated with family, whereas the second is a more overt celebration of distinction characteristically advanced by black Trinidadians. Young (2001) shows that amongst the Anangu of South Australia, cars are utilised to entrench the relationships amongst people, and between people and the land, but may also be used for storage, as a windbreak, a ceremonial prop, a source for light and music, and come to embody other complex cultural meanings.

In a more overt example of the relationship between national identity and cars, O'Dell (2001) provides an insight into the ways in which American cars were viewed in Sweden in the 1950s and 1960s. Whilst Swedes shared the notion that cars were the pre-eminent symbols of modernity and rationality, at the same time the general repudiation of ostentation, the desire to 'fit in' discreetly – in contra-distinction to American individualism and display – meant that the increasingly flamboyant cars from the USA were rejected by most Swedes in favour of more sober European models, notably the Swedish Volvo. Yet American cars were claimed eagerly by the *raggare*, a Swedish youth subculture which defied the normative Swedish preference for the unobtrusively tasteful, as objects which asserted individualism and rebellion. This group (and their cars) was subject to hostile censure from the Swedish media because it supposedly represented a threat to Swedishness by Americanisation, 'in terms of violence, classless gaudiness, superficiality and hedonistic consumption' (ibid.: 123), not to mention the moral decline signified by illicit sexual activities that were believed to take place in these cars. Hagman also observes that, in general, cars were absorbed into Sweden by allying them with the mythical characteristics of Swedishness, namely 'rationality, effectiveness, predictability, harmony, independence, family and love of nature' (1993: 96). Another excellent example of the cultural situatedness of cars is presented by Verrips and Meyer (2001), who show their integration into Ghanaian culture, where they are objects of potential economic reward as taxis and goods vehicles. However, such cars are often ancient, and require considerable mechanical skill and enterprising ingenuity to keep them on the road. Accordingly, an extra-ordinary web of workshops exists whereby these European models are '"baptised into the system", "tropicalised" or "adjusted"' (ibid.: 159), an elaborate social network of money-lenders and patrons supports such endeavours, and cars are enmeshed in rituals which protect them against malign influences.

In order to identify the distinctive car cultures into which these hugely symbolic objects are placed, it is necessary to unravel the whole context: the institutional matrix whereby states regulate and co-ordinate transport; the geographical distinctiveness of roads and roadside cultures, the motorscape; the styles through which cars and drivers interact with other vehicles and road users; the industrial infrastructure which maintains and services motors; driving practices, types of journey and cultural activities carried out in cars; the social relations they generate and reproduce; the range of representations which circulate around and centre upon cars; the economic importance of the symbolic motor industry and its products; and the affordances whereby sensualities of motoring are apprehended – the furnishings, motoring conditions and technical capacities of cars.

To introduce the topic, I will describe the distinctive styles of Indian motoring, before going on to consider more widely the nexus between cars and national identity, looking at national car industries, national 'motorscapes', auto-centric cultural practices, the affordances of cars, and cultural representations which focus upon them.

Characteristics of Indian Motoring

It is apparent that particular rules apply for Indian motorists. There are conventions which are not established by state surveillance – indeed such regulation is distinctly low-level on India's roads – but by common adherence to widespread norms. It is necessary to sound your horn to warn a vehicle that you wish to overtake, for rear-view mirrors are rarely used and often absent. Indeed, most commercial vehicles bear the entreaty 'Horn OK please' to encourage the practice. This adds to the distinct soundscape of the Indian road. Also, vehicles and other road users must obey the maxim that precedence is always given to the largest vehicle. Accordingly, cars must move aside for buses and lorries, auto-rickshaws must defer to cars, bicycles have to permit auto-rickshaws and motorbikes to pass them. For instance, when moving onto a road at a T-junction, cars are not obliged to wait for a break in the flow of traffic for their drivers expect other, smaller road users to stop and allow them to progress unhindered. However, the numerous cows that graze alongside and on the road are not hustled out of the way in the same way as other road users.

The road culture of India has several distinctive qualities. Most roads are bounded by a kind of heterotopic space either side where temporary dwellings, industries and activities reside. A host of services, from bicycle-tyre repair men and telephone kiosk wallahs, to roadside *dhabas* (small cafés and tea shops) alongside other services such as hairdressers, dentists and sellers of all kinds, co-exist with grazing animals and their keepers, rubbish tips, play areas and domestic spaces. Accordingly, life at the roadside is not diminished by regulation but forms part of the habitual motorscape as a source of potential hazard, service and entertainment. It also affords scope for movement, as an unofficial hard shoulder, to avoid accident, or as parking space. I have written elsewhere of the distinct qualities which inhere in the Indian street (Edensor, 2000b). Car drivers in India must take account of the flow of bodies and vehicles which criss-cross the street in multidirectional patterns, veering into courtyards, alleys and culs-de-sac. For busy streets are rarely merely 'machines for shopping'; they are also sites for numerous activities. Disrupting linearity, they are part of complex spatial labyrinths, containing a host of micro spaces: corners and niches, awnings and offshoots. Through the play of children and adults, demonstrations and religious processions, roads may become temporary stages. Accordingly, the scopic concentration afforded to the motorist by many Western streets becomes more difficult, particularly on urban roads in India. Distracted and impeded, the motorist must avoid other vehicles, animals and people, denying smooth, linear progress. The miscellaneous collection of vehicles that use the street: bullock-carts, cars, bicycles, motorbikes, auto- and cycle-rickshaws, buses and other diverse forms of transport, all move at different speeds as they manoeuvre for space, providing a fluid choreography at variance to the controlled flow and pace of traffic on Western thoroughfares.

A distinct sensual experience is thus afforded by these contingencies, a tactile sense of motoring which involves continual manoeuvres: pressing the horn, jerking the wheel and applying the brake. And this is accompanied by the smells of the Indian road: the scent of cooking from the roadside, cow dung and the fumes of distinctive fuel types. Typically, the road's soundscape is not constituted by the uniform purr of cars but by a symphony of different mechanical, human and animal noises augmented by snatches of Bollywood film music, the cries of street traders, and the ever-present cacophony of car horns, to produce a changing symphony of diverse pitches, volumes and tones.

The Indian car industry is often held to exemplify a virile economy. Yet the crises of national identity which have intermittently afflicted sections of Indian society since Independence now find clear expression in what is perceived as a post-colonial reliance on Western modes of governance, politics and culture which have effaced 'traditional' Indian (usually specifically 'Hindu') ways of doing things. Accordingly, India is simultaneously insufficiently modern (underdeveloped by Western powers or too reliant on their technologies and industries) and losing traditional qualities. The Indian car industry is an interesting case where laments are heard about the reliance of foreign technology. The website http://www.cybersteering.com/cruise/driving/indiancar.html contains a litany of complaints about the lack of a properly indigenous Indian motor industry. Though cars are manufactured in India, concerns focus on the dearth of indigenous design and innovation which renders cars un-Indian.

In fact, the car market in India has changed dramatically in the past decade. Formerly, two cars dominated the roads, the Ambassador, produced by Hindustani Motors, and The Premier Padmini (commonly called the Fiat because it was based on a design by that company), produced by Premier Autobackmobile. Only seven companies were granted licences to produce cars until the 1980s, since when the

Ambassador, though still a familiar feature, principally as a taxi and as a politician's car, has been dramatically superseded by a new generation of cars (especially since economic liberalisation in the 1990s) which possess higher status due to their more contemporaneous design. Compact saloon cars now grace Indian streets, by far the most popular being those from the range offered by Maruti, who now dominate the domestic market in economy range vehicles. Formerly the style of motoring in India was synonymous with the affordances offered by the venerable Ambassador, a replica of the 1952 British Morris Oxford, with its low-slung, leather seats.

As far as practices are concerned, it must be added that many middle-class Indians never drive but employ drivers to transport them around. Typically, long-distance journeys are carried out on trains and buses, for cars are owned by a minority of the population and travel across India involves considerable distances. Rather than driving for pleasure in the American sense, cars remain a costly luxury, generally used for functional everyday purposes such as shopping and going to work. Thus in India, cultures of mobility are still dominated by the experience of bus and rail travel, or by bicycle and rickshaw for shorter journeys. The ownership of a car is unthinkable for the great majority of people and this adds to the allure of cars as status symbols and objects of fantasy.

The above discussion is designed as an introductory exemplification of how cars – like most objects – cannot be abstracted from the settings they inhabit. In developing this discussion I will go on to explore how relationships with cars contribute to a sense of national identity.

The Symbolic Role of National Car Industries

The symbolic weight of the car means that the performance of car production has been conceived as a significant measure of national economic and industrial virility and an indicator of modernity. As Ross declares, 'the automobile industry, more than any other, becomes exemplary and indicative; its presence or absence in a national economy tells us the level and power of that economy' (1995: 19). Not only is the automobile industry iconic, but it is associated with a much more extensive 'machinic complex' consisting of a host of other industries; those which service cars, develop roadside leisurescapes, (suburban) housing developments and retail environments. The interlinkages which constitute this vast network also include the subsidiary industries which supply components, refine raw materials like rubber and oil, and build the motor infrastructure of road networks, and these have become extended as never before. Previously, the network supporting the production and servicing of the motor industry and car drivers tended to be more compact, with, for instance, a cluster of small workshops making components being situated close to the large factories. Although car production has always been linked to the import of raw materials, the national identity of products has become evermore denuded by the organisation of production at an international scale, wherein cars are only assembled in a single locality with components brought to these assembly points from far-flung sites of manufacture. Despite the obvious point that cars can no longer be identified with the skills and techniques available in one nation, they continue to be freighted with a national(ist) significance because of their historical emergence in national economies. To exemplify this industrial imbrication with the national, I will examine the British car industry, identifying especially symbolic vehicles.

In 1939, about 2 million people in Britain owned cars, a long way behind the number of American car owners, but an increase on previous years. This partly reflected the gradual transcendence of class associations as cheaper cars were introduced. Car ownership in Britain had previously been the preserve of a wealthy elite, and status continued to be marked by the fact that the gentry owned Armstrong-Siddeleys, Bentleys, Lanchesters and Rolls-Royces, avoiding models such as the Humber, which was associated with mere aspirants (O'Connell, 1998: 23–24). The lack of the American democratic impulse to produce cheap cars for the wider population was also reflected in the widespread, patriotic sentiment that the British manufactured a better class of vehicle than the Americans (ibid.: 16). What counted was quality, not quantity. And this vision of quality was accompanied by accounts which portrayed a kind of heroic masculinity, which O'Connell describes as 'a world of impressive inventions, engineers, manufacturers and racing drivers' (ibid.: 3), a legacy which persists.

The British motor industry developed throughout the 1950s when the six most prominent manufacturers were Austin, Ford, Nuffield, Rootes, Standard-Triumph and Vauxhall, only the latter being a subsidiary of an American company, General Motors. Later Rover and Jaguar emerged, along with British Leyland, consolidating the Britishness of the car industry. In order to give a flavour of the highly charged symbolism of British cars I will focus on three kinds of motor, the Rolls-Royce, the Aston Martin and the Mini, each signifying different definitively British attributes.

The Rolls-Royce has become a byword for quality and luxury, and this is reflected in the price of these cars, beloved by pop stars and self-made businessmen. Moreover, these elite vehicles are commonly cited as the 'best cars in the world', exemplifying apparently native traditions of engineering excellence, craftsmanship and attention to detail, embodied in the arch-engineer Royce, and the energetic entrepreneur, Rolls, symbolically entwining mythic entrepreneurial acumen and technical know-how. Myth has it that in the early years of motoring, Royce took the French Decanville and improved on 'just about everything he could' (Heilig and Abbis, 1999: 11), bettering the best efforts of foreign industrial rivals and signifying pride in Britain as the first and foremost industrial nation. Rolls-Royce cars are owned by notable figures in British institutional life, the most notable being the Royal Family. The Queen owns five, each bearing a solid silver statuette of St George and the Dragon instead of the familiar 'spirit of ecstasy' figurine. Thus the appeal of the Rolls is certainly not based on any democratic availability but rather veers towards a representation of Britain as class-bound and obsessed with status. However, irrespective of class, there is a certain pride in these iconic vehicles which signify excellence in workmanship as well as taste.

In an increasingly competitive world market, the firm went bust in 1971, and after a bail-out operation, its fortunes declined steadily thereafter. Ironically, in 1998, the company was bought by German car manufacturers Volkswagen, and it is intended that the company will be sold to German rivals BMW in 2003. This has caused consternation as another piece of Britain's manufacturing industry declines – and in this case is the subject of a foreign takeover. Rolls-Royce, emblematic of British engineering and entrepreneurial prowess, like other losses, signifies a deterioration in national reputation and worth: 'for the world's most elegant car to be built by a manufacturer of German economy cars comes as a shock' (Heilig and Abbis, 1999: 7). The authors further opine that lessons must be learnt from Ford, who in 1990 took over manufacture of another symbol-ically British car, the Jaguar, but allowed 'the quintessential Britishness of the Jaguar to continue to dominate'. They argue that so long as the cars 'continue to be built in England, and the world's finest craftsmen and craftswomen make the interiors . . . they will survive' (ibid.). Yet there is a hope that BMW and VW will fail to understand the unique qualities of these cars and they will 'throw up their hands after a few years and seek to return Rolls and Bentley to British ownership'. They further claim that 'there has to be a place in the automotive world for these special products that exemplify traditional British craftsmanship' (ibid.: 127).

In a similar vein, the motor of choice of the archetypal British agent, James Bond, the Aston Martin, has also been taken over by American car giant Ford. R. Edwards observes that the Aston Martin has been described as the 'Englishman's Ferrari', but dissents from this description: 'A Ferrari is Italian and can never be anything else. An Aston Martin is British and can never be anything else . . . as British as Edward Elgar or Boadicea' (1999: 7). The car's image is one that, while pertaining to elitism, is very different to the stately Rolls-Royce. The association with Bond ties it in with 1960s social and sexual liberation. Here is a model that connects not only with ideas about 'raciness', pleasure and the pursuit of a hedonistic lifestyle, but also with a certain style associated with British notions of gentlemanly conduct and suaveness.

If the cars mentioned above epitomise a British sense of luxury, the Mini incorporates a host of symbolic traits which operate across the class divide. Again, the conventional stories told about the car's development highlight Alec Issigonis, the vaunted designer genius wrought out of the independent British entrepreneurial spirit. Perhaps most symbolically, the Mini also emerged as a British icon in the 1960s, the decade where Britain showed off the style embodied in its pop music and fashion industries, and apparently discarded many of its post-war, class-bound rigidities. Emblematic of the 'Swinging Sixties', along with the Beatles, the mini-skirt, and symbolic places such as Carnaby Street, the Mini was heralded as a cheap car available to a newly confident working class, but was simultaneously coveted by the fashionable rich. The car operated as a trendy acquisition, which offered status in various ways. Thus, in order to maintain forms of distinction, customising the vehicle was a popular activity especially amongst its wealthier owners; also, its flexible affordances enabled it to be adapted as the Mini-Cooper, a sporting car which won rallies. The accretion of symbolic values was also reflected in the film the *Italian Job* (significantly featuring archetypal English actors from opposite ends of the class spectrum, Michael Caine and Noel Coward) where a 'cheeky' (a term also frequently applied to the Mini) gang of British criminals stage a successful bank robbery in Rome, using a fleet of minis as get-away cars because their small size and steering capabilities were well suited to the winding route used to escape.

This mobilisation of competitive Britishness is beautifully exemplified in the campaign to launch the vehicle, which utilised a spectacular aerial photo of 804 minis in Union Jack formation (see Golding, 1994). And the familiar national rivalry with Germany also emerged. Having created the Volkswagen 'beetle' as the German people's motor car during the Third Reich and later successfully exported it, before the advent of the Mini the lesser charms of the Bubble-car were foisted on the British market. This led one patriotic commentator to announce that 'every engineer wanted to burst the bubble cars that were popping out of Germany' (Scott, 1992: 10).

It is interesting that while the 'high' cultural values of exclusive cars like the Rolls, the Jaguar and the Aston Martin conjure up a traditional Britain, the Mini offers a more democratic world which resonates with the efflorescence of British popular culture and its successful marketing – like the Mini – to overseas markets. Thus we see the reincorporation of a material object into a distinctive kind of national identity, which distinguishes itself from foreigners but draws on a wider range of gendered and class imagery to proffer a more inclusive identity.

The British motor industry has been inextricably linked with the international prestige of Britain as competitor on the world market. Rather than considering companies and cars as regional entities, or as the outcomes of individual enterprise irrespective of nationality, they have been entrusted to represent the nation's economic virility in the world market. Yet the sustenance of the British Motor industry has been particularly fraught over the past three decades. Besides being linked with the masculine virtues of British skill, hard graft and ingenuity, the industry also became associated with the 'British disease', militant trade union industrial activity. In the car industry, the radical activities of mythical shop stewards such as 'Red Robbo', and 'infiltrators' such as 'Red Steph', were the subject of much alarmist commentary in the popular press, being commonly cited by the Thatcherite Conservatives as evidence of the need to return to 'Victorian values' – in other words, a reversion to another imagined Britain. These activities were heralded as symptomatic of the decline of industrial Britain, and accompany other depictions of the loss of those qualities which generated British competitiveness and social cohesion.

Like the decline of the steel, cotton, shipbuilding and coal industries, which constituted the primary elements of the 'workshop of the world', the car industry was part of a symbolic geography and object world in which the links between products, people and places were part of popular knowledge and anchored industrial Britain to a glorious past. The loss of these industries signifies the loss of this symbolic spatial network – an industrial/geographical index which the service and informational industries of the post-industrial economy have yet to replace. In a Scottish context, the disappearance of these large industries is often regarded as evidence of the unsupportive and discriminatory attitude of Westminster towards Scottish industry. In their hit single, 'Letter to America', the avowedly nationalist band the Proclaimers sing, 'Bathgate no more, Linwood no more, Methil no more, Irvine no more', highlighting popular Scottish resentment about the disappearance of these symbolic sites of industrial production, the first two of which hosted car factories.

According to one popular trope, these sites and objects are made by mythic producers: the skilled workers, visionary entrepreneurs and technical geniuses who still exist, but governmental incompetence, devious foreign marketing, and insufficient patriotism have badly let down these heroic characters. This version of events is challenged by Whisler, who argues that the inflexibility of British corporate and national plans in a context of ever-changing markets constituted a 'rigid institutional matrix' (1999: 2) which spelt doom for the industry. More pertinently, he contends that despite the British reputation for 'innovative products and "engineering Culture"', it was this that was the industry's 'Achilles' heel' because amongst those who worked their way up the ranks in time-honoured tradition 'mechanical skill was prized over theoretical knowledge' (ibid.: 179). This will inevitably result, Foreman-Peck *et al.* reason, in British motor production depending 'upon a small number of multinationals headquartered in other countries' (1995: 254).

Nowadays, a vestige of pride in British motoring achievement is echoed in the sporting field, where patriotic pride in the skilled driving performances of Nigel Mansell, Damon Hill and David Coulthard carries on the trend for the worship of skilled speed merchants and the technological back-up they receive. The symbolic cars of yesteryear have not been succeeded by new models but can be found in the popular motor museums which are situated around Britain, transformed into nostalgic yearning for the national(ist) pride instilled by industrial achievement.

National Motorscapes

In a sense, nations have become more available for inspection by the development of the motor industry and the concomitant extension of road systems. The culture of mobility advanced by the car may disembed much activity from local public spaces but it simultaneously opens up wider networks of space. Automobilisation extends human habitats, disperses places across space, enables escape from particular contexts, and facilitates the formation of new socialities (Sheller and Urry, 2000: 742). Accordingly, motoring cultures may be distinguished by how they explore space and link spaces together via car driving. One way of considering these expanded networks of spatial association is to explore the role of motoring in stitching the nation together. The 'democracy' of car travel enables valorised national scenes and sites to be visited, opens up the possibilities for 'knowing' the nation. The development of motoring generated the 'slow meandering motor tour' (Urry, 2000: 60) 'a voyage through the life and history of the land' (ibid.: 61) wherein images were witnessed and photographed (see Taylor, 1994). Compilers of national culture have identified regional features of folklore and customs, historic associations and sites, dialects, dress, styles of building, natural history and landscapes which have subsequently been filtered into popular motoring guide-books and glossy publications.

The car has increased possibilities for gazing upon the nation, especially for 'selected aspects of English heritage and landscape' (O'Connell, 1998: 79). A range of features have been identified for nationals to gaze upon, as both signifiers of regional specialisms and as part of the compendium of national diversity. But while numerous resources exist (books, maps, tourist brochures and information centres, videos), this is an active process – one that requires practice at recognising, representing (for example through photography) and linking landscapes, places and things in familiar ways. In this way, the cultural elements of national space are stitched together by car travel, and utilise particular technologies. In an English context, these include books such as the aforementioned H.V. Morton's seminal *In Search of England*, *I-Spy* books which encourage children to identify pre-assigned symbols of generic roadside Englishness, and a host of more specialised publications, such as the *Shell Guides*, which focus on regional food, natural history, architecture, and so on. The English landscape has become intensively mapped and scrutinised, giving rise to an ethic of knowing one's country 'properly'. Previously remote places can be reclaimed within a national geography. For instance, in the United States the Blue Ridge Parkway has opened up the possibility of gazing upon formerly inaccessible regions, and the national road system provides a huge index of possibilities for potential travel into the 'great outdoors'.

O'Connell remarks that the car is the 'perfect facilitator of the "away from it all" immersion in the beauties of the countryside' (1998: 154). But ironically, the car also threatens this haven of peace and rusticity by its intrusion. Long-standing tension between the rural tradition and the modernity epitomised by the car persists, as arguments rage about the natural beauty of the land becoming desecrated. For despite the almost sacred role the countryside possesses in the construction of national identities, it is also the site of numerous claims about how it should be used and by whom, between rural dwellers, foxhunters and animal rights protesters, commuters and rural inhabitants, conservationists and developers, farmers and eco-tourists (see Macnaghten and Urry, 1998). As part of this conflict, the road protest movement in England has cast its struggle against the car in a nationalist light, by constructing a lifestyle and a set of beliefs that frequently draw on the 'more authentic' Celtic or pre-Christian forms of wisdom which are posited as a more appropriate, ecologically aware heritage, an approach that claims primordiality in the contest over the uses and value of the land.

Besides shaping the experience of the nation, the technologies of the car and its subsidiary service industries have also contributed to the shaping of generic kinds of space. Half the urban landscape in the USA – and two-thirds in Los Angeles – is devoted to cars (Luger, 2000: 9). This concentration of autospace has produced a distinctive landscape, a roadside Americana of drive-ins, malls, amusement parks and suburbia, motels or inns, transport cafés, garages and drive-in eateries that have fed into innumerable representations and fantasies to produce a 'wild mix of cars, girls, drive-ins, bowling alleys, racing, rock and roll music' (Witzel and Bash, 1997: 41). Nevertheless, these images, though nostalgically circulated through popular film, television and music, have, according to Basham *et al.*, largely been replaced by an 'infinitely recurring topography of turnpike, billboard, drive-in, motel and suburb; a world of reassuring sameness or of nightmare repetition' (1984: 129). Now the American motorscape is saturated by signs heralding the Ramada Inn, Wendy's, McDonalds, Holiday Inn and Taco Belle, a sequence of familiar, easily read signs and advertisements. The massive flow of continental traffic has enabled many to see the 'structural commonalities of the US' (Sopher, 1979: 144–145) which inhere in this commercial landscape.

Nevertheless, the nostalgic aura of the roadside is not new. Belasco describes the American roadside as 'a combined theatre and amusement park' (1983: 105) which, since its development in the early years of motoring, has been the site for productions of various forms of nostalgia. 'Auto-camping' or 'motor-gypsying', he argues, emerged as a move to restore a lost American individuality, and public camps developed which harked back to a more communal way of life. Despite the evolution of more privatised cabins, and ultimately motels, during the Depression of the 1930s, 'Americans looked to their road culture for comforting evidence of national solidarity'. For a widespread participation in roadside rituals revealed that there was 'a common American way of life' irrespective of the economic crisis (ibid., 1983: 118). And even since this period, Belasco contends that 'democratic nostalgia' based around the roadside persists, albeit within the realm of style and advertising. Along roadsides, 'New England, Virginian or Spanish colonial architecture' co-exists with signs of homeliness such as 'lace curtains, rocking chairs and window boxes' (ibid.: 120). Even so, other movements try to recapture the original American flirtation with movement across space in backpacking and off-road motoring. And there are extensively mapped highways that search for the sights of the mythical Americana and celebrate those signatures which still exist, as for instance in Marling's homage to the colossal vernacular roadside statues which form part of American motorscapes, many from the 1930s (1984).

The automobile has changed more mundane spatial aspects of American everyday life as well. The growth of automobile ownership facilitated the extension of 'metropolitanism' into rural areas and spurred the 'geographical configuration of a consumer society based on car travel', generating enormous changes in everyday routines (Interranté, 1983: 91). One upshot of this has been the evolution of suburban realms into exurbs and edge-cities far removed from the inner city, a spatialisation that has furthered the institutionalisation of American apartheid and the 'extinction of the walking city' (Gilroy, 2001: 100). But it has also changed the shape of much domestic architecture – for instance, the relationship between the 'garage, the front porch and the parlour' (Kihlstert, 1983: 161) – engendering new domestic choreographies and habits.

Styles of Driving and National Auto-centric Practices

The independent mobility heralded by car culture has been partially desynchronising, disembedding familiar time-geographies from localities. However, the complex systems required for car travel have required a resynchronisation whereby the communal patterns of car use evolve: the routes used (for instance during rush-hours and holidays), parking arrangements in cities, and common rituals. In concrete ways, shared cultures of automobility structure experience of time, and work, leisure and consumption patterns. As Sheller and Urry identify, motoring networks force people 'to orchestrate in complex and heterogeneous ways their mobilities and socialities across very significant distances' (2000: 744). These experiences change as motoring cultures evolve, as new travel options and networks are developed, and the sensual experience of automobility also restricts other, older ways of experiencing space, curbing the sensual possibilities offered by other mobilities (see Urry, 2000: 60).

For Britons, the Sunday drive, driving on busy motorways, getting stuck in traffic jams on holiday trips to Cornwall or en route to Blackpool, getting booked by traffic wardens (national symbols of British petty authoritarianism), and driving to the shopping mall, provide an ensemble of widely recognisable experiences that find echoes across popular culture. For instance, the car has long been a cultural resource in the pursuit of sexual adventure (see Lewis, 1983). An imaginary world of vehicles described as 'passion wagons' and 'love traps' populates the 'low culture' of British comedy (Hunt, 1998), based on familiar strategies devised to facilitate youthful sexual experience and illicit middle-age trysts

In the early years of motoring in Britain, cars pre-eminently became associated with taste and social status, concerns which still surround particular models as has been already discussed. Moreover, a particular gendered construction of motoring evolved and persists to a degree. There are still normative ideas about what constitutes men's and women's cars. For despite the ongoing erasure of highly gendered lifestyles, 'masculine' vehicles remain those which are large and powerful, whereas 'female' vehicles still are portrayed as convenient (usually for shopping in town). Most notable in the early years was the mockery and patronising attitude directed at female drivers, and the persistent association of driving with physical strength and mastery of technology (see O'Connell, 1998: 43–76). The ritual leisure pursuit of tinkering with the car became associated with a particular kind of masculinity (for more on the gendering of car cultures see Scharff, 1997).

Besides this specific form of gendering motoring, the British style of driving placed an emphasis on the 'safe' and 'sensible' – 'playing the game' as it was referred to (O'Connell, 1998: 129). However, in the 1930s, the introduction of speed-traps to ensnare speeding motorists was described by campaigning motorists' groups as infringing national rights and therefore as 'non-English' (ibid.: 133). Driving styles are still held to identify particular national traits and to draw boundaries between national identities. The idea that British motoring remains safe and responsible is echoed in frequent references made to the unsafe driving practices of 'continental' drivers. This conservatism is echoed in the way in which the British motor car became domesticated and is partly evidenced in the design of cars. As Basham *et al.* maintain, although Zephyrs and Zodiacs 'grew tame [tail] fins in imitation of their Yankee cousins . . . the classical lines of the Jaguar or Wolseley' prevailed (1984: 135). Alison Light conjures up this enduring spirit: 'Far from being stuck in the past, conservativism seems to have improvised rather well in the modern period, making something homely and familiar from the brand new: think of the inventiveness of the spirit which could take that futurist symbol of speed and erotic dynamism – the motor car – and turn it into a Morris Minor' (1991: 214).

Despite the contemporary common-sense idea that car ownership is a democratic right for British nationals, aspects of automobility enforce exclusions. For example, widespread poverty restricts car use, effectively disenfranchising a workless or low-paid class. More obviously, institutional racism causes Black male drivers to be disproportionately stopped by the police because of assumptions about the prevalence of black criminality.

Unlike the exclusions marked by car association with an elite in Britain, in the USA 'the car *began* life as a mass product, indeed it was the original mass product, and hence its symbolism is more complex and in many ways intertwined with the "American Dream" and particularly with the ideology of freedom' (Graves-Brown, 2000: 158). Car ownership is often articulated as a right in the USA, as is the right to cheap fuel irrespective of geopolitical and energy-saving imperatives. The entanglement of the car with American identity is captured by the platitude that 'what is good for the country is good for General Motors and what is good for General Motors is good for the country'. This pinpoints the symbolic centrality of the auto industry to the US economy, and it is this which led to the cultural alarm raised when Japan overtook the US as the world's largest car producer in 1980, which lasted until 1994 when America prevailed once more (Luger, 2000: 7).

Kline and Pinch (1993) show that the original reception of the motor car in rural America was far from homogeneous, mixing resistance and use to accomplish diverse tasks and express distinct meanings. However, the contemporary appeal of the car is surely bound up with the possibilities of movement which the development of cheap models opened up. American ideologies often centre on the metaphor of movement (movement westwards, the possibility of social mobility), and the car facilitates trans-American travel and adventure which have become an important motif in constructions of American individualism: the 'freedom of the road'. Long-distance car travel has been a staple ingredient of American popular culture, perhaps best symbolised by Jack Kerouac's *On the Road*, which symbolises the youthful, non-conformist energy of continual adventure and continual movement.

Yet mobility is not only characterised by the endless search across continental USA; it is based in more local activities. The theme of movement and sexuality is beautifully captured in an illustrated book, *Cruisin': Car Culture in America*, which is replete with airbrushed illustrations of sinewy muscled men, but they are out-glamorised by the chrome and steel beasts they attend to. The pleasures of 'cruising' include 'showing off your car, looking for races, or better yet, looking for girls' and following the specifics of a cool appearance low in the seat, and customising the vehicle in particular ways (Witzel and Bash, 1997: 9). Romantically, the authors assert that 'cruising was and always will be an American folk activity that extracts the essence of the early coach builders, blends it with a need for mobility, folds in a hefty dose of good looks, tosses in a dash of exhibitionism' (ibid.: 123). Cruising is also evoked by the Chuck Berry song 'No Particular Place to Go':

Riding along in my automobile
My baby beside me at the wheel
I stole a kiss at the turn of a mile
My curiosity running wild
Cruising and playing my radio
With no particular place to go

Cruising is also symbolically accompanied as a car-centred pursuit by 'hot-rodding', typically a teenage dirt-track racing competition as immortalised in the James Dean vehicle, *Rebel Without a Cause*, and which is described by Basham *et al.* as 'virtually America's unofficial national sport' (1984: 17). These styles and leisure pursuits, mainly emergent and popular in the 1950s, constitute something of a national imaginary, suffused with nostalgic longings for the youthful activities of yesteryear and the mythical small-town America in which they took place.

This mythical 1950s of American car culture is also embodied by the baroque excesses of car design, featuring giant tail fins, and elaborate chrome bumpers and grilles. Such features emphasised luxury and status but also the fantasies stemming from the peculiar modernity of 1950s science fiction. Distinctively American, contrasting with the sleek and restrained shapes of Italian vehicles and the classical refinement of British cars, such exorbitant designs foreground stylistic flamboyance and excess, celebrating unrestrainedly the material abundance provided and promised by American capitalism. These extrovert expressions of Americanness can also be found in the less mainstream, subcultural pastime of customising vehicles, again a tradition that emerged in the 1950s and which is still prevalent amongst marginalised groups such as Hispanic Californians, who devised 'low-riders', huge souped-up cars with enormous wheels and spectacular suspension which afford an alternative form of status for the poor, young men who work on them.

This example points to the exclusions perpetrated by the car's central role as a prop to identity, and as a means to participating in American society. Like Britain, particular notions of gender shape the cultural construction of cars. As Scharff says, the car was 'born in a masculine manger and when women [try] to claim its power they [enter] a male domain' (1997: 13). Whilst this gendering has been somewhat dissipated, the racial coding of automobiles and car ownership is well grounded in history. This is best exemplified by Berger's amazing account featuring Jack Johnson, the black heavyweight boxing champion of the world, who had achieved his title by defeating two white fighters, Tommy Burns and Jim Jeffries. His fondness for motor racing and his ability in this other sport, where he also defeated white competitors, led to a challenge from the world speed champion, Barney Oldfield, to a race. The pernicious racial coding of the contest – pitting black brawn against white intelligence – inevitably won by Oldfield, was intended to teach Johnson a lesson, for having defeated white boxers he refused to adopt the humility white America expected, instead openly pursuing white women and showing off his wealth and fame. His symbolic defeat was thought to reclaim a measure of white American prestige (Berger, 1983). Paul Gilroy explores the marginalisation of black car-owners and drivers in the USA more generally. Where poverty and the refusal of some companies to sell certain models to black customers attempted to debar them from the fruits of the booming economy and its most symbolic commodity, the car was simultaneously appropriated as a sign of black progress. For car ownership could signify social improvement, was a kind of democratic participation via the consumer culture, a movement out of the stasis of segregation imposed in space, and cars became signs of 'insubordination, progress and compensatory prestige' (2001: 94), for instance, resounding through black popular music.

Despite the centrality of the car to national identity, it seems as if the American love affair with the car is threatened. Fear about road deaths, ecological damage, the persistent culture of machismo, the privatisation of experience, segregated cities and the demise of other forms of mobility (Wolf, 1996) have been identified as symptoms of a car-dominated society. And Luger (2000) argues forcefully that the car and its industry also demonstrates the extent to which corporate power continues to shape American economy, politics and culture negatively.

Cars and their Affordances: National Sensualities

To reinforce the arguments about space made in the previous chapter, it is useful to conceive of the car not as a discrete object but as part of 'automobility', a distributed 'complex amalgam of interlocking machines, social practices and ways of dwelling' (Sheller and Urry, 2000: 739). This sort of analysis captures the distinctive national cultures of automobility that I wish to identify. The car driver can be considered as a 'hybrid assemblage', comprising humans, machines, roads, signs, representations, regulatory institutions and a host of related businesses and infrastructural features. Such an assemblage also produces distinctive ways of sensually apprehending cars and car travel for people inhabit, and are institutionally emplaced in, particular webs of affective and sensual experience. The sensuality of motoring and the experience of routinised, mundane forms of travel provide distinct ways of dwelling, moving and socialising in places (Urry, 2000: 59). Like the routines inscribed in the home, modes of dwelling-on-the-road or dwelling-in-the-car suggest that the car is a 'home from home'. Thus distinct sensations are produced by bodily interaction with particular cars, which possess particular affordances – the feel of the wheel, the seats, the rate of acceleration and the ease of changing gears – and they impinge on how the car can be manoeuvred. Particular forms of skill and driving dispositions are thus formed. The Rolls-Royce mentioned above clearly engenders a comfort-oriented drive which minimises the effect of external influences such as bumpy road surfaces. On the other hand, the French Renault and Citroën are less concerned with such matters. Their economy based appeal equates with more compact space, less-plush furnishings and a suspension that lacks the smoothness of the Rolls-Royce. Such sensations also depend upon the road surfaces, the climate and the conduct of other drivers. These bodily experiences, then, are constitutive of a less-heralded form of national identity, as well as a function of the different car models on any market.

Cars can be understood as extensions of bodies, what Graves-Brown (2000) calls a kind of 'exoskeleton'. And the forms of bodily relationships established through car-driver hybrids vary considerably. For instance, the prevalence of automatic gears in American cars means that the driver needs to be less attuned to the noise of the engine and the speed travelled, whereas drivers of most European cars – that largely possess manually operated gearsticks – incorporate a reflexive, bodily awareness of which gears are needed, a practice that barely impinges upon consciousness for experienced motorists. Similarly, cars are customised and domesticated according to nationally shaped conventions. A 'mobile domesticity' is achieved by owners decorating cars with furry dice, stickers signifying nationality, bumper stickers (in the USA), religious emblems and figures, mascots, mini football strips, Garfields, nodding dogs and music facilities (ibid.: 157).

As well as the tactility of cars, particular smells – often associated with the kind of fuel used – can provide a heightened experience of car travel, and so can the sound of motor engines, both one's own car and the noise produced by fellow road users. Bull (2001) has identified the integral role of sound in constituting the motoring experience. The automatic turning on of the radio, or the routine playing of cassettes, provides an internal soundscape which usually covers up the noise of the outside. These intimate pleasures reinforce the homely status of the car, but the nuances of motoring with manufactured sound relate to the particular music or radio programme being listened to. Thus, particular national radio programmes are devised to entertain and inform listeners during this 'drivetime', again constituting a familiar, shared enjoinment in which we, the national audience in simultaneous motion on the way to home or to work, are addressed as a normative community, often reinforced by frequent travel bulletins concerning the state of the nation's roads. Likewise, car journeys in North Africa are more likely to be accompanied by Egyptian pop music than the rock music played by Western stations. The subtle but distinct qualities that such music lends to the journey shape the nationally bounded experiences of motoring.

To explore this further, I want to discuss an episode which occurred in September 2000, when my car radio was stolen. This meant that until I replaced it the 50-minute drive to work was bereft of broadcast music and chat (I usually listen to BBC Radio 1 and Radio 5). It struck me that at first the car seemed devoid of noise, of life, and I experienced the sensation that I was in a vacuum or bubble, and began to long for the journey's end. But after accepting the apparent sterility and sensory deprivation that the trip entailed, the sounds that filled my ears were revelatory. I realised that I hadn't heard traffic for months, or the noise of my own engine, which led me to imagine potential problems in the suspicious noises I was hearing. This attunement to a different motoring soundscape was complemented by a more intense visual awareness: instead of being enmeshed in an auditory experience I switched into a more visual mode. I noticed changes in the mundane features of the M6 motorway, the lushness of the fields and woods. Nevertheless, despite noticing these formerly masked experiences, I continually jerked forward to switch the non-existent radio on, my hands and fingers involuntarily twitching to restore the status quo. Attuned to a sensual norm, my body was unable to de-programme its customary operations and unconsciously performed a regulatory series of movements to reintroduce the missing sound, revealing the somatic embed-dedness of particular routine experiences, where bodies are habituated to customary sounds and manoeuvres which install the body in place.

Representing Cars

Besides the physical interaction cited above, it is evident that the symbolic importance of cars is widely circulated through a variety of media, including painting and photography, poetry, literature, music, adverts, television program-mes and film which contribute to a sense of national identity. This is nowhere more blatant than in the central role of the automobile in twentieth-century film. Hollywood has produced a huge range of films in which cars are a central feature, an iconic role which varies substantially. From the gangster movies of the 1930s to the car chase films of the 1970s (*Bullitt, The French Connection*), cars have been essential components in the making of contemporary folklore. Another particular genre is the rites of passage movie – most prominently *The Last Picture Show* and *American Graffiti* – typically set in an elegiac 1950s, in which youths confront the advent of teenage sexuality and responsibilities of impending adulthood, within a range of social activities organised around automobiles, conjuring up the myth of a common youthful experience. But the best-known car-related genre is the road movie, a genre which encompasses a diversity of treatments. Road movies recycle recurrent geographical and visual themes, including iconographic portrayals of the endless road, spectacular landscapes and roadside garages. Basham *et al.* (1984: 13) cite the 1958 film *Thunder Road* as a seminal movie about cars which captures 'the mystery and elation of driving' and 'the never-ending rhythm of the tarmac and the sublime joy of motion'. At once a metaphor for restless movement across the USA, mirroring the surge westwards of the 'pioneers', the road movie has mutated to encompass a number of themes.

The individualistic, often counter-cultural impulse to escape the sterility of the urban and the control of government (*Easy Rider*), or the search for a better life (*The Grapes of Wrath*), can also be articulated as a route for deviance (*Natural Born Killers, Bonnie and Clyde, Badlands*) (see Cohan and Hark, 1997: 1–14). This ambivalence does not gainsay the power of these treatments for they constitute a recognisable array of multi-interpretable visual signifiers and narrative tropes which provide a shared cultural resource for producing a car-oriented imaginary.

In a fascinating study of French post-war cinema, Ross shows the essentially ambivalent character of the car in its relation to national identity. At first, it was celebrated as heralding modernity and a new, exciting, American-shaped future after austerity, even before cars became a feature of French everyday life. Ross argues that American cinema was hugely influential in projecting a mythical, prosperous America saturated by gadgets, household comforts and cars, as an ideal. French new-wave auteurs also eagerly grasped the car as a modern, rebellious symbol which represented the antithesis of traditional conservative values. Thus the French motor industry and the (French and American) film industry 'reinforced each other' (Ross, 1995: 39). Later, however, films such as *La Belle Americaine* reveal the domestication of an American car, its adaptation to French life, so that 'one can acquire America's good features while avoiding its corruption, one can modernise without losing the national . . . identity' (ibid.: 53). But also, the automobile is represented in later French films as a key factor heralding the destruction of close communities – and hence Frenchness – in its association with the pursuit of individual status, traffic jams and the reordering of experience. Again, this shows how conflicts between traditional and modern versions of national identity are articulated in popular representations.

Conclusion

I have tried to show in this account that objects are part of everyday worlds, symbolic imaginaries and affective, sensual experiences which inhere in forms of national identity. It is true that through travelling cultures, extended commodity flows and diasporic experiences, things are distributed in a more protean fashion than ever before. In this context, Knorr Cetina argues that as individualisation proceeds apace, with the erosion of established communities, objects increasingly displace other people as 'relationship partners' and 'embedding environments' (1997). Sociality, as a form of binding or grouping together, can also be understood by the process of surrounding the self with objects, by interacting with familiar objects in a series of arrangements and by identifying with objects.

A proliferation of objects penetrate our lifeworlds, infest our homes and bodies, and produce 'clusters of consciousness' (ibid.: 3). Their meaning is produced through the ways in which they link to or embody systems of technical knowledge, or are part of wider human–object networks. Knorr Cetina considers that the social is reconstituted through what she calls 'objectualisation'. Through interacting with technologies and things there is 'an increasing orientation towards objects as sources of the self, or relational intimacy, of shared subjectivity and of social integration' (ibid.: 9). The notion that relationships with objects can be created and sustained seems to require reflexive, technically skilled, self-authoritative individuals who construct and reconstruct their identities and lifestyles. As the 'nationalisation of social responsibility' breaks down, and common values and traditions become dissipated, individuals construct *new* links with the nation, in affective and cognitive ways, through alternative networks of association, including those offered by relations with objects. Whilst this is a somewhat bleak portrayal of contemporary material culture, it does point to the ways in which objects are incorporated into contemporary processes of meaning. For the shared resources which already exist means that symbolic objects such as the car can be reincorporated into national identity, can be adopted and adapted in different national contexts, both practically and symbolically, and drawn into particular affective relationships which cohere around ideas about national car cultures.

–5–

Representing the Nation: Scottishness and *Braveheart*

Introduction

National forms of representation articulate the relations between space, things, people and practices, denoting the qualities assigned to them as being distinguished by a common denominator: the nation. This is the context which binds unlike categories together by means of conceptualisation and language, to constitute a shared referential resource, and shared discursive formations. National identity is, then, partly sustained through the circulation of representations of spectacular and mundane cultural elements including those featured throughout this book; the landscapes, everyday places and objects, famous events and mundane rituals, gestures and habits, and examples of tradition and modernity which are held in common by large numbers of people. Importantly, these forms of signification work not because they are realistic but because they 'become naturalised codes whose operation reveals not the transparency of linguistic or visual codes, but the depth of cultural habituation of the codes in operation' (Barker, 1999: 12). These words, images and styles have no essential meaning but represent 'concepts and feelings that enable others to decode our meanings' (Hall, 1997: 5). Yet irrespective of how they are encoded and decoded, these foci provide shared topics for consumption. Through widespread dissemination, they are 'embedded in sounds, inscriptions, objects and images' made manifest in books, TV programmes, adverts and the like (ibid.). They cohere precisely because of their intertextuality, because they form complex chains of signification which provide maps of national meaning, dense clusters of ideas and images which can be connected to other constellations in endless ways. The images we share and are often particularly familiar with occur – and have occurred through our lives – in particular contexts: as pictures in classrooms, on billboards, in relatives' houses, and so on, and are interwoven with the spaces which we have inhabited. Whilst certain iconic images have become detached from the national (Elvis Presley, the moon landing), a host of consistently reproduced images continue to act as a shared resource to underpin national belonging, however recombined and reinterpreted they may be.

   Much of the time, such representations are unreflexively generated and consumed, as Billig (1995) describes insofar as they are manifest in everyday speech and in the deixis reproduced in daily newspapers which assumes that the 'us' and the 'we' referred to in articles require no qualification but will be uncritically accepted by readers. In the same way, images and descriptions can trigger a sense of national belonging without any further explanation being needed. Representations of 'our' national identity become more pointed when used to define 'us' against 'them' – usually other nations in political or sporting conflict – when stereotypes are more likely to be bandied about, and this is also the case when 'exotic' otherness is being sold via commodities and by the tourist industry. As I have mentioned, the constructions of others speaks not of them but of the desires and fears against which we define ourselves. This works in the world of nations as much as it does in the realms of self-identification. Technologies of representing otherness in travel programmes, tourist brochures, natural history magazines and television documentaries are generally produced for and consumed by audiences or readerships that are constituted nationally.

In discussing representation in this chapter, I want to direct attention to media products – films, television programmes and popular literature and advertising. I do not mean to discount all the other cultural elements that have featured throughout this book. In a sense, all these are forms of representation. Spaces are represented by planners and architects; their materialisation and regulation is a form of representing ownership and power over meaning, not to mention the semiotic inscriptions that are engraved onto all spaces subject to human intervention, whether through gardening styles, monumental features or road systems. Performances too are ways of representing ourselves to ourselves and to others, both in terms of shared everyday conventions of enaction, body language, and in large-scale ceremonies. Likewise, objects may be used, placed and bought in order to transmit symbolic meanings. But in addition, the things, landscapes and performances that have been discussed in previous chapters are not discretely consigned to their own realms – all circulate through forms of representation as they become identifiable symbolic cultural elements. And the process of representation adds a further density to the ways in which these are apprehended, producing more points of association through which they accrue meaning. In this chapter, I do not attempt to divorce the material, performative and spatial from the chosen form of representation, the Hollywood epic, *Braveheart*, as will be clear when I look at the rich seam of artefacts, performances and spaces that are intimately related to the themes and mythical elements of the film.

As I have been at pains to express throughout this book, national identity is processed through the realms of affect and sensuality as much as through cognitive processes of meaning construction and transmission. Bodily dispositions, modes of inhabiting space and ways of using things infer a structure of feeling; they can transmit shared emotional and sensual experiences in intangible ways, constituting a shared milieu of feeling and knowing. In looking at representation in this chapter

I do not wish to propose a dichotomy whereby there are realms of representation and non-representation, and similarly to infer that representation can be theorised by a set of tools and that this is separate from what some have called 'non-representational theory'. It should be clear from the foregoing that representation is (always) embodied and embodying, performed and conveying of performance, spatialised and spatialising, and objective and subjective. The problem, I believe, stems from the primacy accorded to the visual and the playing down of the material, spatial and embodied nature of the social world. Accordingly, whilst modes of representation can be identified, they are inevitably imbricated with the various processes of identification which I have discussed throughout the book.

To return to the discussion of national culture in Chapter 1, characteristically privileged forms of national identity have been those assumed to be linked with either a 'high' culture or a 'folk' culture. So national literatures (the 'Great American novel', poetry, national canons), schools of painting, and the pantheon containing Shakespeares, Goethes, Tagores and Matisses are held up as hosting exemplary species of national genius. Besides representing the nation, such literatures, paintings and poems are resources which are called upon to provide images, verses and passages that capture national attributes. Such quotations are brandished by politicians, sports writers and advertisers and circulate throughout popular culture. Yet in contemporary times, the consensus around canon formation and the universal recognition of excellence is no longer tenable. Now national identity is as likely to be identified in film and television products and styles, in popular music, and in fashion. Yet both forms of 'low' and 'high' culture are distributed across mediated cultural forms, in which everyday styles and vernacular cultural practices are represented along with quotations from previously canonical icons. This detraditionalisation and informalisation of culture does not mean that the national no longer exists but rather that it is continually being redistributed in more complex, variegated ways.

The mass media has proved to be the most important way of disseminating representations of the nation. I have argued that writers such as Gellner and Hutchinson have over-stressed the power of an elite in defining what is culturally valuable (high culture) for national identity, and popular culture has now almost entirely absorbed notions of high and low (which is not to say that debates about national cultural values are defunct). For as Thompson has observed, 'a major new arena has been created for the process of self-fashioning' (1995: 43) by the evolution of the mass media. As I discussed in Chapter 2, the experience of the media has been woven into the rituals and routines of everyday life, embedding their temporal and spatial reception in the quotidian, and producing numerous contexts in which they are interpreted. Moreover, as Stevenson states, the arena in which contested representations of the nation are fought out is the media, in which the 'development of a sophisticated array of visual codes and repertoires that interrupt the agendas of more hegemonic institutions and cultures is an essential armament within the semiotic society' (2001a: 5). Morley points to television's potential for examining the 'constitutive dynamics of abstractions such as "the community" or "the nation"' (1991: 12), a facility for reimagining the national community which is promiscuous, drawing on cultural meanings, for instance, about tradition and modernity. Thus, the example of *Braveheart*, the media form discussed here, will show how myth is reinterpreted and recycled, reaffirming old and new meanings about national identity and history. In addition, the mass media also disseminate numerous ways of representing others, and provide cultural forms from elsewhere which are interpreted in cultural contexts far from those in which they were produced. Global news networks, tourist marketing, advertising, films and television all provide often stereotypical representations of otherness which feed into forms of national belonging by providing images which can be reworked in (re)constructing 'our' identity as *not like* this otherness.

Nationally based mediascapes still largely predominate in everyday media experience – people still largely consume national newspapers, listen to national radio stations and watch national television. In certain circumstances, however, this is not so – for instance, with the huge global consumption of Hollywood film. But in all spheres, there has been an enormous increase in the amount of information and imagery available. The globalisation of the media, and the increasingly vast circulation of information, has not diminished the vitality of ways in which national identity is represented, for it has unleashed a torrent of national representations, comprising a welter of stereotypical portrayals and symbols, as well as avenues for dissenting and dissonant representations. Global cultural forms such as the soap opera – which in their British and American incarnations have previously been exported without modification – have subsequently been compressed into a national mould, whilst at the same time pan-continental programmes suited for wider dissemination have been designed to minimise differences (Barker, 1999: 67). Westwood refers to what she terms 'correlative imaginaries' to discuss how the representations produced by South American *telenovelas* – along with football and religion – provide a means to frame the self within a national context, to 'produce a form of identification between the self and the social' (Westwood and Phizacklea, 2000: 42). Plot themes and kinds of character generate shared cultural referents, which are interpreted in multiple ways but nevertheless supply common points of orientation. Crucially, such themes, often dealing with 'sensationalistic' social issues, featuring a range of class, ethnic and gendered characters, potentially undermine official versions of the national story by including marginalised characters and issues. Viewing the *telenovelas* also reveals the forms of scaling by which individuals fit themselves into the nation, connecting emotionally and cognitively with the narratives and representations which offer 'mediations between local and national, big and small worlds' (ibid.: 56).

In fact, within images flows there is great inequality between nations, between those who have a large technological infrastructure and are home to global media corporations which are able to transmit hegemonic meanings globally via visual means, and nations which, lacking the means to produce and circulate a vast array of images of their own, import a larger proportion of representations from elsewhere. This global system of the transaction of images belies a power-geometry whereby the majority of representations consumed by some national subjects are generated from outside. In addition, there has been a growth of 'regional' and 'geo-cultural' markets, such as Chinese, Indian, Arabic, European and other diasporic populations, in which a number of nations must be addressed either specifically or in programming that foregrounds regional 'common denominators' (Barker, 1999: 53).

What I want to emphasise is that there remain identifiable regimes of represent-ation (albeit increasingly unstable, plural and interpenetrated by other regimes of representation) which are shaped around our national identity and our understand-ing of other nations. And I also want to stress that the Baudrillardian nightmare about the production of a free-floating, postmodern sign system within which any possibility of meaning has been lost as images become detached from that which they signify in a welter of signs is a chimera. However, the power to represent means that visual and discursive hegemonies persist across mediascapes, and swarms of images and words offer an increasing range of subject positions. Thus, although attempts are made to fix meaning in the midst of mediascapes and ideoscapes, representations are difficult to pin down, so the attempts of cultural nationalists to retain stable meanings must be ongoing and vigilant, and can only try to limit the potential for undermining hegemonic meaning.

It is with questions about the globalisation of representation that I have chosen to look at *Braveheart*, in many ways a formulaic Hollywood product which deals with (Scottish) national identity but casts the story within a more generic framework designed to appeal to a global audience. I have chosen to look at a global form of representation rather than one that is more obviously located in a national tradition or school. The issues I will explore are different from, but overlap with, those associated with national film traditions. For these latter schools often act as guardians of film heritage, establishing archives and film institutes. Higson has argued that amongst European nations, 'national' cinema has been marshalled to assert a claim for autonomy against the influence of Hollywood and to foster and support a distinctively 'national cultural form, an institution with a "nationalising" function' (1989: 43).

Gledhill (2001) argues that national film can be identified in a number of ways: by a focus on identifiable national narratives and myths; by a tradition of particular genres; by codes and conventions of acting, screenplay, characterisation and so on; through body language and the 'gestures, words, intonations, attitudes, postures' that inhere in performances; by the signs and values which national stars carry (Michael Caine, Sean Connery). It is also distinguished according to the market it is designed for (Hayward, 1999). Gledhill also refers to British cinema as mobilising identifiable kinds of 'story-telling, modes of acting and theatricality, and pictorialism'. These are distinguished by a specific 'cultural poetics' and 'culturally conditioned modes of perception', notably influenced by social divisions of class, region and, latterly, ethnicity. For instance, there is a concern with portraying restraint and passion as distinctive expressions of class which inform and are informed by a broader awareness of acting in a social context. These key elements produce an insistently social cinema which is realised not in 'realistic' representations but 'in the processes of story-telling, lay acting, trying on each other's costumes, listening to each other's accents, quoting each other's stories, mobilising each other's cultural forms and practices' (Gledhill, 2001). Clearly, there are recognisable modes of production and reception which emerge out of particular national identities and preoccupations.

However, rather than explore these undoubted regularities identifiable in national cinemas, I want to examine a Hollywood product to explore how the often formulaic themes it plays with feed back into contemporary constructions of national identity. As an iconic representation of Scottishness *Braveheart* capitalises on popular myth, but the power of this myth, its flexibility, means that the film has been used and interpreted in numerous ways. As such, the example also serves to locate the production of national identity as partly occurring outside the nation, embellishing my concern to show how it is situated in the constellations which are organised within an increasingly global matrix.

Introducing *Braveheart*

The Hollywood blockbuster *Braveheart*, directed by and starring Mel Gibson in the title role, tells the story of the struggles for Scottish independence led by Sir William Wallace, the legendary Scottish warrior, who, although from humble background, assembled a force capable of defeating the occupying English army, and achieved considerable military success until his abandonment by treacherous Scottish nobles led to his capture and gruesome execution on the orders of Edward Longshanks, the English King. Using this film, I will look at the ways in which representations of the nation are contested, the genealogies by which such emblems of national pride are summoned up, and how representations concocted and broadcast at the global scale may become repatriated, and may serve to bolster or question mythic national tropes. My aim is to focus on the response to the movie as an exemplary form of contemporary representation, but then to broaden the discussion by exploring the historical contexts through which the Wallace myth has persisted. Moreover, the role of *Braveheart* in reconstituting forms of Scottishness can be divorced neither from the (re)production of other representations of Wallace, ancient, modern and ongoing, nor the use of Wallace in material culture, and in forms of ritual and performance. My argument will rest upon the contention that representing aspects of Scottishness through the medium of a highly commercial film has not led to a passive consumption of the narrative and images beamed out of the cinema screen, but has dynamically (re)generated a proliferation of other arguments, artefacts, images, performances, phrases and symbolic spaces which (re)produce ideas about Wallace and national identity.

Braveheart emerged at a crucial time for the reconstitution of Scottish identity, in a period which has seen the establishment of a Scottish parliament. Many commentators cite what they call the 'Braveheart effect' in contributing to this renewed national awareness. Yet popular responses to the film highlight many of the ambivalences and conflicts about the constitution of Scottish identity and the representation of Scotland, and these themes are far from recent. The reactions of Scots partly indicate the difficulties of sustaining narratives of national identity in a globalising world.

To explore the various discourses and appropriations of *Braveheart*, I will firstly contextualise the discussion by considering some debates about the representation of Scotland in film and deliberate upon the manufacture of a contemporary Scottish identity in an era in which intensified processes of globalisation – mediatisation, commodification and cultural disembedding – appear to threaten national and local identities. Secondly, I will assess the responses of politicians and commentators to the film, to highlight the debates around Scottish identity. In broadening out the discussion, I will then go on to explore how *Braveheart* has significantly heightened the profile of Scotland in the international tourist market – like film, an important contemporary source through which national attributes and attractions are circulated – and the ways in which this has also been subject to contestation. Furthering my intention to draw on the wider context of representation – and to situate debates about *Braveheart* and Scottish national identity within a wider matrix – I will examine the production of images of Wallace over time, places associated with him, forms of material culture which have been generated by this mythic figure, dramatic rituals organised around him, and briefly discuss the reception of *Braveheart* outside Scotland.

William Wallace is one of the central figures of Scottish history, in official accounts and in popular myth and legend. Commencing with the fifteenth-century book by Blind Harry, *The Actis and Deidis of the Illustere and Vailzeand Campioun Schir William Wallace, Knicht of Ellerslie*, Wallace has been a constant point of identification in popular culture, featuring in the poetry of the national bard, Robert Burns, notably the patriotic anthem 'Scots Wha Hae' (wi Wallace bled) and commemorated at the imposing nineteenth-century National Wallace Monument in Stirling. In 1990, Marinell Ash proclaimed that the power of Wallace (and Robert the Bruce) was becoming irrelevant, yet she conceded that any outbreak of popular nationalism would make it 'surprising if the figures of Bruce and Wallace are not invoked once more' (1990: 92). As the success of *Braveheart* testifies, this is exactly what has happened. The fifth biggest grossing movie in the UK in 1995, Scotland provided 28 per cent of the national audience (its usual share of the British market averaging 8 per cent). The movie was the subject of controversy in the national press, with a profusion of letters, articles and editorials, contributing to a tumult of national self-analysis and definition, as will shortly be discussed. Before that, I want to provide a context for debates about representation, film and national identity by exploring the portrayal of Scotland in film.

Scotland in Film

One may argue that in general the subject matter, characterisation, narrative, pace, action sequence and dialogue in Hollywood films are premised upon the expectations of the international markets at which they are aimed. Forming an integral part of global 'mediascapes' and 'ideoscapes' (Appadurai, 1990), these cinematic flows of images and information contain identifiable tropes which are designed to appeal to an international audience but also bear powerful traces of American ideologies.

Because Hollywood appeals to 'fantasies, desires and aspirations that are not simply of local and national interests' it is, in an important sense, integral to the film cultures of most parts of the world, and hence part of their national cinema (Higson, 1995: 8). Whilst the majority of its films are situated in the United States, Hollywood also casts its net further, often alighting on mythical heroes and epics from other cultural locations (for instance, *The Three Musketeers*, *El Cid*, *Robin Hood*, *Crocodile Dundee*, *Mulan*), disembedding the telling of these stories from localities and encoding them with its own particular themes of stylised romance, versions of masculinity and femininity, and individual liberty and integrity. The circulation of these images and narratives of 'otherness' signify familiar notions of global difference. Such movies are therefore important cultural forms which (re)construct the nation through symbolic ingredients such as traditions, landscapes, histories and myths which are consumed by national and international audiences. Some argue that these commercial strategies which cross national boundaries to create new 'imaginative territories' are destined to dilute national identities portrayed via Hollywood. Indeed, according to German filmmaker Edgar Reitz, Hollywood has 'taken narrative possession of our past' (Morley and Robins, 1995: 93).

To assert cultural identity in response to Hollywood's market onslaught, other independent film projects are devised specifically to articulate a more located sense of identity and repel what are perceived as the denationalising tendencies of this

globalising movie culture. These movies are commonly distinguished from Hollywood as belonging to a 'national cinema' – and in certain cases (for instance, in
France) are part of a defensive reaction against what is seen as 'Americanisation'.
More particularistic films tend to represent other identity formations within
the nation such as race, sexuality, ethnicity, region and class, but there are also
'heritage' films which tap into nostalgic modes of representing the past (Higson,
1995). Alternatively, other strategies exploit their own 'exotic' national characteristics and attempt to sell this difference on the international market, further ensuring
that such productions contain familiar plots based around action adventure, romance
and sexuality, such as the (very) English films *Notting Hill* and *Lock, Stock and
Two Smoking Barrels*, which trade respectively on English reserve and charming
eccentricity, and on East End gangster lore.

Scotland has a particular place in the annals of Hollywood-produced mythology.
According to McArthur, Scottishness in films is represented by well-worn historical
stereotypes. He contends that besides informing ways in which most other cultures
imagine Scots, 'the melange of images, characters and motifs consuming tartanry
and Kailyard' also provides the framework within which Scots continue to construct
themselves. Such films thereby sustain a hegemonic system that interpellates Scots
with a sense of their own inferiority and suffocates attempts to produce alternative
representations (McArthur, 1982: 40). Craig supports this view, asserting that the
reified forms of representation are clichés which 'need to acquire a new historical
significance before they can be released into the onward flow of the present from
the frozen worlds of their myths of historical irrelevance' (1982: 15). The conclusion of the edited collection, *Scotch Reels*, is that 'more politically progressive'
representations of Scotland should be produced in Scottish film (McArthur, 1982).

It is argued that consistent and regressive forms of representation can 'slip into
the national imaginary as familiar identities, and into the international image
markets as tradable symbolic goods' (Caughie, 1990: 14). The key themes of Kailyard, Clydesideism and tartanry indicate the loss of identity and a removal from
'authentic' Scottishness (whatever that might be). McArthur laments that Scotland
seems destined continually to fulfil its role as 'the Romantic dream landscape par
excellence' (1994: 104).

These arguments resonate with wider assertions that Scottish popular culture
is damned by embarrassing stereotypes. Fretting over Scottish television dramas,
popular iconography and commodities as well as films, journalists and intellectuals
attempt to distinguish between 'progressive' cultural products and practices, and
those which stain Scotland's image and promote a 'sense of inferiority'. It is argued
that to achieve a 'mature' or 'modern' national identity, these dismal trappings of
Scottishness – kitsch tartan souvenirs, hard men, romantic scenery and whimsical
locals – need to be replaced by more 'contemporary' representations. This distrust
of 'low' Scottishness is appositely captured by historian T.C. Smout: 'in popular

culture, Scottish history appears as the stuff of heritage industry, colourful and episodic, but basically not serious. It is a poor foundation on which to identify a Scottish nation with a confident and empowered Scottish state' (1994: 109).

Films such as *Brigadoon*, *Whisky Galore*, *Local Hero* and *Loch Ness*, certainly seem to fit into the whimsical, moral stories of kailyard, and have been augmented by representations of folksy Scottishness in TV series such as *Take the High Road*, *Dr Finlay's Casebook* and *Hamish McBeth*. The rural wistfulness and disempower- ing sense of loss that *Scotch Reels* emphasises seems to be evident in other recent films set in the Highlands such as *Ill Fares the Land*, *Venus Peter* and *Another Time, Another Place*.

As far as *Braveheart* is concerned, the preoccupations of Hollywood in general and the imaging of Scottishness in particular appear to follow predictable forms. Some critics maintain that films such as *Rob Roy* and *Braveheart* are fashioned for an international audience by resituating the ethos of the western in a Scottish setting (Royle, 1995). A central theme of the action movie is the fantasy of male control and empowerment through physical engagement (O'Shea, 1996: 244). Moreover, here, as in most Hollywood products, the heterosexual love story is a staple ingredient. Of course, the motif of freedom and the defeat of oppression (connoting democracy, individualism and a dominant American ideology) is frequently integral to Hollywood narrative and needs little further explication here.

In *Braveheart*, these gendered themes are transcoded in an imaginary Scottish landscape populated by the 'wild charismatic men' and 'the fey elusive women' cited in *Scotch Reels*. Wallace and his rugged warriors are fighting to reclaim their land and their masculine dignity from their English overlords – whose (wholly fictitious) practice of *primus nocte* represents the emasculation of Scotland. One figure, Wallace, emerges to claim the right to liberty; the physically courageous hero must be central to the tale whilst the military tradition of Scotland is reinforced. The two chief female characters are grateful recipients of Wallace's hyper- masculine qualities. The romantic interludes are set beneath the stars in pastoral splendour midst trees and rocks. Likewise, the landscape is seen as a source of sustenance to Wallace as he ruminates atop the Cairngorms about the battle strategies he must implement, the camera giddily swirling around him. This mapping of the bodies of the key participants onto archetypal scenery reinforces the importance of the landscape in popular fantasies of Scotland in which Scots are nurtured and strengthened by wild nature.

Despite the persistence of these stories and images, the proliferation of films and TV programmes set in and produced in Scotland means that representations of Scotland are now more complex than in the recent past: 'less than a decade ago, Scottish cinema could be simplified, abstracted and categorised in critical and historical research' (Caughie, 1990: 13). The rise of an independent sector has fuelled the production of smaller-scale, home-based drama which displays themes and images far removed from the kinds of 'stereotypical' films impugned above. Films like *Trainspotting, Shallow Grave,* and *Breaking the Waves* can be evaluated as morally, aesthetically and politically challenging. Moreover, films such as *Small Faces, Orphans* and *Ratcatcher,* TV series such as *Tutti Frutti, Taggart,* and *Bad Boys,* and the plays of Peter MacDougall, all explore themes of urban Glasgow and Clydesideism, deconstructing and parodying the Glasgow 'hard man' and brutal gangs, and the urban culture. These productions underline the diversity of new representations of Scottishness.

More seriously, however, the withering criticisms levelled at the 'traditional' films by McArthur *et al.* miss the contradictions and ambivalences which inhere in their popular reception and the knowing self-mockery which they promote amongst Scots. Ignoring the interpretations of audiences, and the ways such representations are reclaimed, recycled and used to express a wide range of meanings, such analyses presume that films are unproblematically consumed by viewers, that they are encoded with dominant messages which are simply and consensually decoded.

Although it is commonly attributed to popular films that they are formulaic, market-led and predictable, it is necessary to recognise that they are consumed by diverse groups, in particular historical contexts and in specific political cultures. For instance, popular films can stimulate utopian desires through the structures of feeling they concoct, and audiences can imagine transcending forms of oppression and conceive of transgressive and transformational acts. Thus the common filmic representational and narrative tropes around the purposive and efficient expenditure of physical energy, sensual viscerality, the transparent intensity of emotion and its expression, the authenticity of emotional relationships and the sense of community, can promise the transcendence of the quotidian, or of oppressive political circumstances. In this sense, the utopian possibilities suggested by the sensual and narrative intensity of Hollywood movies hint at a transformative appropriation. Films are formulaically encoded with fantasies about 'freedom', individual accomplishment, overcoming inequality, unmasking hypocrisy and corruption, and achieving romantic fulfilment. Moreover, the conventional figure of the doomed hero who 'will not settle for the world as it is' suggests the exemplary nobility of those who struggle to transcend oppression (O'Shea, 1996: 245). *Braveheart* is exemplary in this respect, since it enables particular fantasies about Scottishness and nationalism to be translated into present political struggles.

The political impact of a film is heavily influenced by 'which political currents are in circulation and which discursive strategies they adopt' (ibid.): 'whether particular film viewers connect the pleasures of communitarian transcendence they enjoy in a film to a communitarian politics will depend upon the political culture they inhabit in that historical conjuncture' (ibid.: 259). And in the context of *Braveheart*, the film must have seemed like manna from heaven for many nationalists who have witnessed a rising tide of support for Scottish political independence during the 1990s. For although the Hollywood appropriation and reconstitution of myths exemplifies the disembedding of culture, it also provides new images and reconfigured narratives that can be re-embedded. Rather than losing their significance, the global transmission of disembedded images and narratives may feed back into local discourses, even heightening their power over identity and imagination.

Battles Over *Braveheart*

In order to explore the variety of responses to *Braveheart* within Scotland, I will concentrate on the uses which some nationalists eagerly made of the film, and then look at its negative reception amongst a range of commentators. This is intended to give a flavour of the heated and complex debate which took place, especially in the national press, to further elucidate my argument that popular forms of representation can feed into the reflexive reconstruction of identity, rather than being passively consumed. These debates also highlight the problems of sustaining national identities which depend on 'traditional' forms of representing the nation which appear to clash with 'progressive visions' – again the contest between modern and traditional dimensions of national identity.

Celebrating Braveheart

Although Mel Gibson somewhat disingenuously denied that the film had any political content but was merely a good story (*Scotsman*, 2/9/95), the Scottish National Party (SNP) was quick to exploit the metaphorical possibilities it offered. Former Party leader Alex Salmond claimed that 'the message is relevant today in that it is the Scots who are fighting for their independence the same way they are at the moment' (*Glasgow Herald*, 2/10/95). Skilfully comparing the political project of Wallace with that of contemporary nationalism , he argued that Wallace's 'idea of the "common weal", the common good, is a Scottish spirit that has lasted for centuries; it is that spirit that the modern civic nationalism of Scotland retains' (*Observer*, 10/9/95: 6).

This presumed Scottish quality of a more democratic disposition is intended to compare with the lesser democratic instincts of England, from which Scotland must free itself. As mentioned earlier, notions about the 'double time of the nation' (Bhabha, 1990) and nationalism as 'janus-faced' (Nairn, 1977) reveals how nationalists simultaneously evoke historical events and figures, and optimistic invocations of future glory. What has been achieved can be attained once more. Using archetypal myth to establish precedent, the SNP cite Wallace's exemplary adventures to inform future progress. Out of a long continuous history marked by passages of autonomy and oppression, the present state of affairs merely presages the realisation of the nation, its eventual coming into efflorescence, as prefigured in earlier triumphs. Whilst an appeal to the militaristic characteristics of Wallace's campaign has been seen as crude and triumphalist, the allure of his supposed concern for civil rights, equity and self-determination fit snugly into contemporary political discourse. Others argue that the film addresses other contemporary political and historical issues. For instance, Massie cites the Whig historian G.M. Trevelyan as articulating the popular view that Wallace introduced the 'new idea and tradition' of 'democratic patriotism' into the world (*Sunday Times*, 17/9/95).

Besides this appeal to rational political objectives clothed in the language of modern democracy, the SNP also drew on what Salmond called 'the real power in the emotional appeal' of *Braveheart* (*The Herald*, 11/9/95). This is exemplified in the rabble-rousing parallel he draws by identifying the SNP with the cause of Wallace: 'At the Battle of Stirling Bridge I would have been on Wallace's side and at least [Michael] Forsyth would know he wanted to be on the other side. But Labour would have been in a quandary. I can safely say Wallace wouldn't have been in favour of devolution' (*Sunday Times*, 3/9/95). At the time, Forsyth was the Secretary of State for Scotland in the unpopular Conservative government. In order to capitalise on this emotional and political charge, the SNP distributed cleverly devised leaflets outside cinemas in Scotland in the form of reply-paid postcards. On one side was an image of Mel Gibson as Wallace and 'BRAVEHEART' in large capitals, along with a text, culminating in the words: 'TODAY IT'S NOT JUST BRAVEHEARTS WHO CHOOSE INDEPENDENCE – IT'S ALSO WISE-HEADS – AND THEY USE THE BALLOT BOX'. On the other side is the slogan 'YOU'VE SEEN THE MOVIE . . . NOW FACE THE REALITY.'

The 'head and heart' campaign which the SNP mobilised to cash in on the popularity of the movie had immediate results in opinion polls which recorded a dramatic rise of eight points in those intending to vote for the party, and, according to Salmond, applications for membership were almost sixty a day (*The Herald*, 11/9/95). Even if this contains a pinch of hyperbole, it seems to indicate the powerful impact of the film on Scots – what has been termed the 'Braveheart effect'.

The SNP's belief that *Braveheart* possessed a symbolic significance for nationalists was widely argued by other media commentators and columnists. In line with the imperatives of cultural nationalists, discussed in Chapter 1, who argue that a nationalism bereft of cultural and historical appeal is instrumental and sterile, some commentators acknowledged that the film provided Scots with 'a powerful creation myth which will surely help to focus our national sense of identity' (Brian Pendreigh, *Scotsman*, 4/9/95). Moreover, Mike Russell, Chief Executive of the SNP, contended that the film highlighted a significant historical episode which fostered 'an understanding of the heroic nature of at least one part of our past and a new enthusiasm for the future of our nation' (*Scotsman*, 20/9/95). Such arguments infer that an effective nationalism must have recourse to a set of foundational myths that provide 'roots' for identity. As O'Shea avers in his discussion of the popular consumption of films, political projects need 'affective investment as well as a rational acceptance' (1996: 264). Thus *Braveheart* tapped directly into these transcendent desires for emotional identification with aspects of the nation which connote struggle, history and heroism, and tradition.

One of the most common claims in praise of *Braveheart* was that it highlighted 'wider truths' which hinted at both contemporary inequality and the enduring corruption of a self-serving class of Scots. Maley suggested that 'the triple whammy of anglicisation, inferiorism and anti-Irish sentiment can be addressed at a single stroke, and in an accessible manner' (1998: 78). Mike Russell wrote that the motivation which led Wallace to undertake such a campaign, his decision to embark on a quest for autonomy and freedom, was a positive choice that stresses the importance of independence. For the 'lack of equality and respect between the institutions of Scotland and England' along with the 'thoughtlessness that familiarity, political superiority and dependence have bred' at Westminster, are relevant political analogies that the film arouses (*Scotsman*, 20/9/95).

For others, *Braveheart* raised awareness about how Scottish nobles had consistently betrayed the aspirations of their countryfolk. Lesley Riddoch argued that a class analysis reveals the way the elite – what she terms 'our Uncle Toms' – had sold out the interests of the ordinary Scots: 'the overwhelming lesson of history, and the clear message of Braveheart is that one individual cannot triumph while the so-called professional classes divide their loyalties between themselves and the collective interests they're supposed to serve' (*Scotsman*, 15/9/95). Using the thirteenth-century nobles portrayed in *Braveheart* as an example, she links these betrayals by an aristocratic 'parcel of rogues' to the contemporary betrayals by a Scottish elite in the name of 'enlightened self interest' and warns of the tragic 'prospect of history repeating itself'. This theme is echoed by Pendreigh, who remarks that 'Braveheart does an excellent job in conveying the duplicity of the Scottish nobility, including Bruce, as they seek to promote their own interests' (*Scotsman* 8/9/95). Likewise, Russell accuses the 'deceitful' and 'treacherous' nobility of being 'mean-spirited' and cites the overcoming of these narrow interests as essential in the ultimate achievement of Scottish independence (*Scotsman*, 20/9/95).

In addition to these sentiments, the economic value of the film, and the very fact that Scotland was represented on a world stage, was seen as a source of prestige. Indeed, Michael Forsyth primarily used the film to project an image of himself as touting for business for Scotland (see *The Guardian*, 11/9/95). In this context, the politics and content of the film are irrelevant but its economic potential is not. Others also recognise the economic arguments of projecting a powerful image abroad. As a member of the Wallace clan writes in a letter to the *Sunday Times*, 'A romantic international view can be a good thing and we should not knock the tartan out of Scotland; it has the potential to create many well-paid jobs' (14/6/96).

Widely reported in the press was the request of Ally McCoist, the Scottish international footballer, for a special showing of *Braveheart* before the crucial European Championship qualifying match with Finland to induce patriotic feeling and spur the team on to victory. Whether apocryphal or not, the story evinces the ways in which popular cultural forms and practices are used to express nationalist sentiment, and sometimes operate in an intertextual way so as to reinforce each other. The episode conjures up the war-cry, 'Remember Bannockburn', which resonates when Scotland play the 'auld enemy', England, at football, and testifies to the emotional significance of twinning sporting and celluloid versions of national(ist) achievement. It seems that any Scottish athletic achievement is currently signalled in the press as the feat of a sporting 'Braveheart'.

Finally, the highly charged symbolism of Wallace's exploits in contemporary Scotland was crystallised in the decision to hold the 1999 devolution referendum to decide whether there should be a Scottish Parliament on the date of the 700th anniversary of Wallace's successful defeat of the English at the Battle of Stirling Bridge.

Criticising Braveheart

Despite the celebration of *Braveheart* by numerous patriotic Scots, there were many dissenting voices in the media about the morality of the film, and its suitability as a political and emblematic expression of Scottish identity. It is noteworthy that the arguments identified above by those who lament the regressive and stereotypical representations of Scottishness in popular film and the tourist industry find an echo in critiques of *Braveheart*. The familiar fears about the obsession with tartanry and Highland tales resurface, for instance, in Audrey Gillan's comment: 'Braveheart has encouraged Scotland's lack of knowledge about itself. Greedy for confirmation as a romantically wild nation, our gluttony for feeding on myth and heathery legend reaches worrying proportions when it affects the entire socio-consciousness of a nation' (*Scotland on Sunday*, 16/9/95).

Widespread concern was directed towards the growing nexus between the heritage industry and the media. As the place-marketers leapt onto the *Braveheart* bandwagon, fears about the impact of these attempts to recycle the images of the film for tourists led to complaints about the production of a hyperreal, post-industrial Scotland: 'Sadly, the tourist industry is about the only industry thriving in this wee country today as Scotland gradually moves towards becoming a theme park for wide-eyed romantics' (Miller, *Scotsman*, 7/9/95).

Although I have identified a dominant view amongst Scottish nationalists that the film was a godsend to their cause, for some the importance of presenting a modern, European and progressive image is hamstrung by the persistence of tartan, militaristic and mystico-romantic representations of Scotland. Several responses to *Braveheart* highlight this disaffection with what they envision as anachronistic themes of Scottishness. Counter to the arguments of cultural nationalists, the preoccupation with the motifs of the film was considered by several commentators to be at the expense of rational political debate. As a letter-writer to the *Sunday Times* recorded (15/9/96), 'the SNP should stick to economics, social policies, international policies and its proposals for an independent Scotland. It should forget trying to stir up long dead emotions.'

A major source of discontent about the film was what was perceived as the anti- English sentiment, even hatred, which was believed to encourage a version of patriotism that blamed others for Scotland's own failings. Nationalist strategies of constructing a mythical foe – the English – against which the nation can be contrasted were accused of veering towards exclusivist and hysterical tendencies. According to Gillan, the recourse to demonising the English is a nationalism which has 'at the back of its consciousness . . . imperialist bogeys, redcoats, poll-taxers, and goals by Bobby Charlton' (*Scotland on Sunday*, 16/9/95). The rather homophobic motif running through the film, embodied in the character of the Prince of Wales, was identified by MacAskill, who asserted that 'every Englishman is either completely evil or homosexual, and speaks with a Home Counties accent'. In contradistinction, 'Scots are all kindly, rough hewn souls, mixing courage and humour'. He argues that 'Salmond should be ashamed that his party has benefited from tawdry emotionalism and racism' (*Scotsman*, 12/9/95). Moreover, Massie attests that *Braveheart* panders to popular stereotypes that the English are 'arrogant', less community-minded than Scots, and snobbish, and that these reflect 'old and pointless resentments' that will be rekindled and 'inflame the feelings of animosity which already exist' (*Sunday Times*, 17/9/95). The summoning up of such stereotypical enemies is held to betray a lack of self-confidence and a vilification of a reified 'other'.

Besides fretting about the portrayal of the English and the anachronistic sense of identity that this reproduces, the claiming of a medieval warrior by the nationalist cause was seen as inappropriate and irrelevant by some. Michael Forsyth asserted, 'I think we have to fight the battles of the 21st century, not the 14th century' (*Stirling Observer*, 1/9/95). Later he said that Wallace was a 'loser and a failure' and an example of how Scots tended to celebrate failure. This defeatism, he concluded, signified something about the 'contemporary Scottish ethos', particularly its neglect of celebrating successful figures. Rather predictably, Forsyth cited Adam Smith as a 'more suitable role model' (*Guardian*, 27/4/96). Instead of venerating the attributes of losers, Forsyth recommended that the most estimable qualities of Scots were epitomised by their 'self-sufficiency, education, thriftiness and wealth creation' (*Sunday Times* 21/7/96).

Likewise, Massie insists that Wallace is an 'impossibly remote' figure and that 'the wars of independence are not only a long time ago, but irrelevant to modern Scotland'. His argument is whether an ancient military figure serves as an appropriate icon: 'does it really serve us well to identify as our national hero a man who, however brave and honourable he may have been, has his hands red with English blood?' (*Scotland on Sunday*, 3/9/95). Massie then broadens his discussion by suggesting a list of other Scots who ought to be celebrated with the same fervour as that accorded to Wallace (a theme I will return to shortly), offering those who perished in military conflict to uphold 'democracy and civilisation' commemorated by the national War Memorial in Edinburgh Castle. There is a move here to reclaim the unionist tradition of highlighting those Scots who prospered and made fortunes in the era of empire, and the familiar Victorian litany of heroic inventors and explorers, notably David Livingstone. In a similar vein, historian Richard Findlay argues that the benefits derived from empire go 'against the grain of much of Scottish history that tends to represent Scotland as victim' (*Sunday Times*, 21/7/96). These critiques raise the question of the mythical value of heroic figures, and show how national identity and nationalism is an arena both for radically different interpretations of familiar mythic figures and events and for contests between groups who utilise different mythical elements to stake their political claims through such identifications. As we shall see, more pertinent, perhaps, is the dearth of female Scottish mythic figures, emphasising the masculinisation of Scottish identity as evinced through the film and heritage industries (Edensor and Kothari, 1996).

Two other critical responses to the film are worth pointing out. First is the argument that Wallace's struggle against oppression ought to be identified as a class struggle, an aspect *Braveheart* did not depict. Capitalising on the popular belief that Wallace is a particularly exemplary hero because of his lowly origins, historian J. Mackay averred that 'there is a far better argument that what he did was more Marxist than Scottish nationalist. He was a man of the people. But his struggle was a struggle against the Anglo-Norman aristocracy' (*Sunday Times*, 21/7/95). Likewise, in an academic context, Willy Maley admires the way the film foregrounds class divisions to lambast the 'collaborative national bourgeoisie' and commends its 'uncompromising rebelliousness and anti-authoritarianism' (1998: 71).

A concern with realism is manifest in further critical responses that pointed out the film's lack of historical accuracy and authenticity. Here is evident a conflict between contending forms of narration and representation; namely, between History and Myth. For instance, Miller points out the innumerable 'howlers' of the film, reserving particular opprobrium for the Highland presentation of Wallace – who was apparently a lowlander, Wallace's (Gibson's) Glaswegian accent, the unrealistic portrayal of Edinburgh as a collection of cottages rather than a fortress town, the sound-tracking of uilleann (Irish) pipes as the Highland bagpipes are played on screen, and above all the suggestion that Wallace was the progenitor of the English throne through his liaison with the future queen of England. What is rather more noteworthy here is the implication that the effeminate princely husband of the target of Wallace's affections is inadequate to the manly task fulfilled by the Scottish epitome of masculinity. As Charlotte O'Sullivan notes, 'siring turns out to be the supreme patriotic act' (*Observer*, 16/6/96: 18).

The first lover of Wallace, the elfin Murron, apparently has no basis in documented evidence. Other writers directed particular outrage to the absence of a bridge in the scenes of the Battle of Stirling Bridge, the entirely mythical suggestion that the city of York was captured by a Scottish army, and the inauthentic shortness of Gibson in contrast to the legendary towering height of Wallace. McArthur contends that the film makes no attempt to capture the complicated feudal politics of medieval Scotland (1995: 45). Perhaps most obviously, the sense of national identity, patriotism and self-determination that Wallace seeks in the movie would have been incomprehensible in a feudal era where the ties between lord and peasant were paramount and conflict was typically organised around battles between lords.

Despite these fulminations about authenticity, it is useful to consider Rosenstone's reminder that 'films which have been truest to the past have tended to be visually and dramatically inert' (1995: 7). Moreover, as some nationalists maintain, the wider issues raised by the film transcend the concerns of period detail. The conventions of realism which typify many historical films, motivated by the pretension that 'the screen can be an unmediated window onto the past', are ineffective according to Rosenstone. Instead, he commends what he terms the 'postmodern history film' which 'creates multiple meaning, plays with the past, questions the knowledge on which History is constructed and yet recognises the impossibility of banishing the past' (ibid.:12). Whilst the simultaneous occurrences on screen of image, sound and language often convey contrasting messages and disrupt the flow of meaning, they can convey a more sensual and emotional sense of the past than an arid discourse. In any case, there is no way that the medieval period can be recovered accurately, besides which, claims about inauthenticity mask the ideological and value-laden discourses which inhere in (especially official and authoritative) histories. Effectively, it may be emotional authenticity rather than historical accuracy that satisfies audiences, for the former may more closely relate to the emotional needs and desires of the present. In fact, such popular cultural products may provoke renewed interest in history, as *Braveheart* undoubtedly has, with a greatly increased number of Scottish students applying for places on Scottish History courses.

Recycling Images: The Tourist Industry, Heritage and Film in Scotland

In order to reiterate my general points about the intertextuality of popular culture, its dissemination into an increasingly complex network of connections, I want to look at the tourist industry and the way it also propagates representations of national identity. I also explore the growing nexus between tourism and the film industry, which the former increasingly relies upon to foster its creation of place-images and attractions. For as a symptom of global economic restructuring, the tourist industry exploits 'minute spatial differentiations' (Harvey, 1989: 294) in order to sell 'unique' places and cultures on the global market. Local particularities are exploited and commodified for cosmopolitan consumers, 'torn out of time and place to be repackaged for the world bazaar' (Robins, 1991: 31), so that particular countries stand as metaphors for distinct attributes, such as the 'exotic', the 'erotic', the 'romantic' or the 'classical'.

The fastest-growing sector of the Scottish economy is tourism. Scotland has been subject to a romantic tourist gaze since the early eighteenth century (McCrone *et al.*, 1995: 60), and the tourist industry tends to utilise a repertoire of images with which to attract tourists. And again, the selling of Scotland abroad tends to rely on stereotyped images such as kilted warriors, Highland scenery and romantic castles, constructing what Rojek calls 'an enchanted fortress in a disenchanted world' (1993: 181). Womack has commented that 'all Scots wear tartan, are devoted to bagpipe music, and are moved by the spirit of clanship . . . all these libels live on as items in the Scottish tourist package of the Twentieth century' (1987: 25). These representations emerged in the eighteenth century and solidified in the nineteenth century, when they became enormously popular. Serving as an 'other' realm on the margins of the United Kingdom, a rugged and 'sublime' Highland landscape with its wild clansman garbed in tartan and kilt, Scotland was a romantic dreamscape tailored by and for metropolitan desire. These fantasies were served by the productions generated in the era where folklore and traditions were 'invented'. MacPherson's *Ossian* epic, the Sobieski Stuarts' invention of tartan styles (McCrone *et al.*, 1995: 51), the vast pageant of Scottishness put on for the visit of George IV to Edinburgh (Withers, 1992: 152–153), and the romantic impressions of the Highlands produced by Landseer for Queen Victoria (Pringle, 1988) have all contributed to this staging. Equally, the military significance of tartan was reinforced by its appropriation as battledress for Scottish regiments. To this day, a large proportion of Scotland's tourist sites, like many cinematic portrayals, are military. Tom Nairn mourns that Scottish popular militarism is 'far more strident than anything found in comparable levels of culture in England' (Nairn, 1977: 165).

Pat Kane laments this preoccupation with what he calls 'claymore culture', and he maintains that the construction of Scotland as 'an elemental land of warrior

men and wan maidens, of breast beating heroes fighting the overly rational English'
disempowers identity production, whilst at the same time these tales of 'authentic,
primitive redemption, of direst passions expressed in natural surroundings' serve
the 'tourist agencies perfectly' (*Guardian*, 18/5/95). Similarly, Nairn has attacked
the production of the 'tartan monster', that 'prodigious array of kitsch symbols,
slogans, ornaments, banners, war-cries, knick-knacks' (1977: 162). Of course, any
trip to a tourist centre sees the consumption of such objects in full flow.

Quite clearly, then, there are strong similarities between the ways in which the
long-established tourist industry and the rather more recent film industry represent
Scotland. This circulation of symbols, images and narratives of Scottishness is
protean, operating across various cultural fields, but is especially and increasingly
interconnected between tourist and cinematic representation. Most obviously,
tourist marketing campaigns frequently plunder the images and narratives of
popular films. As part of global 'mediascapes', films also transmit notions of
difference and stimulate the 'desire for acquisition and movement' (Appadurai,
1990: 299); they stimulate fantasies of the 'other' which spark tourist trends. For
instance, a quarter of a million copies of a movie map devised by the British Tourist
Association where tourists can 'follow in the footsteps of their screen heroes' was
produced in 1996. As mentioned in Chapter 3, in such campaigns, touristic
landscapes are promoted as theatres and stage sets where movie episodes can be
reimagined. Popular films can provide important resources in promoting attractions
and boosting the place-images of localities, as has been most evident in the case
of *Braveheart*.

Crucially, particular images and ideological narratives circulate through the
production and presentation of heritage attractions and films. Reconstructions in
costume dramas capitalise on the desire to see the 'other' in the foreign country of
the past (Corner and Harvey, 1991: 49). And as Higson remarks, the construction
of a national identity via the 'heritage film' involves 'the transference of present
values on to the past as imaginary object' (1995: 41). In the case of the English
heritage film, this has typically rotated around conservative images of the pastoral
and the country house, suggesting ideals of a natural, hierarchical community and
historical continuity which are echoed in the popularity of visiting country houses
by foreign and domestic tourists.

Entrepreneurs and politicians have fully attempted to capitalise on the success
of *Braveheart* by intensively marketing Stirling's association with Wallace. As
a marketing tool, the film has proved opportune in attracting tourists and raising
the town's profile. The Loch Lomond, Trossachs and Stirling Tourist Board
acknowledge that the film's success brought in millions of extra tourist pounds,
with the director stating that 'Braveheart has given us the ideal opportunity to
relaunch Stirling as one of Britain's finest heritage towns' (*Stirling Observer*,
20/9/96). The board produced an advertisement which reads, 'Where the Highlands

meet the Lowlands, step into the echoes of Rob Roy, Robert the Bruce and William Wallace – Braveheart Country', and designed an advert for international trans-mission in cinemas before the showing of *Braveheart*. Combining scenes from the film with aerial views of the Wallace Monument and local scenery, the advert ends with the exhortation to 'experience the very heart of Scotland: Stirling is Braveheart Country'. Subsequently, the popularity of the Wallace Monument increased dramatically following the release of the film: in the two years following the film, visitor numbers to Scotland rose considerably and it is estimated that revenue increased between £200 and £300 million (Scott, 2000).

Wollen argues that film and television are becoming a 'kaleidoscope for armchair tourists' (1991: 191). Yet in addition to the marketing and representing of places via cinematic links, heritage interpretation increasingly relies on audio-visual presentations, *son et lumère* shows, dramaturgical re-enactments, and animatronic characters, which offer an experience akin to the cinematic. The Wallace Monument also attracts visitors by advertising their audio-visual experiences and simulacra, altering the relationship between site and visitor by producing an 'experience'. Rather than gazing upon authentic artefacts, the contemporary tourist increasingly enjoys immersion in a mediated, staged experience.

The upsurge in popular movies with a Scottish theme has transformed the selling of heritage attractions in many parts of Scotland as they repatriate and recycle the images and stories from these global media forms. But whilst commercial possibilities for the expansion of the Scottish heritage industry have been expanded, many Scots view these movie-influenced productions with alarm. Pat Kane pro-nounces, 'Some of us feared that the future of Scotland might be as a romanticised, adventure theme park. But could we have guessed that the might of Hollywood would get behind the push so vigorously?' The effect of this recourse to the old signs and stories of Scottishness thwarts Scotland's need for 'a complex vision of its culture and society – a representation that points the nation towards the 21st century' (*Guardian*, 18/5/95).

Here we have returned to arguments similar to those cited above: like the representations of Scotland in film, the heritage industry is replete with dominant stereotypes that curtail alternative versions and imaginative reappropriation. However, in a more populist interpretation, Porter argues that the commodification of the past at tourist attractions and in films decentres auratic, expert versions of history. Subsequently, history enters the realm of public discourse where it is contested and appropriated. He writes, 'the past is not graven on stone tablets, but is a show, constantly being recreated, on the screen, on stage, in the mind's eye. Movie history is moving history' (*Sunday Times*, 30/7/95). His use of the term 'moving' suggests the powerful emotional charge conveyed by dramatised history as well as the ways in which the past is continually reinterpreted according to the politics of the present.

Geographies of William Wallace

To ground the meaning of Wallace geographically, it is notable that there are symbolic sites particularly associated with him, as well as a plethora of subsidiary locations within Scotland and places worldwide, which have rendered a link by erecting monuments. Of particular importance within Scotland is the Stirling area, historical location for the Battle of Stirling Bridge, site of the Victorian Wallace Monument, and venue for several statues of the hero (all in different styles). Describing Stirling as the 'seed-box' of Scottish nationalism, a local historian avers that 'to revive the history of Stirling is to revive the history of Scotland' (Lannon, 1983: 56). Symbolically positioned at the meeting of the Highland and the Lowlands, the historical identity of the town is dominated by the 'Stirling Triangle': Stirling Castle, Bannockburn and the Wallace Monument. Lannon describes how nineteenth-century romantic nationalism culminated in the raising of the flagstaff at Bannockburn and the Wallace Monument, which 'resulted in Stirling becoming a place of pilgrimage for all those who cherish the notion of Scottish independence' (ibid.: 51). These attractions are evocatively described as being 'installed like bits of organic furniture in a spiritual home' (ibid.: 54). Thus the affective tourist geography recently reconstructed by the tourist industry emerges from Victorian times and can be described as a 'memoryscape' whereby representations of Wallace are inscribed upon the landscape to constitute 'points of physical and ideological orientation' which materialise 'circuits of memory' (Johnson, 1995: 63).

A further level of geographical representation is demonstrated by the numerous forests, trees, lakes, summits, cairns and caves throughout Scotland which are associated with Wallace. We can conjecture that over the centuries wandering bards and story-tellers have related stories of Wallace or recited Blind Harry's epic, and that these appellations speak of attempts to translate mythic episodes into local contexts, in a sense commemorating them in the landscape. This local domestication of Wallace and his deeds perhaps illustrates the scaling of national identity whereby the local is connected to the national, showing how shared narratives are locally dramatised within everyday, familiar landscapes.

Other Representations of Wallace

In 1997, 'Scotland's Liberator', an exhibition at the Smith Art Gallery and Museum in Stirling, was organised to coincide with the 700th anniversary of the Battle of Stirling Bridge and to capitalise on the upsurge of interest in Wallace raised by *Braveheart*. The exhibition gathered various artefacts, works of art, texts, videos, and details of rituals inspired by Wallace, to convey his symbolic significance in Scottish art, literature and popular culture over the centuries. The exhibition attracted record numbers of visitors to the gallery.

'Scotland's Liberator' reveals the extraordinary proliferation of visual representations of Wallace, ranging from the medieval to the contemporary. It is evident that no single image of Wallace predominates, for there are many Wallaces – a rugged swordsmen, an elegant statesmen, a neo-classical figure in perfect proportion – differently garbed, some emphasising his masculine physicality, others clothing him in rough cloth or noble robes. Stylistically and ideologically, these depictions epitomise the fluidity of Wallace as a meaningful character, using distinct metaphorical and allegorical ways to represent a range of causes and identities.

Whilst contemporary narratives about Wallace, including *Braveheart*, tend to be contained within a framework of nationalist independence, this has not always predominated. For during the era of nineteenth-century Romantic nationalism, 'British national and imperial identity chimed quite nicely with a strand of Scottish national identity, reinforced by Protestantism, Unionism and militarism' (Nairn, 1977: 209). Strong Scottish patriotic celebrations of Wallace were subsumed within a wider salutation of Britishness. This can be see with regard to the most iconic representation, the aforementioned Wallace Monument, whose founders were predominantly Unionists. The monument contains the most hallowed object associated with Wallace, his mighty sword, recently described as a '15th-century fake' by Toolis (1999). At the ceremony to lay the monument's foundation stone in 1861, Wallace was eulogised as a proto-British figure, and upon inaugurating the campaign to erect the tower, the Earl of Elgin declared 'if the Scottish people have been able to form an intimate union [with the English] without sacrificing one jot of their neutral independence and liberty – these great results are due to the glorious struggle which was commenced on the plain of Stirling and consummated on that of Bannockburn' (quoted in Morton, 1993: 215).

Wallace then, was claimed as an exemplary figure by Unionists, as is borne out by the display on the second floor of the Wallace Monument, the Hall of Heroes. The sixteen busts comprise renditions of Robert Bruce, Robert Burns, Buchanan (poet and Protestant campaigner), John Knox, Allan Ramsey (artist), Robert Tannahill (poet), Adam Smith, James Watt, Walter Scott, William Murdoch (engineer and inventor), David Brewster (inventor of the kaleidoscope), Thomas Carlyle, Hugh Miller (geologist), Dr Chalmers (founder of the Free Church of Scotland), David Livingstone and W.E. Gladstone. Most of these figures – all men – were contemporaries of the monument and supported and served imperial ends through their endeavours in the key areas of literature, painting, scientific invention, Protestantism, statesmanship, economics and exploration. Their presence lends allure to the middle-class values of thrift, industry, religious devotion, enterprise and invention, qualities which were also imagined to be embodied in Wallace himself. Notably, the monument now includes an audio-visual display which features a more contemporary ('politically correct') selection which can be juxtaposed with the idealised marble worthies. This updated selection teems with one hundred Scots from seven fields identified as 'Liberty and Justice', Sport', 'Art', 'Science and Technology', 'Music', 'Literature' and 'Drama'. It includes such popular luminaries as Jackie Stewart, Jock Stein, Eduardo Paolozzi, Jimmy Shand, Lulu, Muriel Spark, Sean Connery and Billy Connolly.

In a similar vein, eighteenth- and nineteenth-century ceramic designs for pottery manufactured in Staffordshire conveyed the key theme of united nationality. A platter embossed with the legend 'Interview between Bruce and Wallace', features the characters 'attired in a manner more suggestive of Roman legionaries than of medieval warriors', signifying the absorption of minorities so that they are rendered 'symbolically safe' (Brooks, 1999: 60).

As I have mentioned, in Stirling and throughout Scotland there are several statues of Wallace, all very different in style. For instance, a familiar neo-classical statue on the Athenaeum in Stirling is markedly distinct from the huge, fierce, thickset warrior looming through the trees at Dryburgh in woodland adjacent to the River Tweed. To this array of statuary has been recently added (as featured on the cover of this book) a controversial 13-foot statue of Wallace at the foot of the Abbey Craig in Stirling, site of the Wallace Monument. It bears a quite obvious likeness to Mel Gibson; across the shield of the figure is embossed the word 'Braveheart', and 'Freedom' is engraved on the plinth. A stonemason, Tom Church, inspired by the film and convalescing after heart surgery, saw the rise of Wallace and the subsequent emergence of an independent Scotland as a metaphor for his own physical regeneration. The placing of the statue led to accusations of 'cultural mediocrity' and banality. The *Stirling Observer* (10 September, 1997) bemoaned that the memory of Wallace was being exploited, and a local SNP councillor declared that the statue would 'detract from the *true*, very important history which the monument stands for' (my italics). The statue has been defended by the marketing manager of the local tourist board on the grounds that it is this image of Mel Gibson that most people now associate with Wallace, and that it will attract tourists and hence create jobs. Fears about the trivialisation of Scottishness are articulated in the notion that a filmic image is not conceived as a fitting form for a heroic piece of sculpture.

I want to explore this response for it seems to articulate several of the concerns in this book. Undoubtedly representative of the most contemporaneous rearticulation of the myth, the sculpture appears to challenge the reified conventions of monumental sculpture. This is a representation of a popular film, an image widely shared in popular culture, but is understood by its many critics to fail to transmit due gravitas to the figure of Wallace because it does not follow the lofty traditions of most monumental sculptures; indeed, it is not a 'proper' sculpture. There are echoes of an increasingly outdated nationalism here, a nationalism which seeks to defy the increasing transmission of national identity via popular culture as being improper, unserious and undignified. As I have tried to demonstrate throughout this chapter, fears about the erosion of national identity concentrate on popular culture as undermining more 'modern' versions that ought to supersede it. These vilified forms might be considered to be too kitsch, commercial, American, senti- mental or inauthentic. Here the arguments against this much-maligned sculpture seem to want to reinstall and secure some sort of essentialised public representation of the Wallace myth – itself an impossible task given the multi-interpretability of successful myths. I understand this to be partially a resistance to the distribution of national identity through popular culture and a desire to produce representations which freeze meaning. Such an aim ignores the fact that such conventions are quite recent reformulated neo-classical expressions in the guise of romantic or civic nationalism. Crucially, since there are so many other, more conventional, monumental representations of Wallace, it is curious that any threat is perceived,

In addition to these sculptural representations, images of Wallace are also found in objects of quotidian cultural production. 'Scotland's Liberator' includes small figurines, models of the Battle of Stirling Bridge, and a marzipan piece of Wallace in combat with an English adversary. The inclusion of these popular creations signifies how Wallace is considered a suitable emblematic topic in the unheralded domestic art of thousands of model-makers, amateur artists, and embroiderers. As a popular motif in the 'grounded aesthetics' (Willis, 1990) of everyday creativity, Wallace circulates through the artefacts of household production, demonstrating that he is not merely passively consumed but actively recreated. These creators must reflect upon his significance and *choose* how to portray him.

The exhibition also includes samples of the vast range of ephemeral commercial products – souvenirs and trinkets that are part of the selling of tourist attractions and commemorative occasions. Commodities such as ash-trays, plates, plaques, postcards, chess pieces, badges, pens and a host of other items are embossed with Wallace's image and are remarkably diverse in form. Stewart (1993: 132–151) remarks that the collection of souvenirs involves the authentication of the tourist's visit, but also domesticates the spectacular, through taking home a representation which is 'appropriated within the privatised view of the individual subject', and rendered enclosable and thus possessed by the body (ibid.: 138). This reinforces a relationship between collector and the symbolic subject of the souvenir, and, furthermore, marks an event that is 'reportable', which, told as a biographical episode of identification, a souvenir of a visit or participation in an occasion, can be situated within a larger narrative of belonging, melding individual and collective identity. Rather than being passively consumed representations, such artefacts might thus be conceived as being worked over in the process of identification and narration.

In addition to these memorabilia, the name and image of Wallace is also used to lend allure to a variety of commercial interests. Wallace/*Braveheart* has recently been used to sell houses, a new shopping centre in Stirling and the Scottish National

Party. Maclays have relaunched their Wallace Pale Ale after a hiatus of several decades. In addition to these commercial uses, Wallace's likeness adds weight to official local documents, such as school certificates, situating the recipient in place by confirming the symbolic importance of Stirling.

The renewed significance of Wallace is glaringly illustrated by the row which broke out after it emerged that the new National Museum of Scotland, which opened in 1998, had no artefacts representing the great man. It transpired that a letter from Wallace was deposited in a German archive but that no effort had been made to claim it for display in Scotland. This provided Alex Salmond with an opportunity to complain that 'for centuries, members of the establishment have been attempting to eradicate all traces of Wallace from Scottish history' (Toolis, 1999).

It may be that Mel Gibson is the most conspicuous Wallace at the moment but he will surely be absorbed back into the mass of other representations, none of which will necessarily predominate. This proliferation prevents the reification of a single image which signifies the views of the powerful or freezes value. Instead, the various representations show that Wallace has been a figure upon whom diverse and contesting meanings and messages can be hung. His flexibility as myth has allowed distinct groups, from different eras, for various occasions and espousing divergent causes, to preserve Wallace's iconic importance. This proliferation of images thwarts a fixing upon any 'definitive' representation, for we confront a range of characteristics which make Wallace elusive, distributed as he is amongst a plethora of cultural settings.

Performances and Rituals: Re-presenting Walalce

To complicate this further, and to expand upon the notion of representation, I want to look at the ways in which Wallace has been represented dramatically in a range of performances – harking back to Chapter 3. I have already alluded to performances shaped around using and interpreting Wallace: through the granting of certificates and qualifications, through the purchase of tourist souvenirs, and also through the visiting of tourist sites and perusal of museum displays.

There are a number of current rituals associated with Wallace, notably the tourist pilgrimage to the Wallace Monument and the more emotionally charged, nationalist Wallace Day march at Elderslie. A good example of a rather more disciplined performance is that undertaken by the Free Colliers of Falkirk, who use Wallace to signify the struggle of their eighteenth-century forebears who were in servitude and used the hero as a talismanic figurehead in their quest for freedom. On the first Saturday of every August, pinkies interlinked, the colliers march to a Wallace memorial they erected in 1810 to lay wreaths and make speeches. This use of

artefacts both materialises the significance of the event and establishes a relationship between symbolic objects and those who use them. The use of music, through
a pipe band, and a flag-waving display, produces an affective ceremony which
ties participants together and expresses the emotive appeal of the colliers' struggle,
and by association reinforces the significance of Wallace.

A more carnivalesque ritual is the guising at Hogmanay, where, typically, four
or more guisers go from house to house enacting a playlet called 'Galatians'.
Formerly popular throughout Scotland but now confined to Biggar, Lanarkshire,
these short dramas always featured Wallace as hero who, with supernatural strength,
slays the villain of the piece. With Wallace at the centre of an ever-changing cast
of characters, the improvisatory performance of these short vernacular dramas
attests to the dynamic ways in which various symbolic elements have historically
been creatively combined and recombined by participants in popular culture.

Besides these rituals, there have also been two theatrical productions staged in
Stirling. A large-scale Battle of Stirling Bridge play was performed on the Castle
esplanade in September 1997, the anniversary of the battle. Featuring a 200-strong
cast, performing in front of an audience of 2,000, the play featured battle scenes
and much music and dance, ending with a singing of 'Scots Wha Hae' and a
fireworks display. This ambitious event was partly devised for a tourist audience
as an impressive spectacle but it made few concessions to a 'balanced' view,
presenting Wallace as an unadulterated hero.

A more challenging, politically engaged drama, *Wallace's Women*, was performed at Lanark and Stirling in October, 1997, by Castlegate Repertory Theatre,
and featured in the 1998 Edinburgh Festival Fringe programme. The play confronts
the gendered nature of national(ist) myths by exploring the role of the women
alluded to in versions of the Wallace myth. The conventional prominence of military
cunning and derring-do in the story of Wallace is supplemented by an attempt to
conjure up aspects of the myth from a female perspective. The play, performed by
an all-female cast, tells the story of Marion Bradefute, Wallace's lover, and other
women mentioned in Blind Harry's *Acts and Deeds of William Wallace*, including
his mother Lady Margaret Wallace, Queen Yolande, Marion's nurse Elspeth and
her daughter Bridget. The reinstating of these characters into the myth reverses
the masculinised characteristics of the tale and imagines a medieval women's
culture which blends Christian and Celtic belief in festivities, pagan cures and
the influence of the environment. Although quite raw in parts, the drama was an
ambitious attempt to critique the invisibilisation of women in the national story
and restore a sense of their participation in great national events.

The play decentres the prominence of Christianity in most versions of the
Wallace myth, and brings out a ribald and powerful femininity at variance to the
stereotypical images of fey Highland maidens. The women share a far from passive
sexuality and are enthusiastic consumers of drink and drugs, which are used in

the wild pagan celebrations in which they participate. *Wallace's Women*, then, represents a struggle which takes place inside the popular myth of Wallace, which tries
to deconstruct its gendered formation, and creatively uses the story to interrogate
notions of Scottishness, masculinity and femininity, and the telling of history.

Theatrical performance is not, as I have argued in Chapter 3, confined to
demarcated events and rituals but is embodied in a host of reflexive and unreflexive
everyday enactions. Overt expressions of identity require that particular clothes
be worn, paraded in conjunction with a physical performance to convey particular
values. The impact of *Braveheart* was particularly influential on a group who
assemble under the title of the Wallace Clan, many of whom acted as extras
and fight arrangers in the film. A key aim is to fund the purchase of 'clanlands' to
replace those taken from them centuries ago so that they may build a village where
they can practise traditional farming and crafts (and receive tourists). They continue
to clothe themselves in costumes from the film that were donated to them by Mel
Gibson. Membership of the clan entails not proof of descent from Wallace, or
indeed any familial connection with anyone called Wallace, but an 'attitude'. This
adoption of a (postmodern) identity is one that does not depend on geographical
or historical mooring but can be freely chosen. Nevertheless, as a seeming example
of individual fluidity, the clan's identity clearly depends on a particular articulation
of Scottishness, sustained by ideas about authenticity, which must be continually
performed to represent a stable identity.

I have discussed elsewhere the ways in which Bannockburn Heritage Site and
the Wallace Monument are (contested) sites of national significance which
nationalist pilgrims visit to pay homage to the mythical heroes of Bruce and Wallace
(Edensor, 1997). The former is the site for the annual nationalist Bannockburn
Rally where Scottish nationalists assemble after a march from Stirling. Participants
at recent rallies, like the football fans who have followed the Scottish team in
football competitions, wore outfits that had clearly been influenced by *Braveheart*.
Rather than donning the immaculate 'white heather club' garb of jacket, kilt, sporran
and shiny shoes, they opted to wear rough leather jerkins, flowing locks and tartan
tunics favoured by Wallace and his followers in the film. This seems to suggest an
informalisation of Scottish identity, reacting against familiar formal signifiers,
which aims to transmit a more 'authentic', down-to-earth identity, which is less
anglified and stereotypical. Such a performance shows how popular movie
iconography may be reclaimed or repatriated by those making symbolic statements
about their origins and identity which challenge traditional expressions.

The Reception of *Braveheart* Outside Scotland

I have discussed the reception of *Braveheart* in Scotland, but as a global product
its impact was wider, and, moreover, in a nationalist sense. This is evidenced by

the large number of large internet sites which are devoted to the movie (Morgan, 1999: 377). Umberto Bossi, leader of the Northern League which was campaigning for secession from the Italian state, acclaimed the movie and was subsequently parodied in the Italian press as 'MacBossi' (Hague, 1999: 78). In the United States, the home of the film's star and director, the effect on particular groups has been well-documented. Hague looks at the Rightist Neo-Confederate League of the South, whose president sang the praises of *Braveheart* since it 'appeals to all the things that New York despises, namely Christian devotion, populism, patriotism, home-rule, self-defense, well-defined sex roles, traditional morality and self-sacrifice for a noble cause' (quoted in ibid.: 78). Likewise, the film was celebrated by white supremacist groups, who, according to a civil rights activist from Alabama, cherish *Braveheart*. Leaders of racist group Aryan Nation esteem what they regard as the racial purity of the Celts, and recommend the use of the Celtic Cross to their members. Thus, they 'create a history for themselves that paints them as bearers of true belief opposed by a remote government' (Seenan, 1999). The story of resistance to a more powerful foe, courage against the odds, and the images of brutal oppression and action-oriented heroics succour the fantasies of empowerment integral to the cultural elements of exclusivist movements. Thus the movie has acted as a spur to these groups, perhaps because its mythic structure and narrative can be adapted to enhance the claims of specific campaigns, despite the Scottish context.

Hague also points out that *Braveheart* was also a powerful ingredient in the constitution of a Scottish-American identity; that is, those Americans who descend from Scottish migrants or believe that they do. There is an interesting slippage between the histories of both countries: both gained independence from the over-mighty British, and the mythic traditions of both countries are grounded in the battle against oppression and the fight for 'freedom'. Moreover, it is argued that the military attributes of Scottish warriors have served America well where Scottish Americans have entered the battlefield (Hague, 1999: 80). Hague argues that the importance of the movie for Scottish-Americans highlights the increasing ways in which diasporic identities and imagined communities are constructed via mediascapes. This 'diaspora dreaming' utilises imaginary portrayals to refresh those parts of the self which have become detached from place (ibid.: 84). Sally Morgan speculates that this myth of Wallace was exported to colonial and national set-tings as a 'ghost in the luggage', for instance chiming with American myths of origin. Moreover, she argues that the Wallace presented in *Braveheart* emerges out of this diasporic re-imagining so that he has been created 'through the lens of an American consciousness' (1999: 385). Thus, like others, she has contended that the film fits into a 'Western' genre, with its emphasis on scenery and steadfast manliness, and also parallels movies about the American War of Independence, where English 'oppressors' are portrayed in similar terms (indeed, Mel Gibson's latest epic, *The Patriot*, similarly demonises the English colonialists and rejoices in the qualities of the American patriots opposing them).

Conclusion

The historical weight of romantic stereotypes around kailyard, Highland tartan-alia, militarism, and the recirculation of these images and themes in the heritage and film industries, might appear to form a formidable obstacle to attempts to rebuild and reconstitute a 'progressive' Scottishness. Nairn argues that the persistent circulation of these representations has produced a deformed national identity which he lambasts as 'cultural sub nationalism' (1977: 156). Apparently, in the absence of any more appropriate cultural resources, Scots seek recourse in prod-uctions such as *Braveheart*, which serve to reinforce archaic, negative versions of Scottishness.

As I have indicated above, certain pundits in the press and academia have inferred that Scottish popular culture is embarrassing and banal. *Braveheart* has been criticised as masculinist, regressively anti-English, irrelevant and inauthentic, and the response to the statue of Wallace/*Braveheart* sited in Stirling has expressed outrage at the degradation of Scottish identity. This response contributes to and partly misunderstands how national identities are dynamically constituted around discursive practices and cultural resources. Whatever the politics and poetics of the movie, and however much experts declaim about historical inaccuracies, the continuing significance of Wallace lies in his flexible mythic qualities. For Wallace, along with Robert Burns, Mary Queen of Scots, Robert Bruce, Rob Roy, the debacle of Culloden, are 'complex icons of cultural, social and political belief' which no amount of historical research can invalidate (Finlay, 1997: 123). By implying that films, narratives and artefacts are encoded with dominant messages which are simply and consensually decoded, the cultural arbiters miss the contradiction and ambivalence in and across the discourses about Scotland and the diverse ways in which representations of myths and archetypes are reclaimed and recycled.

Through visual, literary and dramatic processes of representation, popular symbols and myths of the nation are reworked into contemporary concerns. Because they tend to be ideologically 'chameleon' forms (Samuel and Thompson, 1990: 3) they can be used to transmit contrasting messages and identities. As a 'condensation symbol' (Cohen, 1985: 102), Wallace has been (re)appropriated by a wide range of contesting groups to provide antecedence and continuity to a diverse range of identities and political objectives (Tilly, 1994: 247). Chartists have marched under his banner, suffragettes have used his name, and socialists have claimed him as a common-born fighter for the rights of the oppressed. As I have shown, even Unionists have identified him as an inspiration to the formation of the United Kingdom. And the fact that little is actually known about him extends the symbolic uses to which he can be put. Thus grounded, creative processes have restlessly recreated Wallace in diverse ways, highlighting the dynamic relationship between culture and national identity.

Pessimistic cultural commentators view Hollywood films as imperialistic commodities which decentre local identities and interpellate audiences in predictable ways, and these fears resonate with anxieties about the 'Americanisation' of Scottish culture. *Braveheart* is a global representation of Wallace, in that it is manufactured in the image factory of Hollywood and devised to be marketed worldwide. Whilst it has acted as a catalyst to contemporary forms of political identification outside Scotland, it has also followed the conventional tropes through which Scotland has been represented in films and in the tourist industry – which, it is fair to argue, fix Scotland's marketable identity for foreign viewers and tourists. However, this takes no account of the numerous ways in which it has been repatriated in Scotland, demonstrating that through the proliferating informational and image flows across global space (Appadurai, 1990), national myths are being simultaneously decentred or disembedded, and provide a new impetus for national identification. These responses can be defensive responses, offering succour to essentialist versions of Scottishness, yet the diverse visual representations, dramas and artefacts surrounding Wallace suggest that any exclusive notion of national identity is a fantasy. Rather, a range of identities merge, squabble and ignore each other, but they share a set of cultural resources and themes which are interpreted and used in contesting ways.

The use of Wallace before and after *Braveheart*, even in *Braveheart*, is marked by interpretations which are shaped as much by gender, class, religion and region as by a crude, recursive national identity. Elspeth King makes the point that *Braveheart* is substantially drawn from Blind Harry's epic (1998: 8–9), itself woven together out of the local myths about Wallace that Harry collected during his journeys around Scotland. This work, the *Acts and Deeds of William Wallace*, is exemplary in that like all narratives about Wallace it is constituted out of many strands. *Braveheart* itself is partly a reworking of elements of the Wallace myth, using and supplementing existing narratives, dramatic portrayals and images. The recent development of a Wallace industry has seen the publication of a number of novels, historical texts, books, images, poetry and even a video game, that represent Wallace in various ways, adding to the pool of cultural resources. These representations talk back to history in a dialogic and reflexive environment where Scots negotiate with each other, certainly reproducing and reinterpreting old notions of national identity but also producing new meanings, forms and practices. They feed back into the pool of representations that signify Wallace, contrasting with some and chiming with others in an intertextual circulation of signs.

Nevertheless, as a contested cultural form, the reception of *Braveheart* reveals many of the complexities in the sustenance of contemporary national identities in general and Scottish identity in particular. The imperative to gather together a set of symbols and histories and represent the 'imagined community' of the nation is an ongoing and competitive process. Old symbols fade into disuse, are reinvigorated, are appropriated by different causes and reinterpreted, and new symbols are invented, claimed and circulated. Whilst *Braveheart* was enthusiastically celebrated by many Scots, reinvigorating and adding to the Wallace myth, it caused others to critically assess the desirability of reproducing representations wrought in the era of romantic nationalism. Responses also reveal the tensions between political and cultural strands in nationalist movements. The SNP's development of their 'head and heart' campaign testifies to the need to appeal to an emotional sense of attachment as well as the more 'objective' economic and political arguments. Herein lies the problem of expressions of national identity which are encumbered by anachronistic cultural baggage but nevertheless retain popular appeal. Some politicians therefore recognise the efficacy of foundation myths, notions of historical continuity, a set of shared symbols and myths in sustaining a sense of belonging. They argue that strategies which encourage the nation to loose its historical moorings and set sail for the future deny notions of a shared past. However, such romantic renditions are ripe for ridicule, especially by those who desire to see the nation as moving ever forward in linear progress, towards and beyond modernity. Merging with these debates are those which attempt to retain a version of high culture as the most suitable way in which to clothe the nation, promoting those cultural forms which attempt idealistic, romantic representations. But the era whereby a cultural elite could determine which (high) culture was suitable for the masses has long gone, and as the example of *Braveheart* shows, national expressions of culture are increasingly promiscuous, circulating through expanding networks, where they are utilised by growing numbers of groups. Emphatically, this does not diminish their power; it redistributes it.

$-6-$

Exhibiting National Identity at the Turn of the Millennium

'Self-Portrait' at the Millennium Dome

The Millennium Dome was the national flagship of the millennial celebrations in 2000. Designed to mark the year 2000, and simultaneously provide a celebratory assessment of the contemporary character of the nation, the project seemed to hark back to other grand projects, notably the Festival of Britain in 1950 and the Great Exhibition of 1851. However, the Dome was immediately and continuously surrounded by mockery and criticism, and, as the year went on, to increasing opprobrium. A momentum gathered which allowed few avenues for acclaiming the attraction. It became something of a byword for overweening ambition, and for the ineptitude and self-aggrandisement of the ministers who had so vigorously promoted it and continued to defend it.

This is not the place to go into an in-depth discussion about why the Millennium Dome proved such a fiasco; but a brief contextualisation is needed. The criticisms were fulsome, many arguing that the ensemble of contents in the Dome inevitably produced a senseless jumble of ideas. Others contended that the project should have resembled a conventional theme park. Many maintained that the money would have been better spent on more local, modest projects. And the content of the building, the ideas and displays, were surely compromised by the imperatives of the corporate sponsors, who tended to remove politically sensitive notions and foreground commercial messages about company virtues. There was, it was widely believed, a wholesale 'dumbing down' which resulted in a series of mediocre attractions.

My own opinion is that a grand project on a scale such as this is no longer feasible. Whilst previous exhibitions have managed to persuade most visitors that there was a coherent British national identity, widely recognisable if not shared by all, such an ambition is no longer possible because national identities are fragmenting, as I have tried to argue throughout this book. The elements of national identity, the familiar signifiers, rituals and fixtures, have not disappeared but have proliferated through popular culture and in the diversification of everyday lives. There could therefore, be no singular approach to a project like the Dome.

A grand vision or a set of accepted guidelines seem peculiarly anachronistic. The project therefore reflected the multiple ideas of those contributing to its production, and hence was invariably chaotic, generating an incoherent expression of Britishness.

However, my aim in this final chapter is to look at one zone in the Dome, prospectively called the 'National Identity Zone' but, finally, the 'Self-Portrait'. My aim is to provide a conclusion to the book by way of assessing a contemporary attempt to delineate national identity. It is my belief that the varied expressions of Britishness which the 'Self-Portrait' features, highlight the main arguments that I have been making.

The zone was sponsored by Marks and Spencer, itself a symbolically British company, which despite well-publicised recent problems remains an emblem of high-quality British commodities. The 'Self-Portrait' was devised by the company in association with New Millennium Experience Company (NMEC) – which had responsibility for the overall content of the Dome – and design company Caribina. According to the co-ordinators of the project, primary objectives were to produce a 'non-elitist' version of Britishness, a snapshot of the nation at the turn of the Millennium, and a 'people's view' of the nation rather than an academic or media product. According to visitor surveys, the 'Self-Portrait' was the third most popular zone in the attraction, and *The Times* (Kennedy and Gledhill, 2000) evaluated it as 'absorbing and unpretentious' and gave it 8 marks out of 10.

The 'Self-Portrait' was comprised of five distinct elements: a range of quotes and topics printed on large boards, large satirical sculptures, pre-recorded accounts from local (Greenwich) children and a soundscape of British noises, a huge frieze called the 'National Portrait', and the 'Andscape', a huge collection of over four-hundred images of items identified as typically British. It is this latter feature that I will concentrate upon, but I will briefly outline the other components.

Display Boards

The boards cover a range of topics under the headings of 'Diversity', 'Inventiveness', 'Creativity', 'Fair Play', 'Humour', 'Public Spirit' and 'Language'. It is probably this element of the zone which is most conspicuously self-congratulatory, trumpeting the increasing diversity of British culture and Britain's contribution to literature, high and popular culture and science. Well-known quotes expressing pride in the nation are reproduced, but these are countered by more ambivalent statements about, for instance, the possibilities of alienation. The generally ambiguous and dialogic tone of the zone as a whole is less apparent here, but the sentiments frequently pose contradictions rather than platitudes and are intended for interaction.

The Sounds

There are two dimensions to the production of sounds. Firstly, in a central area of the 'Self-Portrait', visitors were invited to approach a collection of 'reed poles', vertical steel rods with small speakers fitted at their apex, and listen to the recorded voices of children who articulated their hopes for the future and expressed anti-racist opinions, their fantasies and desires. The rather touching sentiments expressed were presumably designed to remind visitors that a future generation was growing up facing a distinctive range of problems and opportunities. The other sonic effect was the background soundtrack of distinctive sounds of Britishness, some of which had been suggested by the 'Andscape' selections. The noises include the anthem 'Jerusalem', ducks, Big Ben chiming, rain, hooting owls, mooing cows, baaing sheep, nursery rhymes at school, birdsong, Kipling's poem 'If', polite applause, sporting commentary on the television, a radio weather report, train-station porters, a jet engine, barking dogs, the sounds of Sunday League football, playground noise, a shop till ringing and horses' hooves. Clearly, this selection is somewhat sentimental and yet, as I will discuss, it co-exists with diverse other elements. Nevertheless, it echoes my earlier comments about the soundscapes that form part of the sensual, affective sense of place.

The National Portrait

This was perhaps the most extraordinary exhibit in the zone. Co-ordinated by artist David Mach, who was commissioned by the NMEC and allowed free rein over the images he produced, it is a huge frieze comprising approximately a quarter of a million images organised into 15 panels, two metres long by one and a half metres high. Described as the world's most complicated collage, it includes landscapes from across Britain, paintings from national collections and images from tourist brochures as backdrops, and in the foreground are photographs of thousands of Britons. Integrated into the mosaic are familiar representations of stereotypical English landscapes and objects, but also some controversial elements. However, the overall effect is one of excess and proliferation, a great seething mass of space and activity peopled by hordes. This carnivalesque profusion decentres central images, drawing them into the chaos and abundance. There is no possibility of fixing an image of the nation, for the presence of so many varied people produces an energy that militates against stasis. After the closure of the Millennium Dome it was planned to take the work around the country, a tour to be launched at the National Portrait Gallery. This will be accompanied by an education pack for primary and secondary schools.

The Sculptures

The coloured, fibreglass sculptures are designed by iconoclastic political cartoonist Gerald Scarfe and are highly satirical, even critical, in content. They were commissioned with a brief to portray the darker side of British national identity, and to act as a counter to the more celebratory elements in the zone. As was written in an introduction to the sculptures, they are intended to 'depict the side of human nature we often do not want to admit'. The sculptures are as follows

1. *Traditional 'Cool' Britain.* The Prime Minister and the Queen are personified as the two emblems in the national crest, the Lion and the Unicorn. The inscription reads, 'The Queen and Tony Blair preside over the joys of traditional Britain: warm beer and cricket, beefeaters and mad cows, late trains and leaves on the line'.
2. *The Racist.* The introductory board opines, 'there is an element of racism in many of us. Beneath the apparently benign figure of a civilised man in his Gabardene raincoat, lurks the monster of racism, which bursts out, raging against what it sees as foreign and different'.
3. *The Couch Potato.* This portrait of a glazed television viewer being absorbed by his chair is similarly self-explanatory: 'How many of us sit lazily in front of our televisions, letting them spew substandard culture over us? This chap has been sitting in his armchair so long, with his beer and remote control, that the upholstery is taking him over'.
4. *TheThug.* Perhaps the most fearsome work, this features a graffiti covered, pot-bellied figure who has a large, spiky boot where his head should be, about whom it is written: 'From football hooligan to road rage, this sculpture shows the violence underlying the thin veneer of civilisation'.

Clearly, these works postulate a critical approach towards national identity; towards the ineptitude of rulers who claim to represent the nation but induce a political culture of mediocrity; towards the exclusivist tendencies of Britishness which are masked behind apparent 'decency'; towards much popular culture – which instead of provoking and informing encourages passivity; and towards an underlying violence which contrasts with the much-mooted virtues of tolerance. The works provoked a strong reaction from some visitors, many of whom were disconcerted by such representations, and complained that they maligned Britain. However, the pieces were further contextualised by the placing of the panels cited above which talked back to these sculptures. For instance, there was a selection of quotes and information on the theme of 'fair-play' directly situated behind the 'Thug', and a panel around the motif of 'Creative Nation' behind the 'Couch Potato'.

This collection of challenging attractions within the 'Self-Portrait' is clearly designed to proffer a multiple, ambiguous, dynamic conception of British national identity. Not only do each of the features described decentre any complacent, zealous expression of Britishness, but also, if they are taken as an ensemble, there is even more of a cacophony of voices, images and sensations. The nation is represented according to no overriding set of themes, an achievement which befits the contemporary characteristics of national identity. The multiplicity of national identity manifested here is further exposed in the final component of the 'Self-Portrait' zone, the 'Andscape'.

The 'Andscape'

The 'Andscape' was devised by asking people all over Britain to respond to leaflets left in Marks and Spencer stores and in public spaces such as libraries, which entailed answering the question: 'What one thing best represents something good about Britain to you and why?' Of the thousands of responses, over four hundred were selected, partly to reflect cultural and geographic diversity. The result was the compilation of an enormous mosaic of photographs representing the entries that were selected, an assortment of positive signifiers of Britain that was accompanied by the reasons given by respondents for these choices. The photographs were reproduced with this text and organised into a linear sequence at waist height along the side of a spiral walkway, but were also hugely enlarged in a larger display to comprise the external and internal walls of the 'Self-Portrait', which was devised as a large cylindrical structure.

I want to use the 'Andscape' as a means to draw out some of the points I have been making about national identity in this book. The hundreds of items, like the 'National Portrait', represent profusion and multiplicity. However, there are innumerable associations that can be made between items, so that forms of constellation emerge. There is no obvious way of representing these constellations, but I have somewhat arbitrarily drawn selections together under my own categories; namely, 'things', 'food and drink', 'geographies', 'institutions and abstract qualities', 'people', 'animals and plants', 'popular cultural forms', 'technology and innovation', and 'cultural practices', primarily to reflect some of the concerns of this book. I invite readers to make their own interpretations about the symbolic values associated with these selections, because my aim is not to suggest that there are self-evident ways of categorising national cultural elements but to assert that such authority ought to be resisted. I also encourage alternative attempts to link these symbols together to make chains of signification. This is why I have cited all the entries. I will draw five conclusions from the exhibit to reinforce the major contentions I have been making throughout the book.

Things

Crossword puzzle
Blackpool tram car
Sandcastles
Red phone boxes
Stamps
Tartan
Wellies
UK/EU passport
The Union Jack
Charity awareness ribbon
Ice cream vans
The map of Britain
Stained glass windows
Lawn mower
Traditional English longbow
The teapot
Umbrella
Marks and Spencer knickers
London Underground map
Blue rinse hair
'House', by Rachel Whiteread
Picnic hampers
The British bulldog
A Ripon horn
Bowls
Graffiti
Red double-decker buses
The Football Association crest
Black cabs
The cup and saucer
Socks and sandals
Conkers
A miner's oil lamp
Beefer acupuncture trainer shoes
An Orange Disabled card
A red letter box
The red poppy
Rocking horse
Embroidery

A knitted tea cosy
Window boxes
My MUFC season ticket
Ordnance Survey maps
The Dove of Peace
The Oxford English Dictionary
The (Churchill) Crown coin
The wake knot
A red rubber ball
An organ donor card
My swimming and football awards
A bicycle

Food and Drink

Cox's Orange Pippin
Chip butty
Cornish pasty
Baxters Soup
Marmite
Gin and tonic
Mushy peas
Fish and chips
Kebabs
Organic/free-range produce
Chicken Tikka Masala
A wee dram
Black pudding
Fair Trade coffee
Baked beans
Cheddar cheese
Seaside rock
Potatoes
Love hearts
Chinese takeaway
Pork pies
Kippers
Seafood
A pint of beer
Liquorice Allsorts
Custard

Victoria sponge
Cream teas
Strawberries
British beef
The *Oxo* cube
The traditional fry-up
Malt vinegar
Dairylea cheese slices
M & S ready-made meals
An IPA can of beer
Candy floss
The Balti
Worcester sauce
Toad in the hole

Geographies

Canals
Traditional markets
Allotments
Drystone walls
War memorials
Public conveniences
Beach huts
Libraries
Pebble beaches
Large windmills
Skateboard parks
Fish and chip shops
The sea
The garden shed
Parks
Mosques
Pigeon lofts
Hedgerows
Hindu temples
Gardens
My church
Bluebell woods
Battersea Dogs Home
Wimbledon

London
Lords Cricket Ground
Cotswolds
Scotland Yard
Belfast Waterfront Hall
Wembley's twin towers
The Palm House, Belfast
Heligan Gardens, Cornwall
The second Severn Bridge
St Albans Cathedral
Dean Clough Mill
Lloyds building
Forth Rail Bridge
Huddersfield Stadium
Carnaby Street
The Giant's Causeway
The Liver Building
Tower Bridge
Cornish tin mines
The White Cliffs of Dover
Speakers Corner
Padstow
The Maharajah's well
Angel of the North
Battersea power station
The Seven Sisters
Blackpool Tower
The Ridgeway, Wiltshire
The London skyline
Bishop's Rock Lighthouse
Yorkshire Sculpture Park
Robin Hood's Bay
Brighton Pier
St James Park
The Elan Valley
Portmeirion
Stonehenge
Bluebell Steam Railway
Tooting Bec Lido
Snowdonia
Stone Lions, Heaton Park

Snettisham
Big Ben
St Ives

Institutions and Abstract Qualities

The royal family
House of Lords
The Red Arrows
National Lottery
Royal Zoological Society
The Royal Ballet
The Royal Marines
MacMillan Nurses
The Open University
NSPCC
RSPCA
The British Lions
The RNLI
The National Trust
The National Health Service
The Inter-faith Network
Greenpeace
Comic Relief
Children's Promise
The Findhorn Foundation
Radio 4
Beefeaters
The Salvation Army
Marks and Spencer
The Family
London marathon
Notting Hill carnival
Guy Fawkes night
Eisteddfods
Crufts Dog Show
The Proms
The Irish Peace Agreement
Equal Opportunities in Sports
Parliamentary democracy
Pageantry

Pub culture
Comprehensive schooling
British pop music
Greenwich Mean Time
The weather
The Queen's head on coins
Competitiveness
Political activism
Politeness
Humour
Enlightenment
Hope
Tolerance
Compassion
Sarcasm
Imagination
Understanding
Spirit
Courtesy
Bloody mindedness
Ambition
Family values

People

Lee Bowyer
Charles Dickens
Roger Bannister
Dougie McLean (Scottish songwriter)
Queen Mother
Stella McCartney
My GCSE class
Quentin Crisp
Oasis
Kate Moss
Our Lady of Walsingham
Thora Hird
Michael Owen
Patrick Moore
The Beatles
Roald Dahl

Harry Enfield
My son
Richard Branson
Nasser Hussein
Mo Mowlam
Terry Thomas
Boat race
Hilda Ogden
Rochdale Pioneers
George Wylie
Michael Barrymore
Oswal Boateng
Kevin Keegan
Jools Holland
Trevor MacDonald
The Dales farmer
Ainsley Harriot
Evelyn Waugh
Tony Blair
Henry Moore
Jarvis Cocker
Vivienne Westwood
Lollipop ladies/men
Michael Caine
Basement Jaxx
Alan Partridge
Ranulph Fiennes
A mixed race couple
Talvin Singh
Our unborn twins
Denise Lewis
1966 World Cup squad
Our 6th form college
Morecambe and Wise
David Hockney
Tricia Guild
Bikers
Gilbert and Sullivan
Cliff Richard
Terence Conran
Iain Banks

Francis Bacon (painter)
Sir Walter Raleigh
My mates
Margaret Thatcher
Paul Oakenfold
Winston Churchill
George Michael
Eddie Izzard
Shakespeare
Tony Benn MP
My son Alistair
Julie Burchill
Stephen Lawrence
British men
Stephen Hawking

Animals and Plants

Seashells
Sweet peas
Skylark
Oak tree
My giant dahlias
Thistle, rose, shamrock, daffodil
The Yorkshire rose
Border collie
Nessie
The native honey bee
My cat
Grey squirrels
Donkey
The house sparrow
Dogs
Salmon leaping
'My school's "Belief and Hope" tree'

Popular Cultural Forms

Thunderbirds
James Bond
Paddington Bear

Billy Liar
The Full Monty
'Kes'
Dad's Army
The Big Issue
Sergeant Pepper's Lonely Hearts Club Band LP
Sooty
The Beano
Rhadamanthus
The saucy seaside postcard
Robin Hood
Basil Fawlty
Mr Punch
Winnie the Pooh
The Mr Men
Mr Bean
'Cats'
Carry On films
The Ministry of Sound
Pudsey Bear
Goon Show
The Sun
British newspapers

Technology and Innovation

Whittle's jet engine
The passenger liner Queen Elizabeth II
The Thames barrier
The internet design industry
CYD (a web language program)
Concorde Leeds Virtual Science Park
The X-ray
The Sinclair ZX81 computer
The Sinclair C5
The Lotus Esprit
The Triumph motorcycle
HMS *Victory*
The Dyson vacuum cleaner
The Hovercraft

The Spitfire
The telephone
The Eurostar train
The Mini Cooper
1907 Rolls-Royce Silver Ghost

Cultural Practices

Pantomimes
Go-karting
Folk dancing
The Edinburgh Festival
Clubbing
Rugby League
Village cricket
Horticultural shows
Car boot sales
The response to the death of Diana
The milk round
Morris dancing
Highland Games
The Ben Nevis race
Glastonbury Festival
Bingo
Orderly queueing
Jumble sales
Rock climbing
Local agricultural shows
Hastings Jack-in-the-Green
Thatching
Golf
Quilting
Sunday morning football
The brass band
Pancake races on Shrove Tuesday
Scouting
Going to the circus
Driving on the left
Trainspotting
Sunday lunch

Interpretation of the 'Andscape'

Locality and the scaling of national identity

I have attempted to show throughout this book that national identity is not only located and experienced at renowned symbolic sites, but equally is domesticated and asserted at local and domestic levels. Whilst in the 'Andscape' familiar landmarks are cited as common-sense geographical signifiers which epitomise Britishness (for instance, Big Ben, the White Cliffs of Dover, Stonehenge), so are the domestic and local spaces inhabited by 'ordinary' people as the centres of their everyday worlds (for example, the garden shed, 'my church' and local or regional attractions such as Bradford's Dean Clough Mill). The connections between these differently symbolic, differently scaled spaces testify to the scaling of national identity. National identity is enacted in homely settings as well as at ceremonial sites and memoryscapes. It is embedded in taskscapes, consumed in the home through the representations shown on television; it is domesticated in the local sharing of national rituals; it is discussed and contested in families, workplaces and pubs. Thus the national is linked to the local in numerous ways; indeed, the local and the national each make sense of each other, are bound together in common-sense enactions, everyday spaces, iconic and mundane objects and in local diversity. This is reinforced by an institutional matrix of places of worship, parks, libraries, pubs and retail outlets, synchronised habits and rituals, and recurrence through national space of serial senses, sights, objects and representations.

The mundanity of national identity

The things, rituals, spaces and representations I have focused upon mix up the spectacular and the mundane, the famous and everyday, the archaic and the contemporary. In each of the chapters I have emphasised the everydayness of national identity, the often unreflexive habits, unnoticed objects and homely spaces that constitute the comfort of identity, conceived in national terms. In the 'Andscape', the milk round, driving on the left, going to car boot sales, playing bingo and Sunday morning football, and eating Sunday lunch are all mundane practices which are identified as epitomising Britishness. National identity is located in the familiar routines and embodied habits that such practices engender. It is perceived in the familiar sparrows and cats that populate local environs, in one's friends, in pigeon lofts and fish and chip shops, Oxo cubes and baked beans, bicycles and tea cosies. These familiar, everyday objects are part of the affective and cognitive structure of quotidian life, the regular, reliable features around which mundane habits and routines are organised. As I have argued, these familiar features may not ordinarily be perceived since they are always there, but any threat to their existence can result in panic and a sense of threat. Moreover, the initial unfamiliarity engendered by confronting others' everyday spaces can similarly result in disorientation and a desire to reinstate the familiar.

The contemporary centrality of popular culture and mediatisation of national identity

It should be clear from the 'Andscape' that national identity is certainly not merely epitomised by what was formerly understood as 'high culture', for there are a host of references to popular music, films, television programmes (especially comedy and children's programmes), comics, tabloid newspapers and sporting celebrities. These popular citations greatly outweigh any of the traditional badges of national identity which are wielded as forms of cultural prestige, although these are not entirely absent. However, the pride afforded by technological innovation appears to echo the symbolic importance that is popularly attributed to the British car industry discussed in Chapter 4. Whilst the high cultural signifiers persist, contestations over value and the importance of particular fields of endeavour mean that there is no longer the possibility of mass adherence to the discriminations of a cultural elite, if there ever was. People engage in multiple ways in the dynamic realm of popular culture, but there is a greater degree of immersion which contrasts with the more distanced appreciation and assessment typical of an engagement with 'higher' cultural forms. Such affective, convivial and protean involvement seems as likely to produce a strong sense of belonging, even national pride, as the marking out of cultural excellence. Everyday hobbies and pastimes (scouting, train-spotting, and attending jumble sales) are as valued as traditional pursuits. The role of the mass media in producing (very rapidly changing) nationally symbolic personalities is also notable, for many of the citations of celebrities are highly contemporaneous.

The intertextuality of national identity – the matrix of associations and their constellations

I have argued that the range and density of connections between cultural elements consolidates rather than erases a sense of national identity. The circulation of ideas and images in the media provides a vast storehouse of interlinked cultural forms, places, objects, people and practices which are associated across time and space. The 'Andscape' provides plentiful examples of these interconnections. For instance, a garden(ing) theme recurs, which includes wellies, lawnmowers, apples, sweet peas and dahlias, allotments and gardens, garden sheds, visitor attractions such as

Heligan Gardens, honey bees and horticultural shows. And these citations conjure up a host of other intimately associated elements which suggest yet others (for instance, I find myself thinking about wheelbarrows, gardening programmes and their celebrities, lawns and nest boxes). These intertextualities do not merely address identity at the level of representation, but also evoke familiar sensations comprising the sounds, smells and tactile experiences which correspond to specific forms and memories of gardening or being in gardens.

Even more apparent is the dense network of associations conjured up by the British royal family through their extension across popular culture and everyday life, which possibly consolidates the continued popularity of the monarchy amongst Britons. Cited in the 'Andscape' are stamps, the Union Jack, several prominent royal persons, the Queen Elizabeth II passenger liner, and other practices (horse-racing) and places (Wembley Stadium) associated with royal presence. In fact, these form only the tip of the iceberg. There are a profusion of places associated with royalty, notably their palaces, but also many historic buildings (Tower of London), towns granted royal charters and titles (Royal Tunbridge Wells), sites where they attend institutionalised functions (London Palladium, Royal Albert Hall, the Cenotaph), and places where they served in the forces or were educated. Many institutions are inflected with royal identity, including charities patronised by royals and state institutions (Her Majesty's Prison Service, the Royal Navy). Moreover, plentiful objects are associated with the monarchy, from the highly specialised (the crown jewels) and the commonly circulated (money and stamps), to the commercial (products purchased by the monarchy and granted permission to display the royal crest, souvenirs and commemorative artefacts). There are numerous rituals and occasions that mark out national time, including historical commemorations; large traditional showpieces such as royal weddings, funerals and marriages, jubilees, the Trooping of the Colour, Laying the Wreath to the Fallen at the Cenotaph, the Changing of the Guard. And there are more intimate, informal events such as the Queen's Christmas speech and, increasingly, television insights into, and press coverage of, royal lives; the playing of the national anthem at a wealth of sporting and cultural occasions; royal visits to localities within Britain and royal tours abroad; not to mention the innumerable references made to the monarchy in the media, and indeed throughout popular culture. The thick network of allusions to royalty in everyday life and popular culture forms a virtually inescapable part of quotidian experience for an inhabitant of the UK.

However, the important point about constellations of national identity is that they are increasingly complex, for a proliferating range of interconnections can be made which stretch across diasporic and virtual space. I have argued that whilst there remain common-sense points of fixity where constellations solidify and hold epistemological weight, it is vital that national identity is understood as continually dynamic, capable of making connections through a persistent rearticulation. It is now the sheer flexibility of ways of making links in the vast, shared cultural matrix that sustains the power of national identity, opening up multiple points of connection. For the old symbols of national identity are increasingly flexible, can be reinterpreted anew where exclusivist attempts to delimit their meaning are less successful. Condensation symbols are more effective than rigid emblems, for they can be interpreted and claimed by different groups, broadening their appeal and constituting a sharing, albeit one that might be contested.

The ongoing contestation, fluidity and diversity of national identity

So it is that a sense of national belonging is increasingly decentred from authoritative, official versions of culture and identity. The 'Andscape' dramatically reveals the contesting and multiple ways in which people assert and assume a sense of Britishness. The 'traditional' is not dead but its power is diminished, for the claims upon Britishness include selections that destabilise reified geographies and performative conventions. Thus Stephen Lawrence and Talvin Singh rub shoulders with Winston Churchill and Shakespeare, mosques and Hindu temples coexist with war memorials, and kebabs are consumed along with mushy peas. Thus the fluid and the hybrid seems to prevail over the 'unchanging' and the 'pure'. For global flows foster conditions for the rearticulation of national identity along more inclusive lines and render impossible fantasies of cultural purity.

Bibliography

Adam, B. (1995) *Timewatch: The Social Analysis of Time*, Cambridge: Polity.

Agyeman, J. and Spooner, R. (1997) 'Ethnicity and the rural environment', in P. Cloke and J. Little (eds) *Contested Countryside Cultures*, London: Routledge.

Allon, F. (2000) 'Nostalgia unbound: illegibility and the synthetic excess of place', *Continuum: Journal of Media and Cultural Studies*, 14 (3).

Alsmark, G. (1996) 'When in Sweden . . . Immigrant encounters with Swedish culture', in J. Frykman and O. Löfgren (eds) *Forces of Habit: Exploring Everyday Culture*, Lund: Lund University Press.

Anderson, B. (1983) *Imagined Communities*, London: Verso.

Ang, I. (1995) *Watching Dallas: Soap Opera and the Melodramatic Imagination*, London: Methuen.

Appadurai, A. (1986) 'Introduction: commodities and the politics of value', in A. Appadurai (ed.) *The Social Life of Things: Commodities in Cultural Perspective*, Cambridge: Cambridge University Press.

Appadurai, A. (1990) 'Disjuncture and difference in the global cultural economy', in M Featherstone (ed.) *Global Culture*, London: Sage.

Appadurai, A. (1993) 'Patriotism and its futures', *Public Culture*, 5.

Archetti, E. (1998) 'The *potrero* and the *pibe*: territory and belonging in the mythical account of Argentinean football', in N. Lovell (ed.) *Locality and Belonging*, London: Routledge.

Armstrong, G. and Giulianotti, R. (eds) (2001) *Fear and Loathing in World Football*, Oxford: Berg.

Arnold, M. (1960) *Culture and Anarchy*, Cambridge: Cambridge University Press.

Ascherson, N. (2001) 'Reflections on international space', in *London Review of Books*, p.10, 24 May.

Ash, M. (1990) 'William Wallace and Robert the Bruce: The life and death of a national myth', in R. Samuel and P. Thompson (eds) *The Myths We Live By*, London: Routledge.

Attfield, J. (2000) *Wild Things: The Material Cultures of Everyday Life*, Oxford: Berg.

Auge, M. (1995) *Non-Places: Introduction to an Anthropology of Supermodernity*, London: Verso.

Bachelard, G. (1969) *The Poetics of Space*, Boston: Beacon Press.

Barker, C. (1999) *Television, Globalisation and Cultural Identities*, Buckingham: Open University Press.

Barnes, T. and Duncan, J. (eds) (1992) 'Introduction', in *Writing Worlds,* London: Routledge.

Barthes, R. (1984) *Camera Lucida,* London: Flamingo.

Barthes, R. (1993) *Mythologies,* London: Vintage.

Basham, F., Ughetti, B. and Rambali, P. (1984) *Car Culture,* London: Plexus.

Bayly, C. (1986) 'The origins of swadeshi (home Industry): cloth and Indian society, 1700–1930', in A. Appadurai (ed.) *The Social Life of Things: Commodities in Cultural Perspective,* Cambridge: Cambridge University Press.

Beckett, S. (1996) 'The new Wallace connection', *The Independent on Sunday,* 12 May, pp. 14–17.

Belasco, W. (1983) 'Commercialised nostalgia: the origins of the roadside strip', in D. Lewis and L. Goldstein (eds) *The Automobile and American Culture,* Ann Arbor: Michigan University Press.

Bell, D. (1997) 'Anti-idyll: rural horror', in P. Cloke and J. Little (eds) *Contested Countryside Cultures,* London: Routledge.

Bennett, T. (1995) *The Birth of the Museum,* London: Routledge.

Bennett, T. (1998) *Culture: A Reformer's Science,* London: Sage.

Berger, J. (1984) *And Our Faces, My Heart, Brief as Photos,* London: Writers and Readers.

Berger, M. (1983) 'The great white hope on wheels', in D. Lewis and L. Goldstein (eds) *The Automobile and American Culture,* Ann Arbor: Michigan University Press.

Bhabha, H. [ed] (1990) *Nation and Narration,* London: Routledge.

Billig, M. (1995) *Banal Nationalism,* London: Sage.

Blain, N. and O'Donnell, H. (1994) 'The stars and the flags: individuality, collective identities and the national dimension in Italia '90 and Wimbledon '91 and '92', in R. Giulianotti and J. Williams (eds) *Games Without Frontiers: Football, Identity and Modernity,* Aldershot: Arena.

Bourdieu, P. (1977) *Outline of a Theory of Practice,* Cambridge: Cambridge University Press.

Bourdieu, P. (1984) *Distinction,* London: Routledge.

Brah, A. (1996) *Cartographies of Diaspora,* London: Routledge.

Brooks, A. (1999) 'Building Jerusalem: transfer-printed finewares and the creation of British identity', in S. Tarlow and S. West (eds) *The Familiar Past? Archaeologies of Later Historical Britain,* London: Routledge.

Bull, M. (2001) 'Soundscapes of the car: a critical ethnography of automobile habitation', in D. Miller (ed.) *Car Cultures,* Oxford: Berg.

Butler, J. (1993) *Bodies That Matter: The Discursive Limits of Sex,* London: Routledge.

Caillois, R. (1961) *Man, Play and Games,* New York: Free Press.

Calhoun, C. (1997) *Nationalism,* Buckingham: Open University Press.

Campbell, N. and Keane, A. (1997) *American Cultural Studies: An Introduction to American Culture*, London: Routledge.

Carlson, M. (1996) *Performance: A Critical Introduction*, London: Routledge.

Castells, M. (1996) *The Rise of the Network Society: The Information Age: Economy, Society and Culture*, Oxford: Blackwell.

Caughie, J. (1990) 'Representing Scotland: new questions for Scottish cinema', in E. Dick (ed.) *From Limelight to Satellite*, London: BFI.

Chamberlain, M. (1999) 'The family as model and metaphor in Caribbean migration to Britain', *Journal of Ethnic and Migration Studies*, 25 (2).

Chaney, D. (1993) *Fictions of Collective Life*, London: Routledge.

Charlesworth, S. (2000) *A Phenomenology of Working Class Experience*, Cambridge: Cambridge University Press.

Chevalier, S. (1998) 'From woollen carpet to grass carpet: bridging house and garden in an English suburb', in D. Miller (ed.) *Material Cultures: Why Some Things Matter*, London: UCL Press.

Claessen, C. (1993) *Worlds of Sense: Exploring the Senses in History and Across Cultures*, London: Routledge.

Claval, P. (1994) 'From Michelet to Braudel: personality, identity and organisation', in D. Hooson (ed.) *Geography and National Identity*, Oxford: Blackwell.

Clay, G. (1994) *Real Places: An Unconventional Guide to America's Generic Landscape*, Chicago: University of Chicago Press.

Clifford, J. (1988) *The Predicament of Culture*, Cambridge, Mass.: Harvard University Press.

Clifford, J. (1989) 'Notes on travel and theory', *Inscriptions*, 5.

Clifford, J. (1992) 'Travelling cultures', in L. Grossberg, C. Nelson and P. Treichler (eds) *Cultural Studies*, London: Routledge.

Cloke, P. (1997) 'Poor country: marginalisation, poverty and rurality', in P. Cloke and J. Little (eds.) *Contested Countryside Cultures*, London: Routledge.

Cohan, S. and Hark, I. (eds) (1997) *The Road Movie Book*, London: Routledge.

Cohen, A. (1985) *The Symbolic Construction of Community*, London: Tavistock.

Connerton, P. (1989) *How Societies Remember*, London: Cambridge University Press.

Cook, I. and Crang, M. (1996) 'The world on a plate: culinary culture, displacement and geographical knowledge', in *Journal of Material Culture*, 1 (2): 131–154.

Corner, J. and Harvey, S. (eds) (1991) *Enterprise and Heritage*, London: Routledge.

Craib, I. (1998) *Experiencing Identity*, London: Sage.

Craig, C. (1982) 'Myths after history: tartanry and kailyard in 19th century Scottish literature', in C. McArthur (ed.) *Scotch Reels: Scotland in Cinema and Television*, London: BFI.

Crang, M. (1998) *Cultural Geography*, London: Routledge.

Crang, M. (2000) 'Between academy and popular geographies: cartographic imaginations and the cultural landscpe of Sweden', in I. Cook, D. Crouch, S. Naylor and J. Ryan (eds) *Cultural Turns/Geographical Turns*, London: Prentice Hall.

Crang, M. (2001) 'Rhythms of the city: temporalised space and motion', in J. May and N. Thrift (eds) *Timespace: Geographies of Temporality*, London: Routledge.

Crossley, N. (2001) *The Social Body: Habit, Identity and Desire*, London: Sage.

Crouch, D. (1999a) 'Introduction: encounters in leisure/tourism', in D. Crouch (ed.) *Leisure/Tourism Geographies: Practices and Geographical Knowledge*, London: Routledge.

Crouch, D. (ed.) (1999b) *Leisure/Tourism Geographies: Practices and Geographical Knowledge*, London: Routledge.

Cubitt, G. (1998) 'Introduction', in G. Cubitt (ed.) *Imagining Nations*, Manchester: Manchester University Press.

Dant, T. (1999) *Material Culture in the Social World*, Buckingham: Open University Press.

Davies, C. (1998) '"A oes heddwch?" Contesting meanings and identities in the Welsh National Eisteddfod', in F. Hughes-Freeland (ed.) *Ritual, Performance, Media*, London: Routledge.

Dawson, G. (1994) *Soldier Heroes: British Adventure, Empire, and the Imagining of Masculinities,* London: Routledge.

de Certeau, M. (1984) *The Practice of Everyday Life*, Berkeley: University of California Press.

Desmond, J. (1994) 'Embodying difference: issues in dance and cultural studies', *Cultural Critique*, Winter, 1993–94.

Dick, E. (ed.) (1990) *From Limelight to Satellite*, London: BFI.

Dinwoodie, G. (1995) 'SNP rides high on back of Braveheart', *The Herald*, 2 October, p.1.

Donnachie, I. and Whatley, C. (eds) (1992) *The Manufacture of Scottish History*, Edinburgh: Polygon.

Du Gay, P., Evans, J. and Redman, P. (eds) (2000) *Identity: A Reader*, London: Sage.

Duncan, J. (1989) 'The power of place in Kandy, Sri Lanka, 1780–1980', in J. Agnew and J. Duncan, *The Power of Place: Bringing Together Geographical and Social Imaginations*, London: Routledge.

Dutter, B. (1996) 'Forsyth's "loser" jibe riles Scots', *The Guardian,* 27 April, p. 3.

Edensor, T. and Kothari, U. (1996) 'The masculinisation of heritage', in V. Kinnaird and D. Hall (eds) *Tourism: A Gender Analysis*, London: Wiley.

Edensor, T. (1997) 'National identity and the politics of memory: remembering Bruce and Wallace in symbolic space', *Environment and Planning D: Society and Space,* 29: 175–194.

Edensor, T. (1998a) *Tourists at the Taj*, London: Routledge.

Edensor, T. (1998b): 'Reading Braveheart: representing and contesting Scottish identity', *Scottish Affairs*, 21, autumn: 135–158.

Edensor, T. (2000a) 'Staging tourism: tourists as performers', *Annals of Tourism Research*, 27: 322–344.

Edensor, T. (2000b) 'Moving through the city', in D. Bell and A. Haddour (eds) *City Visions*, Harlow: Prentice-Hall.

Edensor, T. (2001) 'Performing tourism, staging tourism: (re)producing tourist space and practice', *Tourist Studies*, 1: 59–82.

Edensor, T. and Augustin, F. (2001) 'Football, ethnicity and identity in Mauritius: soccer in a rainbow nation', in G. Armstrong and R. Giulianotti (eds) *Fear and Loathing in World Football*, Oxford: Berg.

Edwards, E. (1999) 'Photographs as objects of memory', in M. Kwint, C. Breward and J. Aynsley (eds) *Material Memories: Design and Evocation*, Oxford: Berg.

Edwards, R. (1999) *Aston Martin: Ever the Thoroughbred*, Sparkford, Somerset: Haynes Publishing.

Elias, N. (1978) *The Civilising Process*. Vol. 1: *The History of Manners*, Oxford: Blackwell.

Enloe, C. (1989) *Bananas, Beaches and Bases*, London: Pandora.

Eriksen, T. (1998) *Common Denominators: Ethnicity, Compromise and Nation-Building in Mauritius*, Oxford: Berg.

Fabian, J. (1983) *Time and the Other: How Anthropology Makes its Object*, New York: Columbia University Press.

Featherstone, M. (1991) *Consumer Culture and Postmodernism*, London: Sage.

Featherstone, M. (1992) 'The heroic life and everyday life', in M. Featherstone (ed.) *Cultural Theory and Cultural Change*, London: Sage.

Felski, R. (1999) 'The invention of everyday life', *New Formations*, 39: 15–31.

Feifer, W. (1985) *Going Places*, London: Macmillan.

Finlay, I. (1997) 'Heroes, myths and anniversaries in modern Scotland', *Scottish Affairs*, 18, Winter, 108–125.

Fiske, J. (1989) *Understanding Popular Culture*, London: Unwin Hyman.

Foreman-Peck, P., Bowden, S. and McKinley, A. (1995) *The British Motor Industry*, Manchester: Manchester University Press.

Foster, R. (1999) 'The commercial construction of "new nations"', *Journal of Material Culture*, 4 (3): 263–282.

Freitag, T. (1994) 'Enclave tourist development: for whom the benefits roll?', *Annals of Tourism Research*, 21: 538–554.

Frow, J. (1995) *Cultural Studies and Cultural Value*, Oxford: Oxford University Press.

Frykman, J. (1996) 'Between rebellion and champagne: festive spirit through three generations', in J. Frykman and O. Löfgren (eds) *Forces of Habit: Exploring Everyday Culture*, Lund: Lund University Press.

Frykman, J. and Löfgren, O. (eds) (1996) 'Introduction', in *Forces of Habit: Exploring Everyday Culture*, Lund: Lund University Press.

Game, A. (1991) *Undoing the Social*, Buckingham: Open University Press.

Gardiner, M. (2000) *Critiques of Everyday Life*, London: Routledge.

Geertz, C. (1993) *The Interpretation of Cultures*, London: Fontana.

Gellner, E. (1983) *Nations and Nationalism*, Oxford: Blackwell.

Giddens, A. (1991) *Modernity and Self-Identity*, Cambridge: Polity.

Giddens, A. (1994) 'Living in a post-tradition society', in U. Beck, A. Giddens and S. Lash *Reflexive Modernisation: Politics, Tradition and Aesthetics in the Modern Social Order*, Cambridge: Polity.

Giles, J. and Middleton, T. (1999) *Studying Culture: A Practical Introduction*, Oxford: Blackwell.

Gillan, A. (1995) 'Brave hearts, forgetful of a troubled past, play the patriot game again', *Scotland on Sunday*, 10 September, p. 16.

Gillespie, M. (1995) *Television, Ethnicity and Cultural Change*, London: Routledge.

Gillis, J. (1994a) 'Memory and identity: the history of a relationship', in J. Gillis (ed.) *Commemorations: The Politics of National Identity*, Princeton, N.J.: Princeton University Press.

Gillis, J. [ed] (1994b) *Commemorations: The Politics of National Identity*, Princeton, N.J.: Princeton University Press.

Gilroy, P. (1994) *The Black Atlantic: Modernity and Double-Consciousness*, London: Verso.

Gilroy, P. (2001) 'Driving while black', in D. Miller (ed.) *Car Cultures*, Oxford: Berg.

Gledhill, C. (2001) 'Class acts: the peculiarities of British cinema style', Professorial Lecture, Staffordshire University.

Goffman, E. (1959) *The Presentation of Self in Everyday Life*, New York: Doubleday.

Golding, R. (1994) *Mini: 35 Years On*, Bath: Bath Press.

Gottdiener, M. (1997) *The Theming of America*, Oxford: Westview Press.

Graves-Brown, P. (2000) 'Always crashing in the same car', in P. Graves-Brown (ed.) *Matter, Materiality and Modern Culture*, London: Routledge.

Gren, M. (2001) 'Time-geography matters', in J. May and N. Thrift (eds) *Timespace: Geographies of Temporality*, London: Routledge.

Guibernau, M. (1996) *Nationalisms: The Nation-State and Nationalism in the Twentieth Century*, Cambridge: Polity.

Guibernau, M. and Hutchinson, J. (eds) (2001) *Understanding Nationalism*, Cambridge: Polity.

Guss, D. (2000) *The Festive State: Race, Ethnicity and Nationalism as Cultural Performance*, Berkeley: University of California Press.

Hagman, O. (1993) 'The Swedishness of cars in Sweden', in K. Sørensen (ed.) *The Car and its Environments: The Past, Present and Future of the Motorcar in Europe*. Luxembourg: European Commission.

Hague, E. (1999) 'Scotland on film: attitudes and opinions about *Braveheart*', *Etudes Ecossaises*, Numero 6: 75–89.

Hall, S. (1980) 'Encoding/decoding', in S. Hall, D. Hobson, A. Lowe and P. Willis (eds) *Culture, Media, Language*, London: Hutchinson.

Hall, S. (1992) The question of cultural identity', in S. Hall, D. Held and A. McGrew (eds) *Modernity and Its Futures*, Cambridge: Polity Press.

Hall, S. (1996a) 'Gramsci's relevance for the study of race and ethnicity', in D. Morley and D.-K. Chen (eds) *Stuart Hall*, London: Routledge.

Hall, S. (1996b) 'Introduction: who needs identity', in S. Hall and P. du Gay (eds) *Questions of Cultural Identity*, London: Sage.

Hall, S. (1997) 'Introduction', in S. Hall (ed.) *Representation: Cultural Representations and Signifying Practices*, London: Sage.

Hall, S. and du Gay, P. (eds) (1996) *Questions of Cultural Identity*, London: Sage.

Handelman, D. (1997) 'Rituals/spectacles', *International Social Science Journal*, 15 September: 387–399.

Hannerz, U. (1990) 'Cosmopolitans and locals in world culture', in M. Featherstone (ed.) *Global Culture: Nationalism, Globalisation and Modernity*, London: Sage.

Harrison, P. (2000) 'Making sense: embodiment and the sensibilities of the everyday', *Environment and Planning D: Society and Space*, 18: 497–517.

Hartmann, D. (1996) 'The politics of race and sport: resistance and domination in the 1968 African American Olympic protest movement', *Ethnic and Racial Studies*, 19 (3).

Harvey, D. (1989) *The Condition of Postmodernity*, Oxford: Blackwell.

Hayward, S. (1999) 'Questions of national cinema', in K. Cameron (ed.) *National Identity*, Exeter: Intellect Books.

Heilig, J. and Abbis, R. (1999) *Rolls-Royce: The Best Car in the World*, London: Apple.

Henley, J. (2001) 'End of the road for emblem of France', *The Guardian*, 6 July.

Herzfeld, M. (1997) *Cultural Intimacy: Social Poetics in the Nation-State*, London: Routledge.

Hesse, B. (ed.) (2000) *Un/settled Multiculturalisms: Diasporas, Entanglements, Transruptions*, London: Routledge.

Hetherington, K. and Law, J. (2000) 'Social order and the blank figure', *Environment and Planning D: Society and Space*, 18.

Hewison, R. (1987) *The Heritage Industry: Britain in a Climate of Decline*, London: Methuen.

Higson, A. (1989) 'The concept of national cinema', *Screen*, 30: 4.

Higson, A . (1995) *Waving the Flag*, Oxford: Clarendon.

Hilton, S. (2001) 'Take the wrap', *The Guardian, G2*, 8 June, p. 2.

Hobsbawm, E. and Ranger, T. (eds) (1983) *The Invention of Tradition*, Oxford: Blackwell.

Hoggart, R. (1971) *The Uses of Literacy*, London: Penguin.

Holliday, R. (1999) 'The comfort of identity', *Sexualities*, 2 (4): 475–491.

Holt, R. (1996) 'Cricket and Englishness: the batsman as hero', *The International Journal of the History of Sport*, 13 (1).

Hooson, D. (ed.)(1994) *Geography and National Identity*, Oxford: Blackwell.

Hunt, L. (1998) *British Low Culture: From Safari Suits to Sexploitation*, London: Routledge.

Hutchinson, J. (1992) 'Moral innovators and the politics of regeneration: the distinctive role of cultural nationalists in nation-building', *International Journal of Comparative Sociology*, XXXIII (1–2): 101–117.

Hutchinson, J. (1994) *Modern Nationalism*, London: HarperCollins.

Hutchinson, J. (2001) 'Nations and culture', in M. Guibernau and J. Hutchinson (eds) *Understanding Nationalism*, Cambridge: Polity.

Ingold, T. (2000) 'Making culture and weaving the world', in P. Graves-Brown (ed.) *Matter, Materiality and Modern Culture*, London: Routledge.

Ingold, T. and Kurttila, T. (2000) 'Perceiving the environment in Finnish Lapland', *Body and Society*, nos. 3–4: 6.

Interranté, J. (1983) 'The road to autopia: the automobile and the spatial transformation of American culture', in D. Lewis and L. Goldstein (eds) *The Automobile and American Culture*, Ann Arbor: Michigan University Press.

Jacobs, J. (1961) *The Death and Life of the Great American Cities*, New York: Random House.

James, P. (1996) *Nation Formation*, London: Sage.

Jarman, N. (1998) 'Material of culture, fabric of identity', in D. Miller, (ed.) *Material Cultures: Why Some Things Matter*, London: UCL Press.

Jenkins, R. (1996) *Social Identity*, London: Routledge.

Johnson, N. (1995) 'Cast in stone: monuments, geography and nationalism', *Environment and Planning D: Society and Space*, 13.

Johnson, N. (2001) 'From time immemorial: narratives of nationhood and the making of national space', in J. May and N. Thrift (eds) *Timespace: Geographies of Temporality*, London: Routledge.

Kane, P. (1995) 'Me tartan, you chained to past', *The Guardian*, 18 May, pp. 6–7.

Kasinitz, P. (1995) Introduction to Part One: 'Modernity and the urban ethos', in P. Kasinitz (ed.) *Metropolis: Centre and Symbol of our Times*, Basingstoke: Macmillan.

Kayser Nielsen, N. (1999) 'Knowledge by doing: home and identity in a bodily perspective', in D. Crouch (ed.) *Leisure/Tourism Geographies: Practices and Geographical Knowledge*, London: Routledge.

Kemp, A. (1995) 'Battling over Braveheart', *The Guardian*, 11 September, p. 13.

Kennedy, D. and Gledhill, R. (2000) 'A Rough Guide to the Dome', *The Times*, 8 January.

Kihlstert, F. (1983) 'The automobile and the transformation of the American house, 1910–1935', in D. Lewis and L. Goldstein (eds) *The Automobile and American Culture*, Ann Arbor: Michigan University Press.

King, E. (1998) 'Blind Harry's Wallace', *Scottish Book Collector*, 5, Spring, pp. 8–9.

Kirkham, P. (ed.) (1996) *The Gendered Object*, Manchester: Manchester University Press.

Kirkham, P. and Attfield, J. (1996) 'Introduction', in P. Kirkham (ed.) *The Gendered Object*, Manchester: Manchester University Press.

Kline, R. and Pinch, T. (1993) 'Taking the black box off its wheels: the social construction of the American rural car', in K. Sørensen (ed.) *The Car and its Environments: The Past, Present and Future of the Motorcar in Europe*, Luxembourg: European Commission.

Knorr Cetina, K. (1997) 'Sociality with objects: social relations in postsocial knowledge societies', in *Theory, Culture and Society*, 14 (4): 1–30.

Kuper, S. (1996) *Football Against the Enemy*, London: Phoenix Press.

Kwint, M. (1999) 'Introduction: the physical past', in M. Kwint, C. Breward, and J. Aynsley (eds) *Material Memories: Design and Evocation*, Oxford: Berg.

Kwint, M., Breward, C. and Aynsley, J. (eds) (1999) *Material Memories: Design and Evocation*, Oxford: Berg.

Lanfranchi, P. and Taylor, M. (2001) *Moving with the Ball: The Migration of Professional Footballers*, Oxford: Berg.

Lannon, T. (1983) *The Making of Modern Stirling*, Stirling: Forth Naturalist and Historian.

Lash, S. (1990) *Sociology of Postmodernism*, London: Routledge.

Latour, B. (2000) 'The Berlin key or how to do words with things', in P. Graves-Brown (ed.) *Matter, Materiality and Modern Culture*, London: Routledge.

Lee, N. and Brown, S. (1994) 'Otherness and the actor-network: the undiscovered continent', *American Behavioral Scientist*, 37: 772–790.

Lewis, D. (1983) 'Sex and the automobile: from rumble seats to rockin' vans', in D. Lewis and L. Goldstein (eds) *The Automobile and American Culture*, Ann Arbor: Michigan University Press.

Lewis, D. and Goldstein, L. (eds) (1983) *The Automobile and American Culture*, Ann Arbor: Michigan University Press.

Liebes, T. and Katz, E. (1990) *The Export of Meaning: Cross Cultural Readings of Dallas*, Oxford: Oxford University Press.

Light, A. (1991) *Forever England: Femininity, Literature and Conservativism between the Wars*, London: Routledge.

Lippard, L. (1997) *The Lure of the Local: Senses of Place in a Multicentered Society*, New York: The New Press.

Lloyd, D. and Thomas, P. (1998) *Culture and the State*, London: Routledge.

Löfgren, O. (1996) 'The great Christmas quarrel: on the moral economy of family rituals', in J. Frykman and O. Löfgren (eds) *Forces of Habit: Exploring Everyday Culture*, Lund: Lund University Press.

Low, G. (1993) 'His stories? Narratives and images of imperialism', in E. Carter, J. Donald and J. Squires (eds) *Space and Place: Theories of Identity and Location*, London: Lawrence and Wishart.

Lowenthal, D. (1994) 'European and English landscapes as national symbols', in D. Hooson (ed.) *Geography and National Identity*, Oxford: Blackwell.

Luger, S. (2000) *Corporate Power, American Democracy and the Automobile Industry*, Cambridge: Cambridge University Press.

Lupton, D. (1998) 'Going with the flow: some central discourses in conceptualising and articulating the embodiment of emotional states', in S. Nettleton and J. Watson (eds) *The Body in Everyday Life*, London: Routledge.

McArthur, C. (1982) *Scotch Reels: Scotland in Cinema and Television*, London: BFI.

McArthur, C. (1994) 'Culloden: a pre-emptive strike', *Scottish Affairs*, 3 (9): 97–126.

McArthur, C. (1995) Braveheart review, *Sight and Sound*, September, p. 45.

MacAskill, E. (1995) 'No Oscar for SNP over Braveheart', *The Scotsman*, 12 September, p. 11.

McCarthy, A. (2000) 'The misuse value of the TV set: reading media objects in transnational urban spaces', *International Journal of Cultural Studies*, 3 (3).

MacClancy, J. (1996) 'Sport, identity and ethnicity', in J. MacClancy (ed.) *Sport, Ethnicity and Identity*, Oxford: Berg.

McCrone, D. Morris, A. and Kiely, R. (1995) *Scotland – The Brand*, Edinburgh: Edinburgh University Press.

McGuigan, J. (1997) 'Cultural populism revisited', in M. Ferguson and P. Golding (eds) *Cultural Studies in Question*, London: Sage.

McGuire, J. and Poulton, E. (1999) 'European identity politics in Euro '96: invented traditions and national habitus codes', *International Review for the Sociology of Sport*, 34 (1).

Macnaghten, P. and Urry, J. (1998) *Contested Natures*, London: Sage.

Maley, W. (1998) '*Braveheart*: raising the stakes of history', *Irish Review*, 22: 67–80.

Mangan, J. (1996) '"Muscular, militaristic and manly": the British middle-class hero as a moral messenger', in 'European heroes', in *The International Journal of the History of Sport*, 13 (1).

Marling, K. (1984) *The Colossus of Roads: Myth and Symbol Along the American Highway*, Minneapolis: University of Minnesota Press.

Martin, I. (1995) 'Expert draws blood in war of Wallace vote', *Sunday Times*, 3 September, p. 3.

Martin, I. (1996) 'Facing up to a bright past', *Sunday Times*, 21 July, p. 14.

Martin-Barbero, J. (1988) 'Communication from culture', *Media, Culture and Society*, 10.

Massey, D. (1993) 'Power-geometry and a progressive sense of place', in J. Bird *et al.* (eds) *Mapping the Futures*, London: Routledge.

Massey, D. (1995) 'The conceptualisation of place', in D. Massey and P. Jess (eds) *A Place in the World? Places, Cultures and Globalisation*, Oxford: Oxford University Press.

Massey, D. (1998) 'The spatial construction of youth cultures', in T. Skelton and G. Valentine (eds) *Cool Places: Geographies of Youth Cultures*, London: Routledge.

Massie, A. (1995a) 'Pride, prejudice and the birth of a hero figure', *Scotland on Sunday*, 3 September, p. 12.

Massie, A. (1995b) 'The scars of battle that centuries have failed to heal', *Sunday Times*, 17 September, p. 13.

Matless, D. (1998) *Landscape and Englishness*, London: Reaktion Books.

May, J. and Thrift, N. (eds) (2001) *Timespace: Geographies of Temporality*, London: Routledge.

Meinig, D. (1979) 'Symbolic landscapes: some idealisations of American communities', in D. Meinig (ed.) *The Interpretation of Ordinary Landscape,* New York: Oxford University Press.

Melucci, A. (1989) *Nomads of the Present*, London: Century Hutchinson.

Michael, M. (2000) *Reconnecting Culture, Technology and Nature: From Society to Heterogeneity*, London: Routledge.

Middleton, T. and Giles, J. (1995) *Writing Englishness 1900–1950: An Introductory Sourcebook on National Identity,* London: Routledge.

Miller, D. (1994) *Modernity: An Ethnographic Approach*, Oxford: Berg.

Miller, D. (ed.) (1998a) *Material Cultures: Why Some Things Matter*, London: UCL Press.

Miller, D. (1998b) 'Coca-Cola: a black sweet drink from Trinidad', in D. Miller (ed.) *Material Cultures: Why Some Things Matter*, London: UCL Press.

Miller, D. (ed.) (2001) *Car Cultures*, Oxford: Berg.

Miller, E. (1995) 'Schoolroom howlers that make Braveheart a travesty', *The Scotsman*, 7 September, p. 13.

Mitchell, D. (1995) 'The end of public space?: People's Park, definitions of the public, and democracy', *Annals of the Association of American Geographers*, 85: 108–133.

Moores, S. (1988) 'The box on the dresser: memories of early radio', *Media, Culture and Society*, 10 (1).

Morgan, P. (1983) 'From a death to a view: the hunt for a Welsh past in the romantic period', in E. Hobsbawm and T. Ranger, (eds) *The Invention of Tradition*, Oxford: Blackwell.

Morgan, S. (1999) 'The ghost in the luggage: Wallace and *Braveheart*: post-colonial pioneer identities', *European Journal of Cultural Studies*, 2 (3): 375–392.

Morley, D. (1991) 'Where the global meets the local: notes from the sitting room', *Screen*, 32 (1): 1–15.

Morley, D. (2000) *Home Territories: Media, Mobility and Identity*, London: Routledge.

Morley, D. and Robins, K. (1995) *Spaces of Identity*, London: Routledge.

Morse, M. (1999) 'Home: smell, taste, posture, gleam', in H. Naficy (ed.) *Home, Exile, Homeland: Film, Media and the Politics of Place*, London: Routledge.

Morton, G. (1993) 'Unionist Nationalism: The Historical Construction of Scottish National Identity, Edinburgh 1830–1860', Ph.D. thesis, University of Edinburgh.

Nairn, T. (1977) *The Break up of Britain: Crisis and Neo-Nationalism*, London: New Left Books.

Nash, C. (1993) '"Embodying the nation": the West of Ireland landscape and national identity', in M. Cronin and B. O'Connor (eds) *Tourism and Ireland*, Cork: Cork University Press.

Nash, C. (2000) 'Performativity in practice: some recent work in cultural geography', *Progress in Human Geography*, 24 (4): 653–664.

Nordström, I. (1996) 'Manners and meals: on cultural imprinting, the power of rules, and changing habits', in J. Frykman and O. Löfgren (eds) *Forces of Habit: Exploring Everyday Culture*, Lund: Lund University Press.

Nowotny, H. (1994) *Time: The Modern and Postmodern Experience*, Cambridge: Polity.

Nugent, J. (2001) 'Networks of Ethnicity: A Cybernetic Study of the Second-Generation Irish in Birmingham', Unpublished Ph.D. thesis, University of Staffordshire.

Nurse, K. (1999) 'Globalisation and Trinidad carnival: diaspora, hybridity and identity in global culture', *Cultural Studies*, 13 (4): 661–690.

O'Connell, S. (1998) *The Car and British Society: Class Gender and Motoring 1896–1939*, Manchester: Manchester University Press.

O'Dell, T. (2001) 'Raggare and the panic of mobility: modernity and hybridity in Sweden', in D. Miller (ed.) *Car Cultures*, Oxford: Berg.

O'Reilly, K. (2000) *The British on the Costa del Sol: Transnational Identities and Local Communities,* London: Routledge.

O'Shea, A. (1996) 'Modernity, cinema and the popular imagination in the late twentieth century', in M. Nava and A. O'Shea (eds) *Modern Times: Reflections on a Century of English Modernity*, London: Routledge.

O'Sullivan, C. (1996) 'In the name of the father', *Observer*, 16 June, p. 18.

Østby, P. (1993) 'Escape from Detroit: the Norwegian conquest of an alien artefact', in K. Sørensen (ed.) *The Car and its Environments: The Past, Present and Future of the Motorcar in Europe*, Luxembourg: European Commission.

Palmer, C. (1998) 'From theory to practice: experiencing the nation in everyday life', *Journal of Material Culture,* 3 (2) 175–199.

Palmer, G. and Jankowiak, W. (1996) 'Performance and imagination: toward an anthropology of the spectacular and the mundane', *Cultural Anthropology*, 11 (2): 225–258.

Parker, D. (2000) 'The Chinese takeaway and the diasporic habitus: space, time and power-geometries', in B. Hesse (ed.) *Un/settled Multiculturalisms: Diasporas, Entanglements, Transruptions*, London: Routledge.

Pendreigh, B. (1995) 'Gibson turns Wallace into Mad Max', *The Scotsman*, 4 September, p. 8.

Pickering, M. (2001) *Stereotyping: The Politics of Representation*, London: Palgrave.

Porter, R. 'Animating histories', *Sunday Times*, 30 July, p. 2.

Pringle, T. (1988) 'The privation of history: Landseer, Victoria and the Highland myth', in D. Cosgrove and S. Daniels (eds) *The Iconography of Landscape*, Cambridge: Cambridge University Press.

Rapport, N. and Dawson, A. (1998) 'The topic and the book', in N. Rapport and A. Dawson (eds) *Migrants of Identity: Perceptions of Home in a World of Movement*, Oxford: Berg.

Rauch, A. (1996) 'Courage against cupidity: Carpentier–Dempsey: symbols of cultural confrontation', *The International Journal of the History of Sport*, 13 (1).

Rausing, S. (1998) 'Signs of the new nation: gift exchange, consumption and aid on a former collective farm in north-west Estonia', in D. Miller (ed.) *Material Cultures: Why Some Things Matter*, London: UCL Press.

Renan, E. (1990) 'What is a nation?', in H. Bhabha (ed.) *Nation and Narration*, London: Routledge.

Riddoch, L. (1995) 'Getting to the heart of the matter', *The Scotsman*, 15 September, p. 13.

Ritzer, G. (1993) *The McDonaldisation of Society: An Investigation into the Changing Character of Contemporary Social Life*, Thousand Oaks, Calif.: Pine Forge.

Robins, K. (1991) 'Tradition and translation: national culture in its global context', in J. Corner and S. Harvey (eds) *Enterprise and Heritage*, London: Routledge.

Roche, M. (2000) 'Citizenship, popular culture and Europe', in N. Stevenson (ed.) *Culture and Citizenship*, London: Sage.

Rojek, C. (1993) *Ways of Escape*, London: Macmillan.

Rojek, C. (1995) *Decentring Leisure*, London: Sage.

Rojek, C. (2000) *Leisure and Culture*, London: Macmillan.

Rorty, R. (1991) *Objectivity, Relativism and Truth: Philosophical Papers, Vol. 1*, Cambridge: Cambridge University Press.

Rose, G. (1993) *Feminism and Geography: The Limits of Geographical Knowledge*, Cambridge: Polity.

Rosenstone, R. (1995) *Visions of the Past: the Challenge of the Film to our Idea of History*, Boston, Mass.: Harvard University Press.

Ross, K. (1995) *Fast Cars, Clean Bodies: Decolonisation and the Reordering of French Culture*, London: MIT Press.

Royle, T. (1995) 'The fate of little nigger', *Scotland on Sunday*, 10 September, p. 10.

Russell, M. (1995) 'Braveheart points up positive nature of independence', *The Scotsman*, 20 September, p. 13.

Rybczynski, R. (1988) *Home: A Short History of an Idea*, London: Heinemann.

Samuel, R. and Thompson, P. (eds) (1990) *The Myths We Live By*, London: Routledge.

Sarup, M. (1996) *Identity, Culture and the Postmodern World*, Edinburgh: Edinburgh University Press.

Savigliana, M. (1995) *Tango and the Political Economy of Passion*, Boulder, Colo.: Westview Press.

Scharff, V. (1997) 'Gender and genius: the auto industry and femininity', in K. Martinez and K. Ames (eds) *The Material Culture of Gender, the Gender of Material Culture*, London: University Press of New England.

Schechner, R. (1993) *The Future of Ritual*, London: Routledge.

Schieffelin, E. (1998) 'Problematising performance', in F. Hughes-Freeland (ed.) *Ritual, Performance, Media*, London: Routledge.

Schiffer, M. and Miller, A. (1999) *The Material Life of Human Beings: Artefacts, Behaviour and Communication*, London: Routledge.

Schutz, A. (1964) *Collected Papers: Vol. 2*, Den Haag: Martinus Nijhoff.

Scott, G. (1992) *Mini: A Celebration of the World's Ultimate Small Car*, London: Hamlyn.

Scott, K. (2000) 'Scotland to boost tourism with searches for ancestral roots', *The Guardian*, 17 February.

Seenan, G. (1999) 'Klansmen take their lead from Scots', *The Guardian*, 30 January.

Sharp, M. (1996) 'Braveheart helps Stirling capture top tourist award', *The Scotsman*, 16 September, p. 3.

Sheller, M. and Urry, J. (2000) 'The city and the car', *International Journal of Urban and Regional Research*, 24.

Shields, R. (1991) *Places on the Margin*, London: Routledge.

Short, J. (1991) *Imagined Country*, London: Routledge.

Shurmer-Smith, P. and Hannam, P. (1994) *Worlds of Desire, Realms of Power: A Cultural Geography*, London: Edward Arnold.

Sibley, D. (1988) 'Survey 13: purification of space', *Environment and Planning D: Society and Space*, 6: 409–421.

Sibley, D. (1997) 'Endangering the sacred: nomads, youth cultures and the English countryside', in P. Cloke and J. Little (eds) *Contested Countryside Cultures*, London: Routledge.

Silverstone, R. (1994) *Television and Everyday Life*, London: Routledge.

Silverstone, R. (1997) 'Introduction', in R. Silverstone (ed.) *Visions of Suburbia*, London: Routledge.

Smith, A. (1991) *National Identity*, London: Penguin.

Smith, A. (1998) *Nationalism and Modernism*, London: Routledge.

Smout, T.C. (1994) 'Perspectives on the Scottish identity', *Scottish Affairs*, 6, Winter, pp. 101–113.

Sopher, D. (1979) 'The landscape of home: myth, experience, social meaning', in D. Meinig (ed.) *The Interpretation of Ordinary Landscape*, New York: Oxford University Press.

Sørensen, K. (ed.) (1993) *The Car and its Environments: The Past, Present and Future of the Motorcar in Europe*, Luxembourg: European Commission.

Sørensen, K. and Sørgaard, J. (1993) 'Mobility and modernity: towards a sociology of cars', in K. Sørensen (ed.) *The Car and its Environments: The Past, Present and Future of the Motorcar in Europe*, Luxembourg: European Commission.

Spillman, L. (1997) *Nation and Commemoration: Creating National Identities in the United States and Australia*, Cambridge: Cambridge University Press.

Spooner, B. (1986) 'Weavers and dealers: the authenticity of an oriental carpet', in A. Appadurai (ed.) *The Social Life of Things: Commodities in Cultural Perspective*, Cambridge: Cambridge University Press.

Stevenson, N. (ed.) (2001a) *Culture and Citizenship*, London: Sage.

Stevenson, N. (2001b) 'Introduction', in N. Stevenson (ed.) *Culture and Citizenship*, London: Sage.

Stewart, S. (1993) *On Longing: Narratives of the Miniature, the Gigantic, the Souvenir, the Collection*, London: Duke University Press.

Stewart, S. (1999) 'Prologue: from the museum of touch', in M. Kwint, C. Breward, and J. Aynsley (eds) *Material Memories: Design and Evocation*, Oxford: Berg.

Stokes, M. (1996) '"Strong as a Turk": power, performance and representation in Turkish wrestling', in J. MacClancy (ed.) *Sport, Ethnicity and Identity*, Oxford: Berg.

Storey, J. (1993) *An Introductory Guide to Cultural Theory and Popular Culture*, Hemel Hempstead: Harvester Wheatsheaf.

Susskind, J. (1992) 'The invention of Thanksgiving – a ritual of American nationality', *Critique of Anthropology*, 12 (2).

Swingewood, A. (1998) *Cultural Theory and the Problem of Modernity*, Basing-stoke: Macmillan.

Tacchi, J. (1998) 'Radio texture: between self and other', in D. Miller (ed.) *Material Cultures: Why Some Things Matter*, London: UCL Press.

Taylor, J. (1994) *A Dream of England: Landscape, Photography and the Tourist's Imagination*, Manchester: Manchester University Press.

Thompson, A. (2001) 'Nations, national identity and human agency: putting people back into nations', *Sociological Review*: 18–32.

Thompson, J. (1995) *The Media and Modernity*, Cambridge: Polity.

Thrift, N. (1997) 'The still point: resistance, expressive embodiment and dance', in S. Pile and M. Keith (eds) *Geographies of Resistance*, London: Routledge.

Thrift, N. (2000) 'Still life in nearly present time: the object of nature', *Body and Society*, 6 (3–4).

Tilly, C. (1994) 'Afterword: political memories in space and time', in J. Boyarin (ed.) *Remapping Memory: The Politics of Time Space*, Minneapolis: University of Minnesota Press.

Toolis, K. (1999) 'Scotland the vainglorious', *The Guardian*, 24 April.

Tuan, Y.-F. (1974) *Topophilia*, Englewood Cliffs, N.J.: Prentice-Hall.

Tulloch, J. (1999) *Performing Culture*, London: Sage.

Urry, J. (1995) *Consuming Places*, London: Routledge.

Urry, J. (2000) *Sociology Beyond Societies*, London: Routledge.

Valentine, G. (1997) 'Making space: lesbian separatist communities in the United States', in P. Cloke and J. Little (eds) *Contested Countryside Cultures*, London: Routledge.

Verrips, J. and Meyer, B. (2001) 'Kwaku's car: the struggles and stories of a Ghanaian long-distance taxi-driver', in D. Miller (ed.) *Car Cultures*, Oxford: Berg.

Vlastos, S. (ed.) (1998) *Mirror of Modernity: Invented Traditions of Modern Japan*, Berkeley: University of California Press.

Walton, J. (2000) *The British Seaside: Holidays and Resorts in the Twentieth Century*, Manchester: Manchester University Press.

Warner, M. (1993) *Monuments and Maidens*, London: Verso.

Watkins (2001) 'Moving home', Unpublished conference paper.

Weber, C. (1998) 'Performative states', *Millennium: Journal of International Studies*, 27 (1): 77–95.

Westwood, S. and Phizacklea, A. (2000) *Trans-Nationalism and the Politics of Belonging*, London: Routledge.

Whisler, T. (1999) *The British Motor Industry 1945–1944: A Case Study in Industrial Decline*, Oxford: Oxford University Press.

Williams, E. and Costall, A. (2000) 'Taking things more seriously: psychological theories of autism and the material–social divide', in P. Graves-Brown (ed.) *Matter, Materiality and Modern Culture*, London: Routledge.

Williams, R. (1961) *The Long Revolution*, London: Chatto and Windus.

Williams, R. (1981) *Culture*, London: Fontana.

Williams, S. and Bendelow, G. (1998) *The Lived Body: Sociological Themes, Embodied Issues*, London: Routledge.

Willis, P. (1990) *Common Culture: Symbolic Work at Play in the Everyday Cultures of the Young*, Milton Keynes: Open University Press.

Wilson, A. (1997) 'An English tea party in the heart of darkness: a critique of the cultural practices of an expatriate enclave in Nigeria 1983–1989', unpublished undergraduate cultural studies dissertation, University of Staffordshire.

Wilson, F. (1997) 'A bunch of Wallies?' *Stirling Observer*, September 10.

Withers, C. 1992 'The creation of the Scottish Highlands', in I. Donnachie and C. Whatley (eds) *The Manufacture of Scottish History*, Edinburgh: Polygon.

Witzel, M. and Bash, K. (1997) *Cruisin': Car Culture in America*. Osceola, Wis., USA: Motorbooks International.

Wolf, E. (1982) *Europe and the People Without History*, Berkeley: University of California Press.

Wolf, M. (1996) *Car Mania: A Critical History of Transport*, London: Pluto.

Wollen, T. (1991) 'Over our shoulders: nostalgic screen fictions for the 1980s', in J. Corner and S. Harvey (eds) *Enterprise and Heritage*, London: Routledge.

Wolschke-Bulmahn, J. (1996) 'The mania for native plants in Nazi Germany', in M. Dion and A. Rockman (eds) *Concrete Jungle*, New York: Juno Books.

Womack, P. (1987) *Improvement and Romance: Constructing the Myth of the Highlands*, London: Macmillan.

Wood, R. (1998) 'Tourist ethnicity: a brief itinerary', *Ethnic and Racial Studies*, 21: 218–241.

Young, D. (2001) 'The life and death of cars: private vehicles on the Pitjanjatjara lands, South Australia', in D. Miller (ed.) *Car Cultures*, Oxford: Berg.

Young, I. (1997) 'House and home: feminist variations on a theme', in *Intersecting Voices: Dilemmas of Gender, Political Philosophy and Policy*, Princeton, N.J.: Princeton University Press.

Index

Printed in the United Kingdom
by Lightning Source UK Ltd.
115920UKS00001B/241